THE MANAGEMENT OF IDEAS IN THE CREATING ORGANIZATION

THE MANAGEMENT OF IDEAS IN THE CREATING ORGANIZATION

John E. Tropman

Foreword by Gersh Morningstar

Q

QUORUM BOOKS
Westport, Connecticut • London

Library of Congress Cataloging-in-Publication Data

Tropman, John E.
The management of ideas in the creating organization / John E. Tropman ; foreword by Gersh Morningstar.
p. cm.
Includes bibliographical references and index.
ISBN 1-56720-168-7 (alk. paper)
1. Creative ability in business—Management. I. Title.
HD58.T76 1998
858.4'03—DC21 98-4947

British Library Cataloguing in Publication Data is available.

Library of Congress Catalog Card Number: 98-4947
ISBN: 1-56720-168-7

First published in 1998

Quorum Books, 88 Post Road West, Westport, CT 06881
An imprint of Greenwood Publishing Group, Inc.

Printed in the United States of America

The paper used in this book complies with the Permanent Paper Standard issued by the National Information Standards Organization (Z39.48-1984).

10 9 8 7 6 5 4 3 2 1

Contents

Foreword

Gersh Morningstar

This is a terrific book. I worked with John Tropman in writing an earlier book (*Entrepreneurial Systems for the 1990s*), and I regret that my business schedule kept me from participating in this one. It is full of good ideas. Let me stress two. The first is the importance of innovation—its messiness and unorganization. An old mentor of mine explained it to me, after a company I owned and cared a lot about went bankrupt: "Listen! Organization is the death of creativity. All successful enterprise is born in chaos. The real trick in success is knowing when not to create mechanisms to achieve well-defined objectives." This lesson came from the man who developed the loved, hated, and universally misunderstood organizational tool, Management by Objectives.

Creativity, then, is the genesis of all enterprise. It provides the seed from which a company will grow. As the company grows, it is necessary to impose ever-expanding structures upon it in order to organize and track its activities. As the organization becomes more complex, constraints and restraints arise in the form of rules, policies, charters, corporate by-laws, traditions, and history. Finally, creativity diminishes the further it moves away from chaos. Negative entropy is its ultimate enemy. This book helps make creativity a daily event, not an occasional one.

John sees the organization as balanced between chaos and structure. He elected to look at a business enterprise as a living system and attempted to examine the forces that affect its critical subsystems, without which no living thing can continue to live. While he did not recreate the detailed subsystems schema that characterize the work of others (James Grier Miller, for example), he did arrive at the same final understanding of why some living systems (businesses in this case) continue to live and why some die. Traditional vectors of strength and weakness, incentive and enthusiasm, capital and research, even goal setting and business planning, appeared to be diminished by two unrelated constellations of processes.

One of the constellations defines what can be called success behavior, and the strength of its primary vector is a general measure of the extent to which success may be predicted. The other constellation is made up of processes inimical to the continued existence of one, some, or all the critical subsystems; and it is a general measure of the extent to which failure may be predicted. While the two behaviors may have some reciprocal modifying effect, they operate independently each from the other. Exciting organizations do two things—they do right, and they do not do wrong. Failure is not the opposite of success. Failure is an entirely different set of processes, in the sense that failure has an absolute vector strength of its own, which, if achieved, will cause an enterprise to die—regardless of the extent of its success. Thus, although it is important to watch the success behavior of a company or organization very carefully if the enterprise is to grow and prosper, it is even more important to watch the failure behaviors—for it takes the death of only one out of a great many critical subsystems to kill the whole company.

To me, this way of looking at business makes wonderfully good sense, and I put it to the test every day of my working life.

Preface

An earlier organizational book I wrote (with Gersh Morningstar), *Entrepreneurial Systems for the 1990s*, was developed at a time of lagging American productivity. It was widely believed that the American engine had stalled. A headline in the *New York Times* screamed, "America: Snap Out of It." The article showed a graph of the productivity of three economic regions—America, West Germany, and Japan—from 1960 to 1980. If you hold up the three fingers of your left hand vertically in front of you, that is what the graph showed: Your third finger is the United States; your second finger is Germany; and your index finger is Japan. We were dead last. But we were not dead yet.

The *New York Times* was not alone. Lester Thurow (1992), in his influential book *Head to Head*, looked at the same three economic powerhouses (except that Germany became Europe). He concluded that the European economy would be the victorious one. Japan was too ethnocentric, and we in America would not be able to get our act together.

It turned out that it was not over till it was over; that the fat lady had not sung yet. American organizations have sprung back with a vengeance. How did this happen?

One answer was the spur of competition. Up to a point, competition is beneficial. It causes you to look closely at yourself and want to be better. Competition provides the jolt of energy needed to overcome inertia. A second answer was energy, or the drive to change. The sleeping giant indeed woke up. A third answer involves focused action. Just wanting to be better, however, does not mean you will be better. Actually being better requires areas upon which you take action. There were two major ones.

One focused on better processes. It is reengineering. Reengineering refers to the processes through which you work. Processes became leaner and meaner.

Whatever they are called, reengineering is the process of "work-out"—taking work out of the system. This is one kind of efficiency: doing things right.

Competition also causes you to re-architect. Re-architecting refers to the structure of the organization, as opposed to its processes. The major problem here was that many organizations had a vision, but did not have "alignment"; that is, their organizational parts would not set up to drive the vision. The vision was new, but the organizational house was old. We became, then, more efficient. We were doing things right, well even. But much of this improvement involved the implementation of what we already knew; fixing the house we were already in.

Organizations require three kinds of resources: money, people, and ideas. When you go into a firm and ask about its money, you are quickly taken to the CFO or someone like him (though there are a few hers). Everyone knows about money.

If you ask about people, you will, more slowly, get to a CHRO. Already one wonders, "CHRO?" Of course, it is the Chief Human Resources Officer. Some firms have such people (much more often women than the CFO). Many have "directors," "managers," or "departments," but the message is clear: People are a lot less important than money, even though it is through people that money is made. Many CEOs have had CFO experience; it is frequently a requisite. On the contrary, few individuals would say, "I have to have CHRO experience if I am ever to make it to the top!"

When we come to ideas, "It's a puzzlement." If you go into an organization and ask, "Who handles your ideas?" they might say, as one firm did say to me "No one. We don't have any ideas!" The premise of *The Management of Ideas in the Creating Organization* is that ideas are the fundamental driving force in organizations and firms. Ideas excite (or enervate) people; products and services are ideas turned into money.

This is a book, then, about idea development and idea management. The idea of ideas reorganizes much organizational thinking through a common thread. Firm policy, for example, is a set of ideas, written down and approved by firm officials. The approved part means choice. Choice means decisions. Hence, decisions are all about ideas. Strategy management is idea management.

Culture is the set of values that drives the firm; values are ideas to which commitment is attached. Culture management is idea management. Change from change in the system (transactional) to change of the system (transformational) is, at root, change in ideas. A "paradigm shift" is just a change in really basic ideas.

This book takes off from the central idea that ideas matter, and that they can and must be managed. Regrettably, Gersh Morningstar was not able to join in the direct writing of this volume because of other commitments. It is the poorer for it. But his ideas and energy infuse every page.

In this book I have been concerned primarily with the idea of IdeaManagement—developing and implementing the new, the creative, the innovative—

and you, as the IdeaManager and IdeaLeader—the person who helps and makes that happen. Without an adequate supply of new ideas, the American organizational community, whether it is business or government or some non-profit undertaking, is doomed to ever-decreasing productivity and to ever-increasing disappointments and failures in the world competitive community. The tragedy of this situation is twofold. First, it occurs. Second, it is completely *unnecessary*. All we have to do is look around us to see the abundance of creative and interesting ideas in our shops, our organizations, our firms, our agencies, our offices, and our bureaus. The concept and process of IdeaManagement rests heavily on the need to develop, orchestrate, promote, follow-up on, or implement—use whatever terms you prefer—these ideas so that some kind of organizational and behavioral change results from them. There can be no more important issue before this society. Those who are able to achieve progress toward this goal will have achieved IdeaLeadership. IdeaLeadership differs from organizational management in that the leadership component involves envisioning and enabling in ways that management often does not achieve. The IdeaLeader is the one who *develops* and *implements* new ideas repeatedly and who *enables* others to do so as well.

IdeaLeadership is desperately needed today in our three major organizational systems: business, government, and the nonprofit sector. A look at the erosion of the American competitive position in the world today ought to be sufficient evidence that such leadership is badly deficient at the present time. The current problems of American business do not need retelling here. We are all familiar with them.

The problems of federal and state government activities and programs are also well known. Our education system seems to be working very poorly. The criminal justice systems seems, if anything, to be counterproductive. The nonprofit system seems replete with crises, from adoption agencies to symphony orchestras. And these by no means exhaust the list.

IdeaLeadership encompasses IdeaManagement, but it goes far beyond it, extending organizational management concepts to other spheres and other arenas. The IdeaLeader, in effect, spreads the word. Where IdeaManagement harnesses and directs good ideas, IdeaLeadership extends, expands, and interlinks them. It is this capacity that must be recaptured in American enterprise, and it is this capacity that will reenergize the systems where it is applied.

Acknowledgments

It is always important to let readers know that most authors, are, in a way, editors and orchestrators. The work of others—their help, their perspectives, their energy—is vital to any project. This one is no exception. First, of course, is my esteemed coauthor of *Entrepreneurial Systems for the 1990s*, Gersh Morningstar. Other commitments prevented him from joining as fully here as he did in our previous volume, but his spirit and intelligence have been a source of constant inspiration. I would like to mention others who have made their presence felt here, through conversation, presentation, and evaluation: Bill Birdsall, Jim Duderstadt, Jeff DeGraff, Ejner Jensen, Diane Kaplan-Vinokur, Bill Phillips, Bob Quinn, Noel Tichy, Karl Weick, and Joe White are *premus inter pares* among those who have been of constant help and inspiration.

My family—my wife Penny, daughters Sarah and Jessica, son-in-law Matthew, and son Matt—have provided me with encouragement, humor, and a constant supply of anecdotes of organizations running on empty concepts. My thanks to you all. Penny especially deserves appreciation. As a reader, she obviously appreciates authors; it is much tougher when the author is your husband who is "always" in front of his computer. Still, she was excited about the project, encouraged me, and reviewed and improved the text countless times.

I must also mention Dan Madaj. Dan worked through two phases of the project. An editor of extraordinary talent (unusual for a man who is a writer in his own right), he was a continual source of support and improvement. Finally, Rick Lane checked the manuscript, processed and did more editing on it, and was hugely helpful in the final stages of its creation. Finally, Seth Reichgott, editor extraordinary, pulled the text into shape.

PART I

Ideas and Organizations / Organizations and Ideas

THE POWER OF THE PEN

The question of which is stronger, the pen or the sword, has been on the lips of philosophers and practitioners for hundreds of years. Naturally, the philosophers have argued for the pen; practitioners have stressed the sword. This is not surprising. But in spite of personal and professional interest, the issue is a key one. Do ideas come first—are they "the real thing," and structure follows? Or, on the other hand, does structure come first, and ideas follow. Which, after all, organizes which?

The "greats" have taken different positions. Plato was a "pen" guy; Aristotle a "swordsman." Sigmund Freud was another pen guy; B. F. Skinner, the Harvard behavioral scientist, took the other side, like Pavlov. Max Weber was an "ideas first" person; Karl Marx took the other perspective. For Marx, where you stood in the social structure (capitalist or proletarian) was the key. Ideas, like religion, came later—and second. These may seem like abstract concepts, but today, ideas—we call it information—is key. Consider this *Wall Street Journal* (Kaufman, 1997) observation in an article called "Gray Expectations" about Chris Toal, a software company manager, who at age fifty-four in 1997 was "staying alive" in his firm: "The intensity of his work has grown exponentially in recent years. Mr. Toal, like most managers, used to manage mainly people. He now spends much of his time managing information" (p. 1).

Nike's ad, "Just Do It," was written by a swordsman. America itself is oriented that way. Planning is out; action is in. But "Just Do It" becomes "Do It—Fix It."

Information management—IdeaManagement—is going to be the key to the future, or at least the near future. We have had "action"—downsizing, rightsizing, resizing, outsourcing, insourcing, resourcing, and so on. We have merged, purged, urged, regurged, and you name it. We have TQMd, PDQd, SOBd, and RSVPd and FOWd (fad of the week). We have proacted, enacted, and reacted. And the result of all this? In the words of the Roman poet Horace, "A mountain roars, and a mouse comes forth."

That is, perhaps, unfair. America has regained dominance in productivity, but it was a catch-up game. We were in the fourth quarter, well down. The future may not allow us that much time. We need, in the beginning of the next century, to emphasize thought over action. We do not have, and will not have, the resources to "Do It—Fix It." We must, in the words of Westinghouse, do "the right thing, the right way, the first time." That means think, then do. If the human species is distinguished by anything, it is the ability to learn from experience—to codify, to organize, and to transmit in a variety of forms experienced from one generation to the next. And new ideas change things.

Chapter 1

The Energy of Thought

Our caveperson ancestors, the Neanderthals, were able to accumulate and transmit their knowledge. This gave our species an incredible advantage. Think for a moment about the difference between sewn clothing and the simple use of skins unattached to one another. Consider, too, what is required to sew clothing; namely, a needle and thread.

The needle is a commonplace item in our daily lives now, but that has not always been the case. Sometimes concepts are most readily understood when presented in their simplest form, so suspend your disbelief for a moment and travel back to a time without needles.

It is winter. It is cold and gray. Our ancestors—a whole group of them—are rocking back and forth around a fire on the balls of their feet. They have all just finished a lunch of roast Pterodactyl wing. All except the chief are covered with small skins, but they keep falling down. They are very cold. The chief is covered with a bearskin: His head is nicely covered by the top of the bearskin, and the bear face, jutting out over the top of his head, gives him a fearsome appearance. Also, he is warm. And he does not mind, actually, that his tribesmen's hands are busy putting their skins back; after all, if their hands were free it would be easier to attack him.

But one of the members, in putting his skins together, accidentally sticks a sliver of wing through two of them and into his hand. The bone sliver is attached to a sinew, he looks at the result, and the two skins are sort of joined together, held by the sinew which runs through a small spear hole in the skin, a spear hole made by the pointed bone fragment. Something is about to emerge that will change the course of human history.

He pokes the pelt again and makes another hole in it with the bone. It takes some doing, but he finally manages to make a nice small hole. Using a rough stone, he sharpens the end of the bone still further. It does not take nearly the effort to make the second hole. He makes holes in the edge of a second pelt. Now comes the hard part—he is out of sinew. But there is plenty around. The hard part is getting the sinew through the holes when it is not hooked onto the little spear. It is tough going until it occurs to him that if he cuts a small notch in the other end of the bone with his flint knife he can tie the sinew there and pull it through the pelt as he makes the hole.

Very excited, he says, "Hey, have I come up with a great idea. We take a tiny piece of bone, see, and we put a little notch in one end, and we attach a long piece of sinew to that piece of bone. Then we pass the pointy needle from one skin through to another and in that way fasten each skin to a different skin. We can make whole blankets."

Other of our Neanderthal uncles—and indeed the rest of the fire council—respond as they would, no doubt, today. "The gods don't like it. If God wanted to make a tiny point with a notch in the end attached to sinew, he would have done so," one says.

Another adds, "And it is unnatural to join the skins of one animal to another."

Then a third chimes in, "Besides, such a tiny spear would break."

The chorus of complaints, comments, and criticisms goes on around the fire for hours. Needless to say, the chief does not like the idea at all. Team participant after team participant speaks against his idea.

Our ancestor tries to change their thinking. "But we could trade these superpelts for things we need from other tribes."

The chants of derision grows even louder. "Who would want them?" "It would be too complicated." Then he says, "The women could do it. If we bring home the pelts, they could put them together." Suddenly the tenor changes, the idea is beginning to take hold.

Through the years the response to organizational concepts and suggestions has probably changed little. There is always some god that will be offended by the new idea. Of course, as a general rule, gods always tend to disapprove of new things.

Scientific American (1987 March), quoting from their March 1887 issue, comments on one spectacular case of missing the boat: "When the last census was taken, to wit 1880, the census man did not consider the electric lighting investment of sufficient magnitude to warrant him collecting the data. Today [1887] the investment is worth one hundred seven million dollars—that is, $107,000,000. And how long has it taken for this vast sum to be attracted to the electric lighting field? Only six years!" (p. 10).

Still, these same new ideas—from a needle with a sinew attached, to the domesticating of animals, to writing and alphabets, to horseshoes—demonstrate clearly that the energy of thought is one of the most powerful forces that exist. IdeaManagers and IdeaLeaders are major developers and users of that energy. They harness it, structure it, and take the initiative in forcing us to confront the validity and integrity of new ideas, products, services, plans, and policies. This was true of our ancient relatives sitting around their campfires in the middle of a freezing European winter. And it is true for those who develop Post-it™ Notes for the 3M Company who must try to convince a company that has made most of its money by creating and marketing products that stick that there is money to be made and a service to be performed in providing products that do not stick very well.

Harnessing the energy of thought is amply demonstrated by a principle developed by the inventor of the modern machine gun, Sir Hiram Stevens Maxim, the expatriot American inventor and fixer (Slade, 1986). He was perhaps a classic in at least two regards. He conceived a number of important inventions—inventing an electric light at the same time as Edison (and later losing out in a patent fight with Edison)—and he was unable to carry through on many of his inventions. Though he had the idea for the light, for example, Edison had the idea of the light *and* the system of power to generate the light. This gave Edison the edge. Maxim likewise lost out to the Wright brothers, though he experimented with a steam-powered airplane that actually lifted off the ground ten years before the Wright brothers. But it is in the development of the modern machine gun that Maxim provides the perfect metaphor for the energy of thought. For many years individuals had known that guns recoiled when fired. No one had been able to harness that energy. In his design, Maxim was able to capture the energy from the gun's recoil and, using a spring, transfer that energy to the performance of another function: loading the next shell and cocking the gun preparatory to firing.

Though it is not our intention to extol the virtues of the machine gun, the principle that Maxim used is one that we can all learn from. Maxim thought of the problem as one of energy transfer, or saving of wasted energy. In his book, *High Output Management*, Andrew Grove (1983) calls a similar process leveraging. Whatever the process is called, it involves capturing the available energy of a system and using it to expand and enhance the system's activities. Ideas do this job for us quite well. It is ideas, in fact, that give the organizational system its zest—whether that system is the place where we work, or a family, clubs, lodges, or other places where we spend our time. The kinds of systems that we find exciting are those where new things are happening. The paradox is that while we enjoy the excitement of the new mixed with the tradition of the old, we tend at the same time to be resistant to the new. Consequently, we need help in overcoming these conservative tendencies.

New ideas are structured by two main sources. They are either *needs* driven or *means* driven. The needs-driven idea is something that comes from a pressing requirement or problem for which there is no existing solution. Such a solution is called an *invention*. A new vaccine, a completely new product, or a new service can be considered in this category.

Alternatively, there are means-driven developments or innovations. These arise as a current product or service is offered, perhaps with only minor modifications, perhaps with none at all, to a new market or market segment or is assigned to a new function that it has not yet played before in the system—the use of dried corn cobs as a fuel, for example. Nothing is invented, but the application is new.

IdeaManagers and IdeaLeaders are people who energize systems. They either develop them or revitalize them. They harness the energy of thought. Engaging in the harnessing process essentially involves the management of three tasks simultaneously: (1) doing your regular job, (2) understanding the problems of negative energy within an organization and finding ways to diminish its impact, and (3) introducing positive energy within the organization. Sometimes this introduction occurs by transforming negative to positive energy, as Maxim did with his machine gun. Sometimes totally new sources of energy must be introduced. Ideas are energizing elements. They can be negative or positive. Much of the success of organizational effort comes from harnessing and directing the energy of thought. The ability to introduce innovations successfully within an organization is a similar process.

In thinking about this harnessing or redirecting process, you cannot simply wait for some "big idea" to come along, or the right job, or the right position. Rather, you must make energy-harnessing activities a normal part of your everyday routine in your home and family, in the microenvironment of your work area and work station, and in the macroenvironment of the organization as a whole.

The problem—one problem—that faced the small company was the following: They assembled motors which flowed along an assembly line. At several points along the line, washers had to be slipped over protruding bolts. Many men and women sat on high stools in front of the line and performed the washer task. Washers came in small burlap sacks of about 100. The employee dumped them out on a small steel work table in front of him or her, picked them up, and slipped them on the bolts. Here is where the problems began. As the washers were dumped out, many of them bounced off the steel table onto the floor. Loss was heavy. Management was angry, and screamed and yelled at the workers to be more careful. It was also hard to pick them up and many workers moved the washers to the edge of the table to grab them more easily. Some additional ones dropped. Management then riveted a lip at the edge of the steel table to prevent this. Workers injuries, a kind of knuckle shock, was very common. Management called the workers sissies, but the knuckles were actually quite swollen from the day-in, day-out trauma of hitting the tips of your fingers on the steel table. Tension was running high, production low, scrap high, morale low. Management complained about "workers today," "Generation X," "lack of a work ethic," and so on. One day a young woman came to work—a new employee. She worked the first day at her job without saying much. The next day she arrived at work with a one-inch piece of foam rubber cut to fit the space of the steel table. It cost a buck. It revolutionized that workplace.

CONCLUSION

Change is necessary in order to keep current, in order to keep alive, in order to keep things fun, in order to keep things moving. And the forces of change are continually pressing us to think of new ways to do things. Those forces are the subject of the next chapter. The energy of thought is released through planned, proactive steps. Maybe no one will come up with something as revolutionary as the needle, but there are lots of ideas out there that can help an organization achieve its goals, help introduce new products, new services, improvements, and refurbishments. The idea alone, however, is not enough. In new ventures, special attention needs to be given to intellectual, interpersonal, and organizational aspects if the idea is to bear fruit and not be relegated to some dumpster of "crazy suggestions" that is perennially full.

The first step is to recognize the energy of thought. The next is to enhance, increase, and legitimize the supply of new ideas in order to create an organization that welcomes new approaches and perspectives. There is much more than this, of course; but without the supply, little that happens later makes much difference.

At the front end, ideas are the resource that is "machined" by the organizational structure into some kind of policy or product at the back end. It is a process parallel to financial processes or the human resources process. In financial processes, money comes into the organization and is, in effect, "turned into" products and services. Raw materials are purchased, people are hired, machines are bought, and they are all orchestrated and connected together to work in a synchronous way so that a product or service might result. A human resource process is similar. Organizations hire people to be *transformers*. These transformers exchange their transformational services for money and perform operations on business materials (such as raw materials and documents) so that they can become products and services.

The idea management system is similar to money and people. As the firm's third central resource—and most important in the future—it is the ability of an organization to generate a range of ideas on a continuous basis concerning both fundamental aspects of the organization (how to do the right thing) and process aspects of the organization (efficiency, or taking work out of the system). Everyone in the organization is tasked to come up with big and small ideas about what the organization should do, and how it might do it.

This whole process can be organized around the KSS system—Keep, Stop, Start. In KSS, everyone from the CEO to the CCO (Chief Clean-up Officer, or janitor) is tasked with addressing the following questions on a continuing basis:

Keep—What is the organization doing that we should keep? What are the processes, approaches, papers that are useful to us?

Stop—What are the things the organization processes (like paper) that we are no longer using but still somehow retaining? What, in effect, should be stopped?

Start—What are the things we are not now doing that need to begin?

Many people erroneously think that ideas only fall into the "start" area—something new. But appropriate continuance, and making that case, is an idea. Suggesting some things that we are now doing that ought to stopped—that is also an idea.

The successful organization of the future needs to be a cauldron of concepts. Many of the ideas will not stand scrutiny or will not be able to be pursued. There is, after all, a high death rate among ideas. That should not, however, keep organizations from working in the area. In fact, it should cause firms to redouble their effort. Idea generation is a lot like mining—a lot of excess rock, constant production, and few real nuggets. It is both the constant production and the nuggets which sustain the organization and help it to grow. It is ideas that direct money and people.

Most firms regard ideas as random events that occur occasionally. The purpose of this book is to suggest that they are absolutely necessary and vital, and that attention to the idea management function which garners, shepherds, organizes, stores, recycles, and in general manages ideas within firms big and small will be a "success driver" function for the future.

Chapter 2

The Forces for Change: Diversity, Speed, and Magnitude

New ideas are becoming the driving forces of change. Let us begin by looking at the forces driving change.[1] What are some of the elements that are changing the organizational workplace and creating constant change? In a few words, pluralism, multicentricity, customization, and complexity. One might even call it diversity.

DIVERSITY

Pluralism refers to the many-ness of things: many kinds of customers, many kinds of employees, many kinds of vendors and suppliers, many kinds of computer languages, many kinds of needs, and many of this and that with which the twenty-first-century firm must deal.

Multicentricity refers to the many decision centers that now characterize the organization. It is not as lonely at the top, and there are many more tops to bring into the loop.

Customization points to the necessity of optimizing the product—albeit from a large base—for the customer in question. Customization is the organizational response to choice. One-for-all fringe benefit programs are turning into cafeterias. Indeed, the entire compensation system might become a series of spigots which employees adjust to their own desires. Everybody is Frank Sinatra, and wants it "their way."

Complexity is the natural result of these three forces—if we are lucky. Otherwise we have chaos. Some argue you can thrive on chaos, but most of us would rather thrive a bit better on complexity and keep the chaos outside the door.

There are a number of key changes working toward increasing the complexity of the organization, and, hence, change.

From Money-Centered to Idea-Centered Organizations

The bottom line will be ideas—as has already been said. It used to be, in some organizations, phrases like "If I need an idea from you, I'll give you one," or "My way or the highway" were the norm. Now, the broadest range of intellectual input will be needed to compete.

From Means Control to Ends Control

Older organizations were convinced that if they structured the means, the ends were a given. It is probably the case that this was never as true as we thought. But today, it is not true very much. For one thing, it is almost impossible to control means so completely. That effort can lead to what Robert Merton (1957) called "means ritualism," which occurs when old means are enforced and used regardless of their appropriateness. For another thing, means regularity assumes sameness of input. A system set up to process one kind of customer problem does not work so well on another kind of customer problem. Means control, therefore, tends to restrict inputs to those which the organization could actually deal with. The newer organization needs just the opposite approach. It specifies ends, and helps the workplace and individuals in that workplace configure the means to deal with them, depending upon a variety of factors, including local setting, skills of the workers, particularities of the customer or supplier, and so on. It is assumed that different means can, and will, lead to the same, and satisfactory, ends.

From Thing Centered to People Centered

Organizations in the past were dominated by "the harder side" of their environment—product, machines, forms. Consistent with ends-control development, organizations of the future are going to be driven by people. It has finally come to be recognized that it is people who make organizations run. The mechanical or nonhuman elements of the organization are seen in their appropriate support role. This change is forcing organizations to look more closely at human pluralism—and to embrace such pluralism within themselves—because increasing human variety is needed to attempt to deal with and solve the various additional problems with which humans are being tasked.

Multiple Decision Centers: From Fixed Structures to Burrows, Spiderwebs, Lattices, and Networks

The very structure of organizations is changing. Older organizations were heavily structured, deriving, no doubt, from the old "span of control" idea that suggested a supervisor could only supervise (i.e., micromanage) five direct reports. Frequently, a triangle was used to describe such a fixed structure. The "boss" was at the "top," there were fixed positions below the boss, fixed positions below that boss, and so on and so forth. This is a kind of organizational chart, and it is still driven by concepts like span of control and "reporting relationships." Newer forms of organizations are more fluid. As the burrow, spiderweb, or lattice suggests, they are not without structure, but they have a different structure—a multicentric structure. Burrows are networks. So are spiderwebs. Lattices have many places of intersect. A multiplicity and plurality of intersections—bunches of nodes, in fact, as opposed to reporting relationships—will be needed by and characteristic of the new organization.

Many Sizes and Distances: From Boxes to Bubbles

This metaphor is perhaps another way of talking about new organizational forms. The old box-like organization, emphasized in the organizational chart mentioned before, had fixed faces, both vertically and horizontally. VPs were a certain distance from the CEO and from each other. Box-pictures did not communicate any interaction, any mutuality, any interdisciplinarity. And, in fact, many organizations were apparently driven by the pictures in their heads and on their pages. The people in those boxes did not interact. Each jealously guarded their own box, their own turf, and sought, if possible, to have boxes reporting to it. Today, of course, departments need to work together. Perhaps a different way of thinking about them would be to use a "bubble" idea.

The concept of organizational bubbles is one way in which the idea of dynamism and merging then separating can occur. Anyone who has blown bubbles out of a jar knows the bubbles flow together in large clumps, then sometimes separate, breaking apart and floating away on their own, only to rejoin other bubbles. If one were to think of organizations represented by this level of dynamism, then one would have the "bubble-ized" organization. An advantage of such a metaphor is that is may actually produce what it represents, in the same way that the box metaphor tended, in the view of many, to produce what it suggested as well.

Many Decision Makers: From Office-Centered to Decision-Centered Organizations

In older, rigid organizations, decision makers were those who were officially authorized: To make decisions, you had to get to the right box. You could not go "above" the box "above" you (occasionally there were skip-level team meetings). Whether they knew anything about the issue, or were the right person, often seemed irrelevant. Contemporary organizations start with a decision set that needs to be made, and then look to see who needs to be involved. Typically, it is functions, not offices, that are the focus. Nobody in those organizations mistakes compliance for good judgment. This emphasis reveals not only a plurality of decision points, but also a plurality of decision makers.

Many Tasks at the Same Time: From One at a Time to All at Once

Organizations of the past, and of course many today, focused on doing, making, and accomplishing one thing after another. The phrase "one day at a time" communicates this idea as well. The assembly line was and perhaps is the perfect example of this *ad seriatim* approach. Step H could not be completed before Step G, and must be completed before Step I, and so on. Today's organizations thrive on simultaneity. If B, H, I, and K can be done today, well, "hey, let's do it." The fact that K may need to await the completion of J for final assembly is okay. We are taking advantage of something that is present and capturing a previously lost opportunity. One of the best "owe me" examples of this simultaneous process is the set of pots and pans that has recessed lids with a buried handle, such that another pot can sit on top of and use the heat from a lower pot. Hence, simultaneous cooking is possible, rather than waiting for one pot to finish before starting another one. Simultaneity is diversity in time, and it is an important presence in today's organization.

Many Energies: From Either–Or to the Sprint–Pause Cycle

It used to be that in organizations you were either working or you were not. Work was work, and non-work was non-work. But work itself was never as structured as the job suggested. There has always been "on" periods and "off" periods. However, as Arlie Hochschild (1997) has pointed out in her new book *The Time Bind*, many bosses have become fixated on the idea that work and "time in the office at your desk" are one and the same. This concept led to busywork (appearing to be working), face time (showing up so the boss can see you and think you were working), to self-promoting work (being busy on your computer with your resume for your next job). Perhaps these several ersatz working ideas are captured in a joke from the Eastern Bloc countries: "We'll pretend to work, and you'll pretend to pay us." The more flexible organizations of today recognize what might be called the sprint–pause cycle. Most organizations really are not on or off, it is just a matter of sometimes adjusting the pace. The sprint pace often occurs when a contract is near deadline or a product is near launch, and all talents need to roll up their sleeves and work together. Here diversity blends into uniformity, as distinctions are dropped, subcultures set aside, idiosyncrasies interdicted, and everybody works to get the product out on time. In the pause cycle, diversity flourishes again in more manifest ways. The pace slows, individuals are working, but nowhere near as hard or as frenetically. Everybody relaxes a bit and does more of their own "thing," but that piece of their own thing which is still linked to the organization. In time, sprint will come again. That is the sprint–pause cycle (Mintzberg & Waters, 1982).

Many Rewards: From Enervation to Energizing

The older workplace, given some of the characteristics of rigidity, means-ritualism, anti-self, and social distance, tended to be an enervating place. It was not a place to which one really looked forward to going. It was a place where, to paraphrase Robert Frost, you went there because, since you worked there, they had to let you in.[2] The new workplace is designed to provide, in addition to cash compensation, a measure of psychic income, a place where one actually wants to go, a place from which one draws energy rather than one to which one is given.

Many Worlds: From Local to Cosmopolitan

One change that is pushing against organizations perhaps deals most directly with the diversity issue. It is the change of local points of reference to more cosmopolitan ones. Cosmopolitanism comes to organizations in many ways. Obviously, heterogeneity of the workforce is one way, but given the global links required to put together today's complicated products, other kinds of diversity include linking with workers in Canada, Mexico, Hong Kong, Singapore, Poland, London, as well as perhaps customers in some of those same countries. The idea that global emphasis is only the prerogative of large organizations is certainly not true. Small organizations as well are experiencing similar kinds of connections and context. With the Internet and the World Wide Web developing quickly, contact is easy.

Many Identities: From Self versus Community of Work to Self in Community of Work

One way to look at the workplace is as a kind of community where people come together and have unity around common tasks or common goals. Historically, as represented by labor–management conflict, the worker cells were viewed as "opposed to" management cells. Implicit in all of this discussion was that the worker community was a place where one had to protect oneself. In the case of management, one could protect oneself through politics, kissing up, and the like. In the case of worker cells, organizing or threatening to leave, jump ship, and go to another organization was a way to produce a raise. The workplace was a coliseum community, and the "lion managers" and the "Christian workers" contested daily. And the score always seemed to be Lions 28, Christians 0. With this historical perspective, it is no wonder that the worker cells sought communal solace elsewhere—in the bowling alley, in the saloon, in non-work, ethnic, and other enclaves, where "people like them" could share support.

The new organization seeks to break down these barriers—to emphasize that partnership is, after all, the emphasis, and that the competition is with those outside, not with those inside. So bloody is the organizational history here, that it might be a long time, if ever, before a majority of organizations achieve the communal status that the more successful organizations seem to have constructed. The paradox is, it is not that hard. All that is required is the development of common goals and a willingness to truly share the product—the results from common energy being applied to those common goals. In this particular case, the diversity of community previously excluded from the organization is brought into the organization, structured, and harnessed around a common focus.

Many Locations: From Shop Here to Shop Anywhere

Firms are being pushed to offer the services from a variety of locations. Catalog and computer-driven technologies allow one to shop from any phone, to consult with a physician from any place.

Many Minutes: From Nine to Five to Around the Clock

Given globalization, time take on a different meaning. Organizations increasingly need to be available twenty-four hours a day, 365 days a year. Holidays here are not holidays there. Organizations need to adapt to a round-the-clock mentality.

Many Forms: From Theme and Approved Variations to Theme and Your Variations

As will be indicated later, Americans like choice, and people around the world like it too.[3] Corporations are going to need to customize, and tweak, core models to the individual tastes and preferences of the customers, and do so quickly.

Many Perspectives: From Photograph to Kaleidoscope

Organizations of the past had a photograph culture. There was one picture, one way to view things, and it was captured in "the photo." Today's organizations have what might be called a kaleidoscope culture. While they have the same stones, a twist here and a twist there creates diverse combinations. There are thus many views about what the organization is, might be, does, and could do. It is from this kaleidoscope that "pictures of our disposition" are assembled.

SPEED AND MAGNITUDE

Structures of the twenty-first century will change faster than the they did in the twentieth century. While we have always had to cope with change—tough enough on its own—the situation is made more difficult by the fact that change is coming faster and with greater magnitude than ever before. Global connections and instant communications mean that what took weeks can now take minutes; those same connections mean that what might have had a limited effect in the past can now have a global effect.

Speed

Speed is a fact of life with which all managers, leaders, and organizations must contend. As a *Newsweek* headline intones (in an article about Montgomery Ward stores), "You Snooze . . . You Lose." In the twenty-first century, it will come in two velocity packages: fast and really fast (DeGraff, 1997).

Magnitude

Magnitude, the impact things have or can have, is also a factor for organizations. Boundarylessness also means that what used to be contained cannot now be contained. Everybody knows your business; everybody wants to know your business.

Two levels of magnitude are important as well: large and really large. What is important for the IdeaManager and IdeaLeader is the intersections of those forces, and the different kinds of ideas are needed.

SPEED AND MAGNITUDE CONFLUENCE AND THE IDEAS THEY REQUIRE

	Speed of Change	
	Fast	Really Fast
Magnitude of Change		
Large	Innovations	Inventions
Really Large	Inventions	Reinventions

As a standard practice, innovations will be constantly needed just to remain competitive. Most organizations do not have a system for producing regular innovations in their ongoing operations. They will experience stress.

But doing what you do better (an innovation) is not enough. Inventions will be required at twice the rate as innovations. Inventions mean doing something different, something you have never done before. In that sense, it is new. The double-rate requirement comes from the ratchet effect: If change is fast and magnitude is big, an innovation can probably handle it. But if either one of them changes—if the magnitude of change increases or if the speed of change increases—then innovations will not suffice. Inventions are needed.

And, of course, if speed and magnitude are at their highest, then transformational ideas—a total reinvention of the enterprise—will be required. Activities in this last cell are what Bob Quinn (1996) of the University of Michigan points to in his book, *Deep Change.*

CONCLUSION

Many organizations will not be able to undertake any of these activities and will die. Others will experience what Quinn calls "slow death." Slow death occurs when organizations know they need to change, they see change coming at them, and they choose (a decision) not to engage the system. This is usually because they have a paucity of ideas; they are conceptually bankrupt, and do not know what actually to do. Terrorized and without innovations, inventions, or reinventions available, they busy themselves "changing the deck captains on the Titanic."

NOTES

1. This pluralism of pressures comes at all levels of the Five Cs.

2. The original expression dealt with going home. In "The Hired Man," Robert Frost says, "Home is the place where, when you go there, they have got to take you in!" (1971, 156).

3. For more on "anytime, anyplace and mass customization," see Davis (1987).

Chapter 3

The Five Cs Theory of IdeaLeadership and IdeaManagement

The signs of the times are, as Chapter 2 suggested, all around us. Ideas, new ideas—information, concepts, theories, proposals—will be the key resource of the twenty-first century. Peter Senge (1990) has talked about the Learning Organization. What he assumes is that there is something to learn. That something is ideas.

IDEAMANAGERS AND IDEALEADERS: WHAT DO THEY DO?

What does it mean to "expand" entrepreneurship to include a focus on ideas? After all, the entrepreneur is a thinker and a doer. The problem is that action—the urge for action, the press for action—can and does drive out thought. Action is capturing! Action excites! We are more likely to get drawn into action without thought as we "Just Do It!" When that happens we slip into rework. Expanding entrepreneurship means emphasizing the idea part of the organizational package. But it means more than this; it means that ideas—as the shapers and molders of action—require their own management, their own leadership. We not only need ideas, we need good ideas.

The Internet is providing us with huge new sources for ideawork. It may not be the information highway, but it sure is the data highway. Getting the data organized into information, the information shaped into concepts and proposals, and sculpting the concepts and proposals into decisions will be the primary work of the twenty-first century manager and leader. He or she will be the IdeaManager or IdeaLeader. Leading and managing these processes is what the leaders and managers of the future will work on.

DATA, INFORMATION, KNOWLEDGE, AND IDEA PARADIGMS

There are a lot of terms that one hears today that relate to the idea of ideas: data, information, organizational knowledge. Peter Senge (1990) talks about the Learning Organization. Some organization of these terms might be helpful.

Data are the simplest of the terms. Data are measurement aggregates—how many sick days have been taken; how many returns. The huge reports that the accounting department often churns out, page after page of tractor-feed printout represent (indeed, are) tons of data. The problem is converting data into information. Indeed, it may be the case that we can have data overload or glut, and information deficit. People mistake data for information. They provide this table and that table. For people who use the World Wide Web to search, there is another example. One can type in "leadership," and ask one of the search engines to find what is out there. It is not uncommon to get several hundred thousand documents popping up. That is a lot of data, but little information. It is physically impossible to go through 300,000 pieces of data to find what you find. That leads us to information.

Information, from my perspective, could be defined as "patterns of data." Central to patterns is the concept of organization. So one looks for a variety of measures around absence (sick days), or a variety of measures around sales (sales per hour, sales per square foot). Readers may have noticed that it requires ideas to convert data into information. If you do not think to ask about sales per square foot, the data may be present but the information is not.

A key concept that is important for data is reliability. Reliability essentially means accuracy, low error rates in the measures. It does not mean that the measures are right, in the sense that they are the right ones for you, nor that they are appropriate. When you are driving in your car, a reliable speedometer will actually read 70 mph when you are going 70 mph. That is reliability.

Indexes are another kind of information. Various statistical and analytical processes are applied to data, combining and recombining data bits to find out what combination of measures is useful, predictive, and economical. In short, validity and reliability matters.

Information is affected by validity. Validity asks if the measure measures what you really want to measure. You can have a lot of reliable data, but the ways in which they are combined into indexes, proportions, and ratios may or may not tell you anything of use.

Knowledge, then, is information which is valid over time. Knowledge has a permanency to it. While not infinite, it certainly has measures that have stood the test of time, that allow for comparison, that seem to explain things.

Notice that the amount of material in each category is decreasing. There is a huge amount of data, much smaller amounts of information, and still smaller amounts of knowledge that results from the information. Ideas are concepts that relate data in ways that provide new information. The reorganized pieces of information produce new knowledge, and that reorganized knowledge becomes innovation and invention. One might think of them as new paradigms.

Paradigms are fundamental patterns of knowledge which are assumed to be true or which are fundamentally unquestioned at a given point in time. There are only a few competing paradigms at any given time, and in most cases one of them is dominant. For example, when somebody says "winning isn't everything, it's the only thing"; that is a paradigm. It may be true or not true, just as knowledge may be true or not true. But it is nonetheless accepted and serves as a fundamental basis for action.

Ideas, then, are concepts which serve functions at each level. One is an intra-level function, the second an inter-level function. Within levels, ideas serve to reorganize and reshape data, information, knowledge, and paradigms. Hence, at the data level, some ideas call forth new kinds of data to be collected, and some call for the cessation of the use of certain kinds of data. At the information level, ideas serve to define new combinations of data and create new kinds of information from existing data. Similarly, at the knowledge level, ideas propose recombinations of information that produce new knowledge. And finally, at the paradigm level, ideas cause a reorganization of knowledge that leads to fundamentally new paradigms and ways of thinking about the ways things "really are."

It is ideas, then, that organize, drive, and reorganize data, information, knowledge, and paradigms into tools which not only represent the environment, they indeed create the environment. In a slower changing environment, discovery probably works well. In an environment that rapidly changes, creation is what is necessary. It is for this reason that ideas, the fundamental creators, are essential to the success and prosperity of the organizations of the twenty-first century.

From Data to Decisions—Part 1: Organizing Data into Information

Ideas, therefore, come in various forms, and are buried in a sea of data to be crystallized and focused as a decision. The IdeaManager and IdeaLeader need to undertake essentially two tasks. One of them is to assure that there is a flow of ideas into the organization—that means a flow of information from external sources keeps coming and coming. In this sense, the concept developed at General Electric of "The Boundaryless Organization" is very apt, because it reduces the barriers to new ideas.

The problem is to organize the information that comes in. Let me give an example.

The Gerontocar

Several years ago I was head of the Institute of Gerontology at the University of Michigan. Our institute did a number of surveys of seniors around things like health and home concerns. As always, though, we asked "Is there anything else?" To this question, many seniors responded that, yes, there was. They did not like their car. Interviewers were programmed to probe for more information, and they did. Senior respondents gave many specific examples. For one thing, the dashboard was a problem. Dials were too small, and they needed something that could be read with trifocals. The interior lights were too dim. They wanted a TV audio channel (so that they could listen to their favorite programs and not be homebound by a TV schedule). Many remembered from their youth that there had been a little knob that stuck up on the steering wheel. They wanted this back. (Of course it would be unsafe; it would have to be redesigned and recessed. What they were telling us is that it is easier to grasp a knob than a wheel if you have arthritis.) Others complained that cars were hard to get into. Several remembered, and mentioned, that there had been a car in the 1950s with a seat that turned around (Chrysler 300) so that you could sit down and then you and the seat could turn to face front. Others did not like the trunk. (Those were the days when the trunk lid attached to a lip; that meant you had to bend over to lift things out of the trunk, and lift them up over the lip. It was a strain on your back.) There were other things: Older women especially complained that they had to use a pillow to sit on. The list goes on. Anyway, an idea struck me. I thought that the university could work in collaboration with the "Big 3" to design a car package especially for seniors that would have these and other features they especially would like. I even had a name for it (friends told me later the name alone was the kiss of death): the Gerontocar! I wrote to the CEOs of the Big 3 and proposed that we all meet, their company and the university, and begin a collaborative project that would, I was sure, result in a useful product and healthy sales. Needless to say, no letters ever came back, and the project wilted.

I am sure that auto companies get thousands of letters every day from folks like me telling them how to build cars. The problem is that some of them are actually good. There needs, therefore, to be a sifting and sorting function, people who put data together with needs. Sifting and sorting will become key organizational processes. Information specialists who know the needs of the organization and can catalog and categorize the blobs of data bobbing around in the boundaryless organization will be continually in demand. Leading and managing functions like this will be part of the job of the IdeaLeader and IdeaManager of the new organization.

From Data to Decisions—Part 2: Shaping Information into Concepts and Proposals

The next step is to create concepts and proposals from the information. Let us say that an information specialist at one of the auto companies notices that there are several pieces of data pointing to a senior market—demographic trends, letters from customers, proposals from crazy professors, and so on. There needs to be IdeaLeadership and IdeaManagement to create the process through which concepts—with better names than Gerontocar—and proposals move into the organization for discussion, consideration, and improvement. Someone has got to take the puck down the ice.

From Data to Decisions—Part 3: Sculpting Concepts and Proposals into Decisions

But concepts and proposals are just that—concepts and proposals. Nothing may happen to them or with them. Many great concepts lie around because they cannot "get" to the next step—the decision. Of course, concepts and proposals do not have "little cat feet," they do not do anything by themselves. They need sponsorship, assistance, and help in getting into the proper councils. Ides about cars for seniors need to be acted upon. And of course one hopes for good decisions and decisions of high quality. IdeaManagers and IdeaLeaders will need skills and systems to help the organization actually take action on proposals before it. And the decisions need to lead to action. One organization I worked with had an important council that used to pretend to act on things. Proposals would be discussed, and then someone would say "Well, let's put this on the list." Everyone would agree, and felt as if something had been done. The list, at one time, had over sixty items on it. Nothing ever happened to anything on the list. They substituted the appearance of action for the reality of action (and were paid six figures each for doing it).

THE FIVE Cs THEORY OF IDEALEADERSHIP AND IDEAMANAGEMENT

The Five Cs Theory of IdeaManagement and IdeaLeadership involves five basic components: *characteristics, competencies, conditions, context,* and *change*. They are all interlinked.

Characteristics points to the individual temperaments required to be an IdeaLeader or IdeaManager. *Competence* suggests that there are certain skills that can be learned and must be practiced. IdeaLeadership is not an accident. There are managers who are good at it, and those who are less good. It is better to be good, and even better to be really good! *Conditions*—within the family, within the firm, within the community—refer to the elements that are favorable to the development of new ideas and the introduction of new products and new services, and the elements that will be in opposition. These are in part given, but they can also be sculpted. There are also *contexts*—larger-scale macroenvironmental forces—that can be similarly favorably disposed toward being supportive of new ideas or not. Though less amenable to influence, these can also be shaped; and aspects of them can be used and exploited. Finally, there is *change*. Change may be of many sorts. In the case of characteristics and competencies, we are creating things by adjusting, adapting, and modifying our own personal repertoire, approaches, and skills to meet different opportunities available in the environment.

In the case of the conditions we are far more likely to be controlling change than creating it. The conditions in the workplace and in the organization are always changing. The difficulty, as we have observed with many of America's large companies, is that the direction of change is frequently negative. Bureaucracy increases. Communication channels and systems become clogged. The process of innovation declines. What is needed, therefore, with respect to conditions is averting negative change directions and developing positive ones.

Finally, with respect to context, it is certainly possible to capitalize on change. Capitalizing on change means adjusting the conditions of your organization; changing your competencies or (to the extent possible) your characteristics to align them with the ever-changing context in which your organization works and in which you live. Such adjustment will prevent failure and may enhance success. Such adjustment involves the perception of the environment, which is always changing. Firms and businesses die. In part, they do so because they are unaware of changes in the context, changes to which they need to adjust.

Tichy and Devanna (1986) talk about this phenomenon as "the boiled frog effect." They point out that if you place a frog in a pan of water over a Bunsen burner and let the temperature of the water rise extremely slowly, ultimately the frog will boil to death. This example is not a pleasant one, but the message is powerful. Slow changes in the environment are just as real as rapid ones. The fact that we cannot recognize them as changes at any particular point in time does not mean that change is not occurring. In fact, it is for this reason, Tichy and Devanna argue, that whole sectors of industry, living in what they call "cultural cocoons"—steel, motorcycles, and consumer electronics are a few—experience the boiled frog effect because they did not recognize the changes in their own business environments.

But capitalizing on change can involve other aspects, as well. The large number of women in the wage-labor force has created a boom for the restaurant and prepared food industries. The increasing number of "chronologically gifted" Americans (those over sixty-five) remains to be exploited by merchants catering to the needs of that particular age group.

These examples can be multiplied many times over. However, the point is that as awareness of context becomes sharpened, opportunities for products and services become clearer. Unexplored niches develop where none existed before. But before new ideas for products and services can be addressed to these evolving markets, their potential must be recognized. It is the recognition of the reconfigurations of context created by change that allows you to capitalize on it.

Each of these elements can favor idea development, but they can also work against it. Some individuals may not have the requisite characteristics or enough of them. Or, they may have the right characteristics but not the competence. Or, the context or the conditions may be negative. You need to look, therefore, not only at the presence of each of these five components, but at their simultaneous interaction. IdeaLeadership and IdeaManagement activity will be at its highest when each of these five elements is in the positive column. Such activity will be at its lowest when each is in the negative column. For the most part, though, there will be a mixture. Thus, a good part of IdeaLeadership and IdeaManagement involves the orchestration of characteristics, competencies, conditions, context, and change.

Many ideas fail. In part, that failure is due to a lack of attention to characteristics, competencies, conditions, context, and change and to a failure to orchestrate these appropriately within a given situation. Many times, even though a new idea has been introduced, a new product or service offered, its possibilities remain largely undeveloped because the conditions were wrong or the context inappropriate. Similarly, businesspersons, managers, or leaders may not get from their employees the kinds of creativity and imagination that are needed. This may have nothing to do with any specific deficiencies on the part of the employees. Instead, it may result when the businesspersons, managers, or leaders themselves do not know how to structure work conditions and context to generate the required productivity. We focus, therefore, on the structure, creation, and management of idea systems and the importance of the concept of IdeaManagement along with the ability to manage innovation and new ideas creatively. One way to orchestrate the Five Cs and help the organization move toward becoming an idea-centered firm is through a Five Cs conference.

THE FIVE Cs CONFERENCE

The conference is geared to a collective, group-oriented process, designed to provide information on each of the Five Cs. It also encourages questions about the ways in which change can be created, controlled, or capitalized on with respect to a particular firm or venture.

Individuals are assigned and are responsible for one of the Five Cs. All individuals prepare a *characteristics assay*. This is a report on their own characteristics and on the kinds of improvements and changes in these characteristics that they can consider making. All individuals prepare a *competencies assay*. In this they outline the competencies that they have developed and suggest areas in which they would like to learn more. The *organizational* or *conditions assay* looks at the culture of the organization and its structure, and asks if the firm has a supportive enough set of values and a flexible enough structure for new ideas to germinate and flourish. Finally, teams are assigned to examine the context from an environmental scan, a *context assay*. This assay focuses on the environmental structure and the kinds of changes and developments in it that are most noticeable, as well as the environmental culture where the beliefs, values, attitudes, and opinions are most prominent (or most characteristic) of a contemporary time. Finally a change team looks at the most powerful currents of changes—changes in the workforce, changes in characteristics (e.g., temperaments of Generation X as opposed to earlier generations), changes in the organization itself, and changes in the needed competencies, and builds a picture of the dynamics of the situation. It also, like the others, looks to needed changes as opposed to existing changes. (Almost every change one discovers means that additional changes are required.)

All this work is done *before* the conference. The conference itself always follows the same three-step process in the same order. At each step, each of the Five Cs is examined, focusing first on facts, second on problems, and third on opportunities. Ideally, though it can be done in less time (as little as a day, if all details are carefully attended to in advance), the conference is organized to take place over a three-day period. For the purposes of this discussion, we assume that you have scheduled it over a three-day period, which really works best.

The conference begins with Day One dedicated to reviewing the contextual facts, conditional facts, competency facts, and characteristic facts, as reported by the assays. Teams and individuals share their particular views of the factual situation. Discussions are limited to the factual situation. Regardless of whether individuals perceive those particular facts as relevant or not, helpful or not, useful or not in subsequent discussions, it is important to begin at that point.

Day Two focuses on problems. These will be problems either with respect to the facts or with respect to gaps in communication and other missing pieces that seem to have caused organizational problems in the past.

Day Three focuses on opportunities. These may come in any of three areas: (1) the needs, as represented by environmental changes; (2) the competencies and characteristics, as represented by the self-reports (individualized personal assays); or (3) the conditions of the organization, as represented by the conditions assay. Given any of these three, it is then possible to reconfigure and reposition the organization to create necessary change at the characteristics and competencies level, to control change at the organizational level, or to capitalize on change in the context.

Usually, the Five Cs Conference will end with a set of plotted new directions for the organization over the next eighteen to twenty-four months. Sometimes, as in very high-speed, high-development industries—computers and computer-related electronic products, for example—a Five Cs Conference might be held as often as every six months because the relevant changes, competencies, conditions, and contexts are in that much flux. In other organizational settings a longer time frame could be developed.

Key Requirements of the Five Cs Conference

There are several requirements that a Five Cs Conference needs to meet for greatest success. IdeaManagers and IdeaLeaders work toward having all of these present. Ten are especially worth mentioning here.

1. *Mind Frame*—A Five Cs Conference requires a different frame of mind from "business as usual" or any other kind of group problem-solving process. In particular, openness to new ideas is imperative. So, too, is the willingness to deal simultaneously (and perhaps sloppily) with all of the ills of the organization at the same time and with all the people present.
2. *Commitment*—A Five Cs Conference requires a willingness to commit time. It does not fit into the business-as-usual mold. A time commitment of several days is usually involved. Provision might be made, therefore, for temporary organizational help to perform the essential services while most members of the organization are at the conference. The procedure we have outlined fills three days and works very well. A shorter or a longer program can also be used.
3. *Mind Float*—A Five Cs Conference requires members to set aside their usual search for "quick fix solutions" or "adequate enough answers." These represent the vein of most organizations. It satisfies us most of the time, and usefully so. Those methods are not sufficient, however, for long-term organizational reconfiguration and repositioning.
4. *Nice, Neutral Facts*—The Five Cs Conference needs individuals to put aside perceptions, explanations, justifications, history, reasons, understandings, lore, and all of the organization's mental activities that explain why the current situation is the best possible. Rather, there needs to be a focus on nice, neutral facts—and facts alone! Judgment must be suspended as to whether these facts are right or wrong, good or bad, brilliant or dumb. Furthermore, one starts by talking about problems, not solutions. In fact, early discussion of solutions is prohibited. All too frequently, leaping from a limited array of facts to a solution forecloses adequate discussion of problems.
5. *Options*—A Five Cs Conference requires commitment to the discussion process at least long enough to come up with two or three better ideas about what is being done or how it is being done as a result of current practice and policy. If nothing emerges, you can always return to business as usual or decide that business as usual is, in fact, the preferred choice. But if this is true, it must be a conscious, proactive selection, not something that occurs just because one did not spend the time to think up anything different.
6. *Suspension of Negative Judgments*—In many organizations (and in families and small teams, for that matter), the power of a negative is strong. Negative comments on an idea often generate defensive reactions. This can cause the scenario of overcommitment and collapse. In the Five Cs Conference, therefore, negative judgments are suspended as much as possible. Such suspension is necessary because of this defensiveness. The energies of the participants are focused automatically on solutions rather than on problems. Negativism is a line of least resistance—a passive process—that nine times out of ten generates a destructive

outcome. Little thought or involvement is required to engage in condemnation. Instead, a positive climate is fostered. In a positive atmosphere, ways in which ideas can be used rather than what is wrong with them can be explored. Positivism requires special effort—a virtual active process—that is dedicated to the generation of constructive outcomes. Much thought and considerable involvement are required to cast circumstances in a positive mode.

7. *Ambiguity Tolerance*—A Five Cs Conference requires a willingness to live with ambiguity and uneasiness. These are the inevitable results of standing back, looking at what we do, and questioning it. Particular uneasiness comes from the discomfort of a question rather than the comfort of an answer. Our natural tendency is to take any answer as the answer, thereby bringing an end to the examination of further alternatives. Not having an answer, even for a short time, is very discomforting for most people. When we have an answer, we do not have to live with the discomfort of having a problem. Quick-fix, short-term solutions may be stimulated, in part, less by bottom-line concerns than by the psychological pressure to reduce ambiguity and to come with a decision, any decision, that appears to solve the problem or resolve the issue. To avoid this, individuals have to be convinced to live with ambiguity. That is not easy. There is no really good way. A step in the right direction, however, is to tell people in advance that (1) the situation will be ambiguous and (2) that such ambiguity is okay. Indeed, because one person's ambiguity is another person's excitement, you can try to refocus the group's processes on the positive aspects of ambiguity: the openness that it implies and requires and the fun that it can generate.
8. *Presence of Confidence*—The problem with asking questions is that one may not know the answers. It is often better, therefore, to follow the sage advice, "don't ask." Unfortunately, such a strategy contains a dangerous precedent. If we do not ask, if we do not inquire, we will never be stimulated to think of things that are different or better—things that are improvements on what we have. Some managers lack confidence in the group's ability to generate possible answers. In situations of uncertainty and ambiguity, you *must* have confidence that answers will emerge to the questions. A particular answer may not be the answer, but at least it will be a good one.
9. *The Natural Superiority of Teams*—In addition to confidence in the answers the questioning process generates, you must have confidence in the natural superiority of teams. You need the conviction that teams, working together, challenging questions, debating, constructively disputing, can emerge with higher-quality perspectives and decisions than individuals can themselves.
10. *Challenge Existing Assumptions and Presuppositions*—Most organizations are full of lore about why things happen, what the organization or societal forces are that make that an absolute certainty, and why nothing can ever be changed anyway. In consulting with organizations, I have often been impressed with the positive certainty with which organizational lore is shared. The face that it is lore seems to escape the comprehension of the individuals sharing it. The following exercise illustrates the point. Consider the following phrase:

The Friendly Fellows, men and women of distinction, and of great competence, filed scientific reports frequently and faithfully.

Scan that sentence for ten seconds. Count the Fs. Check your work. Here is the answer: The Friendly Fellows, men and women oF great distinction and oF great competence, Filed ScientiFic reports Frequently and FaithFully. There are nine Fs. Seven sound like F and two are "ofs." If you did not get it right, do not worry. The accuracy rate on this little quiz runs about 20 percent in groups I have worked with. So the next time someone says such and such is true, challenge them in a diplomatic way. Ideas get stuck, and we become attached to them.

Potential Benefits of a Five Cs Conference

Going through this process on a regular basis has a number of potential benefits. The following are seven of them.

1. *A Broad Picture*—A broader picture of what the organization is doing emerges from the Five Cs Conference than can be obtained from the usual "one-at-a-time" assessments common in most firms, where one issue is examined independently of or differently from the whole.
2. *Common Perception*—Because everyone is in a room together, the Five Cs Conference opens up the factual base for assessment and presents the challenge to everyone. All too frequently, organizations fail because one individual knows something and another individual knows something else, each piece of information crucial to the other, and they are not sharing. Still other individuals may know other sets of facts. There is no real opportunity for everyone to get together and share all their perceptions. Working together allows all the facets to be presented, explored, and challenged.
3. *Sharing Identification*—Everyone being in the room together creates a sense of common fate and community. It increases the likelihood of generating common practical suggestions that can lead to success.
4. *New Resources*—If a common problem focus develops, a common sense of the resources needed and available also emerges. Gone is the common refrain, "I need more cash," and in its place can emerge a sense of the creative potential already present in the existing staff.
5. *Specificity*—Specific, measureable ways to assess results also are needed. These frequently emerge from a Five Cs Conference. As one example, short-term and longer-term tradeoffs can be explored.
6. *A Range of Options*—An additional important benefit of the Five Cs Conference is that a range of options is developed. Though ultimately one is selected, the provision of a range insures the greater likelihood that the ultimate decision is a good one. Furthermore, the unselected options may be useful at a later date or for other units in the organization, or they can be called in when the environment changes. Consequently, the Five Cs Conference generates a veritable stable of ideas and approaches.
7. *Team Building*—Bringing people together creates a sense of team building, what Akio Morita (1987) called a "family feeling" among the staff. This sense of common commitment to a shared purpose will pay off well in terms of the accomplishment of any tasks that are later decided on and any goals that are to be developed and implemented.

In summary, the Five Cs Conference has some requisites and some benefits. Sometimes a facilitator—a guide who knows the Five Cs ropes—is useful in order to help put this whole package together. Other times, regular staff can be involved. The Five Cs Conference provides an exceptionally valuable total look at what a business is doing, where it might go, and what problems it might be having. It is this look that is the essential feature and virtue of the Five Cs Conference. It permits a combined look, focusing on facts and all of the components of the organizational matrix, not just the consideration of one or another set of ideas. From this point of view, you should not be hesitant to undertake such a conference without facilitation. What matters is that the time is set aside, preparation is undertaken, and people have a frank and open discussion using the three-step method. It is a recipe for success.

THE CONCERT OF COMPONENTS

American society is very individualistic. This is common knowledge. We also tend to emphasize—and this is odd—ascribed rather than achieved statuses. This is a little different wrinkle on the individualistic theme, but an important one. Illustrative of this is a common answer to a common question. Here is the exchange, between parent and child:

Parent: Johnny does so well in school; Why is that?

Child: Johnny is so smart.

We have all been through many discussions like this. But think for a moment about that answer: smart. "Smart" is an internal quality or characteristic, almost a given. Almost no child replies, "Because Johnny works like a dog!" Smart, individualistic, internalistic. In places of business, when employees are asked why Frank has so many ideas, they reply, just like the child, "Because Frank is so creative, individualistic, internalistic." There is no "Frank works at it," or "Frank works in a unit which supports his work," or "Frank is close to the customer." No, it is "Frank is creative." Individualization and internalization have two very bad sequalae. One is that they push our attention to the person to the exclusion of the system; two, they mean that we, as speakers, are removed from any obligation. Since Johnny is smart, he gets good grades (and the unspoken, but very real, "and I am not that smart therefore you can't expect me to get good grades," or the equally unspoken, and equally powerful message, "and I am not as creative as Frank so do not expect me to give you what he gives you"). There is no doubt that characteristics are important. But so are competencies, conditions, context, and change. IdeaManagers and IdeaLeaders need to create a balance. That is where the concert of components comes in.

Overemphasis on characteristics leads to ignoring the other elements in the

Five Cs scheme. This in turn leads to a limited and blunted perspective of what is needed for organizational success. The IdeaManager and IdeaLeader not only need to develop the elements in each of the vectors but to develop them simultaneously so that each articulates with the other. It does little good to develop specific business strategy plans, for example, when the context is changing rapidly in the area in question. A more flexible strategy is needed. All the competencies in the world will not help if the conditions of work are not developed and structured in such a way as to make innovation productive.

Of the Five Cs, two—characteristics and context—are less able to be influenced than others. Even with these, however, there are ways you can be proactive. With respect to characteristics, you can seek to inventory your characteristics. There are books and programs that can help you think more creatively, tolerate ambiguity a bit more, and so on. Similarly, there are ways to take advantage of, if not change, the context. Little attention is paid to the need for bringing all these components together in concert. There are certainly ways to make this happen. One of the most effective is the Concert of Components Conference.

The Concert of Components Conference

In this conference, IdeaManagers and IdeaLeaders schedule a day or a half day for themselves and their staffs (and here I mean all staff, not just professional staff) to review their ventures in light of the Five Cs Conference decisions. Staff are assigned to review progress (one each if there are five staff members) and asked to research and present the area. Others challenge. The day is spent looking at characteristics, competencies, conditions, contexts, and change with respect to the particular firm in question. The norms or rules of the game for the conference are that problems and positives are brought up, both to continue the positives and to learn from the problems (or failures). You may think of this conference as a kind of "mid-course" correction conference. It supplements the Five Cs Conference in that it looks at progress and integration while retaining a proactive (rather than a reactive) posture.

In preparation for this conference, staff members are asked to make suggestions at any point throughout the Five Cs plan period. One staff participant has the job of Five Cs Coordinator. That individual receives suggestions and comments and helps in the specific planning of the conference. This assures that ideas and topics that people think about throughout the year are not lost. They are kept and organized by the coordinator, who distributes packages of assignments and issues to the individual staff members or staff teams as the time for the conference nears.

How it is actually organized is of less importance then the fact that at least every six months—and once a quarter in turbulent, high-growth sectors—time is spent in proactive assessment. That investment will pay off well, not only in profits but in satisfaction and pride in the organization itself. All too often IdeaManagers and IdeaLeaders become successful and then fail to see the problems lying in their path. In the December 12, 1986 issue of the *Wall Street Journal*, Allen Michaels comments on the prelude to the failure of his firm, Convergent Technologies, Inc.: "Yes, it was heady. In retrospect I can see what was happening; a guy who always questioned what he did, who wanted to sleep on decisions suddenly began to believe that all his decisions were right—because they were his. The normal apprehension that goes with decision making gave way to the dangerous conviction that we were always right. In fact, invincible" (p. 26). Though there is no guarantee that the Five Cs Conference and the Concert of Components Conference will prevent things like this from happening, they most assuredly give the firm a better chance than the usual ways.

One of two perspectives is usually associated with writings about management and leadership. The first emphasizes the individual personality (*Five Traits That Lead to Success*). The second emphasizes environment (*Anyone Can Make Money in Real Estate*). Neither takes in the kinds of competencies and conditions that IdeaManagers and IdeaLeaders need to make a venture successful. Neither deals with ways existing firms can become more organizational. We have suggested that the Five Cs perspective takes in more of the variables that need attention. These are (1) characteristics of you, the entrepreneur; (2) competencies of you, the IdeaManager and IdeaLeader; (3) conditions of the organization you develop; (4) the context in which you and the organization live and work; and (5) the changes that are affecting the other four.

Each of these elements—the *Organizational Quintet*—needs to be in place and attended to if you are to achieve success. You may not fail right away if any of the Five Cs are ignored, but the weakness of inattention builds up. Problems appear. The balanced (and successful) organizational leader keeps an eye at all times on each of the Five Cs. He or she will move among them, always working on the one that is least developed at any moment in time. The Five Cs Conference is the key to monitoring the strength and weakness of each part of the firm. The purpose of the conference is threefold:

1. To insure attention to the Five Cs on a regular basis.
2. To involve the whole organization in those considerations (because it is the whole organization that must work together to make the adjustments that are necessary to keep current).
3. To create an articulation of components such that all are considered together, at the same place and time, by the relevant people. Otherwise there will not be the kind of commonality needed to effect change.

In addition to the Five Cs Conference, the Concert of Components Conference is an extremely valuable tool for achieving balance among the components.

CONCLUSION

The idea-driven organization has to think of itself in that way, and create processes to get there. Doing things the same old way, or even thinking that the same old resources will have the same old meaning, will be less than successful in the twenty-first century. But there are problems. Part II outlines some of the more common problems, in the hope that readers, recognizing them, can avoid them.

PART II

The Fatal Glass of Beer

Given the importance of ideas, their structure, and management, something of a no brainer in today's world, what makes them so hard to introduce and why are they resisted so strongly when they are suggested? One would think that all organizations would be devoting part of their resources to idea management. But of course we know that is not so. There are a lot of reasons why these difficulties exist, but they fall mainly into three sets. One is practical: We do not know much about the process of idea processing and changing. We know more, perhaps most, about materials processing and changing, a bit about people processing and a bit less about people changing, and least about idea processing and changing.

To this set of problems two more need to be added. New ideas are destructive of old ideas. Indeed, that is their main virtue. However, old ideas create attachments, and while organizations dislike the discomfort of the new, they abhor the destruction of the old. Hence, a blizzard of opposition.

Third, new ideas embody, and actually become, decisions that reallocate goods and values in the system. Somebody gets the car phone; somebody else gets the car phony (just an aerial you can put on your car, and an empty plastic phone shell with a cord attached—you can pretend you are on your car phone even if you do not really have one). New ideas also destroy relationships based on the old allocation of goods and values. Again, organizations abhor this destruction, and oppose the new. The three chapters in this section address these three kinds of problems.

Chapter 4

Pernicious Procedures: Problems of Processing New Ideas

In thinking over a strategy of change, the late Ron Lippitt, with Watson and Westley (1958), talked about change forces and resistance forces—those that promote and support new products and services and those that caution and sometimes rage against the introduction of the new and the different. Resistance forces are legion. Galbraith (1982) writes, "New ideas are never neutral. Innovative ideas are destructive; they destroy investments in capital equipment and peoples' careers. The management of ideas is a political process. The problem is that the political struggle is biased toward those in the establishment who have authority and control of resources" (p. 11).

A REPERTOIRE OF RESISTANCES

Tom Fitzgerald (1987), an organizational consultant and former GM manager, summarized what some of them can be:

- inability to plug into the change system
- the difficulty of linking microactions to macrogoals
- social distance of management over worker
- protection from the need to change
- vested interests
- self-comforting patterns in organizations
- control as a key value

- self-cloning techniques in organizations
- lack of understanding about the true and important mechanisms of change

To these, as related but independent factors, I add the following:

- lack of conceptual energy
- the inertia of institutions

What do these mean? A little detail might help us.

Inability to Plug into the Change System

In many organizations employees at all levels of the firm's hierarchy are job oriented rather than work oriented. They tend to identify their tasks with some version of the job description, usually the more specific and concrete aspects of that job description. And management expects them to be job oriented ("If I want an idea from you, I'll give you one!"). As such, they have no influence on the change system, cannot change the job they are doing (even if they have perfectly good ideas about how to change it), and are stuck.

In the Red Beads experiment, developed by W. E. Deming (1986), this exact problem arises. Five workers are assigned to make white beads. They have a scoop and a tray of 1,000 beads, of which 200 are red (a supplier problem). When I saw Deming do this, he specifically instructed the workers how they were to do their job: Insert the scoop, lift, shake excess beads off (they fell in little indentations in the scoop), and present the scoop for checking. They could not change the structure of work in any way (e.g., to have three workers scooping and two workers reorganizing the beads in the box). It was clear to the audience that there were a lot of things the workers could have done to be more efficient, even given the 200 red beads already there, but they were prohibited from taking any action whatsoever.

The Difficulty of Linking Microchanges to Macrogoals

Change is also resisted because it is hard to link microactions to big goals. Rosabeth Kanter (1983) makes the point that this link is important. Looking at the problems of their whole organization, workers have a hard time feeling that what they do would make any difference, even if they could change things. As one worker told me, "After all, what can just one person do?"

Protection from the Need to Change

I recently saw a cartoon involving two men talking in an office. The office had a cushy appearance. One of the men was saying, "Of course it's cozy in here Hoskins; we are insulated by layers of bureaucracy!" (Frank Cotham, in *The New Yorker*, 17 March 1997, 82). Both management and worker are often protected from the need to change. Management is too far away from the problems, so often does not think there are any problems. An auto plant executive from Flint, Michigan, said to me not that long ago, "I think the Japanese car thing is really overrated. Look out there; do you see many Japanese cars?" It was, of course, his own parking lot! (No wonder Ross Perot proposed to move GM headquarters out of Detroit.)

Workers are protected from the need to change because nothing they do really matters. If they are excellent workers or poor workers, the pay is the same or very close. They either do not have performance appraisals or the appraisals are personalistic and problematic. No wonder stability looks good.

Social Distance of Management over Worker

Then there is the "social question." Despite the fact that management and workers need to cooperate in the achievement of more successful products and services, social distance between workers and management creates problems in achieving this goal. In American society we receive status by association. That is why we "dress up" when we go to work. Interacting across social boundaries has a number of special problems associated with it when one is talking about organizational change and the introduction of new ideas. The new operation or procedure carries with it a social baggage. If a worker suggests something to a manager, the social structure of that communication makes it less likely that the manager will accept it. Similarly, communication going the other way carries the negatives of authority and office. Workers are, as a result, more inclined to reject managers' suggestions.

Vested Interests

In addition to not being able to change much, workers at all levels have vested interests. Though almost all of us have such interests, most of us fail to see the extent of our own involvements. We mask actions that advance our own personal interests justifying them as being necessary in some larger, impersonal sense. These kinds of justifications are made for the very high salaries of corporate executives by those who will receive the salaries. Thus, our own ability to deny that our interests are self-serving further compounds the problem. As Robert Myers, Canadian author and consultant told me once, "Nobody goes in to be fired who doesn't believe she or he is being promoted." Arguments against a new product or service are therefore likely to be couched in terms that make it seem as if it is wise and sound for the organization to avoid investments and risks in these areas. The fact that such investments and risks may have profound negative consequences for the individual making the argument is set aside as an incidental grace note. In this way, individuals are protected from the need to change. For many persons, organizational structure serves much the same function as the shell does for the turtle: It protects the individual from the slings and arrows of outrageous fortune. In part, at least, this protection is to the good. If you are living on adrenaline's edge all the time, the likelihood of making innovative and imaginative new contributions is surely lessened. On the other hand, overprotection is as much of a danger as underprotection. In both cases, you fail to experience sufficient outside stimulation to motivate change, adaptation, and advancement as an organization grows in size. Self-confirming styles emerge, fueled by the self-fulfilling prophecy.

Self-Comforting Patterns in Organizations

The self-fulfilling prophecy, a well-known self-comforting organizational (and personal) pattern, begins with a statement or belief about the condition of the world, which at the time it is made is neither true nor false. Statements such as "We can never penetrate that market," "I can never stop smoking," or "I can't do anything with my teenage son" are typical examples. The person who utters such statements then begins to act as *if* the statements were true. Because market penetration "cannot" be established, no efforts are made to do so. Because the drinking or smoking behavior "cannot" be stopped, no efforts are made to stop it. Because truculent, recalcitrant sons "cannot" be handled, they are not handled. Indeed, it is not unusual for efforts of a contrary nature to be taken: "I wash my hands of the whole affair." Often the result of these activities is the very event that was feared in the first place. In other words, though nothing was necessarily true at the beginning of this intellectual scenario, as the individual begins to believe that a certain thing is true, he or she acts as if it were true. This in turn creates the reality, and the last step in the self-fulfilling prophecy takes place. The market penetration has not been achieved, drinking and smoking have not been controlled, the offspring's behavior has not been altered. The observer uses these results as proof that his or her original suppositions were correct.

In a nutshell, the self-fulfilling prophecy is a reality creating and confirming procedure. With it we create those things we believe to be true and use that creation as proof that we were right in the first place. Members of organizations engage in this behavior both in their personal lives and in their organizational lives. But entire organizations can engage in self-fulfilling prophecy. No one wants small cars. Therefore, small cars are not made. The few that are introduced do not sell well. Based on the assumption that no one really wants them anyway, they are badly manufactured and poorly appointed. After people take a look at them, no one *does* want them! Those who predicted that result in the first place are self-comforted and self-confirmed.

Control Is a Deep American Value

Change is also resisted because control is such a deep value in American society. Control is important because it represents the other side of freedom. In a society that is as open as the American society, in a society that has as many opportunities as American society has, there are a number of problematic aspects that go along with that openness. Manfred DeVries (1985) wrote a piece called "The Dark Side of Entrepreneurship." In a sense, control may be thought of as the dark side of freedom. All of the openness and opportunity in American society generates anxiety. It creates uncertainty. That is probably why *The Gong Show* is so quintessentially American: There is always opportunity to go up, to improve, but there is also opportunity to go down, to fail at any moment you might be "gonged." It follows, therefore, that the antidote to uncertainty and anxiety is control. The social structure of our society makes change in organizations difficult, because having once established a certain amount of control, some amount of certainty within their life space, individuals are loath to reject it.

Organizational Cloning

Organizations tend to reproduce themselves. Armies are always preparing for the "last" war. Units and subunits are set up like the parent unit. Field offices are structured in a similar way. It is often thought that what has worked in one setting, in one instance, in one time period, for one problem, or with one kind of employee mix, will work again in other sites, with other employees, and so on. Hence, new ideas, as introduced through new organizational forms, tend to be rejected by organizations and firms.

The True Mechanisms of Change

Organizations also miss the true and important mechanisms of change. Simply put, these are people. People at all levels of the organization have ideas and, if the structure is right, will contribute that wisdom. When the structure is not right, organizations fail to use that inherent creativity.

A Lack of Conceptual Energy

Many firms have a lack of conceptual energy, or the excitement and fun of new ideas flowing around, being considered, being tried, being improved, being rejected, and so on. The climate and culture of the organization, therefore, becomes a problem for the introduction of new ideas simply because of what might be called "the inertia of institutions." This inertia is both structural and intellectual in nature. Old structures, old ways of doing things, and old equipment all represent one aspect of organizational inertia.

Inertia

A second and, perhaps, less obvious form of inertia is embodied by old ideas, old assumptions, and old precepts captured in concrete in some organizational lore. Overcoming this inertia is one of the more important tasks of the entrepreneur. This is true whether the entrepreneur is already in an organization and seeking to change it, or seeking to change an interorganizational team participation which he or she must depend on for supplies, equipment, capital, personnel, and so on, in order to do business.

These ideas create a repertoire of resistances which mean that the very process of idea generation and processing is likely to be cut off at the knees. It is not something people intend; actually, it is just the way the organizational system works. The IdeaManager and IdeaLeader of the future will need to address these impediments in order to free up the organization's ability to innovate, invent, and reinvent. The bad news, though, is that those actions will not be sufficient. Apart from the general resistances delivered by the organizational and social structure itself, there are other, more mundane problems which deal with the processing of ideas themselves.

PROBLEMS OF IDEA PROCESSING

There are a number of difficulties with ideas generally and new ideas specifically that relate to the way they are handled within the organization. Some of the most common are the following:

- No Good Way to Assess New Ideas
- Organizational Ghosts
- The Polarization Problem
- The Politics of Acceptance or Rejection
- Erroneous Acceptance or Rejection

No Good Way to Assess New Ideas

One problem with new ideas is that they are hard to judge. It is fairly common practice among employees in firms that use the "suggestion box" to espouse the belief that the box is mounted firmly atop a chute leading directly to the furnace (or paper shredder or wastebasket). Despite the truth behind such suspicions, the new idea is actually a bountiful commodity. The real problem is that we do not have any good way in most organizations to take a look at possible new products or services. In fact, it is the intransigence of most existing firms to new ideas that leads to the development of many ideas outside the organization. It is for this reason writers talk of the need for product or organizational champions who follow up new ideas and approaches personally (Daft & Bradshaw, 1980).

Organizational Ghosts

New ideas clash with old ideas. This problem is part of the vested interest difficulty that Galbraith (1982) noted and Fitzgerald (1987) mentioned in a somewhat different guise. The new approach, the new product, the new service not only displaces old products and services, it displaces old ideas about what the company is, what the organization is about, and what its mission and purpose has been historically. The organizational priests tend to oppose new ideas, not on grounds that those ideas will not be productive or profitable, but that they are somehow in violation of the rules and rituals of "what we are." Old ideas represent the "ghost in the machine," ready to haunt those who strive to introduce something new. They trap us in ways we do not even understand in the same way that old routines imprison us.

The Polarization Problem

Because effective mechanisms do not exist in most organizations for assessing new ideas, and because some form of vested interests resists their introduction, new ideas often get polarized into a "them or us" mode within the organizational structure. It is this either/or dilemma that Fisher and Ury warn against in their book, *Getting to Yes* (1981). Though John Naisbitt (1982, 1990) sees us moving from an "either/or society to a multiple option society," polarization is still a major difficulty.

A typical scenario involves someone in the organization introducing a new idea. Naturally, because the idea is new the organizational environment is a somewhat hostile environment. Now the problem begins. It starts with the natural vulnerability of the new idea.

There are several features of new ideas that make them vulnerable initially. To begin with, they are fledgling and incomplete, with parts missing. Because they are new, new ideas do not have thoroughly worked-out answers to all the problems that individuals reviewing them may see. This leaves them more open to attack than standard operating procedures.

New ideas are often working in uncharted territory. It is for this reason that market research is not always the best guide. Indeed, at any given moment in time a market may not exist for a particular product or service and will not until the product or service is introduced.

Because individual workers and managers do not know how to respond to these problems, they tend to adopt traditional modes, images, and methods of assessment—comfortable postures and conventional comparisons. In a new idea conference, the flaws and vulnerabilities of a new idea are used as a point of attack by opponents.

Attempts to deal with these attacks may—and often do—lead to exaggerated claims by the one who introduces the idea. The proponent is committed to the idea; obviously, he or she thought it up. Criticism sounds like an attack—and it often is an attack. And because it is a new product or service, the proponent cannot prove that all of the concerns raised by opponents are invalid. Some may be viewed as correct. Counterassertions tend to be made, and once this scenario has begun to develop a spiral of attack and response is difficult to stop. Each phase contains more exaggeration: "The proposed product is awful" versus "The proposed product is great."

Clever—even sinister—opponents of new ideas exploit these exaggerated claims as a next step and propose tests or assessments based particularly on them. The exaggerated claims are now likely to prove false, which in turn may lead to the whole idea being rejected erroneously. Keep in mind that the failure of the claims for innovation does not necessarily mean that the idea is wrong, any more than their acceptance proves that an idea was right.

The Politics of Acceptance or Rejection

In general, ideas for new products and services are either inappropriate or appropriate, wrong or right. Their quality of correctness or their merit, however, does not necessarily insure their appropriate rejection or acceptance. Politics play a part. In the best of all possible worlds, poor ideas are always rejected and good ones are always accepted. In the world we live in, that is not always the case. Instead, acceptance or rejection is often controlled by one of two pernicious errors that cloud the business mind—and that IdeaManagers and IdeaLeaders must seek mightily to avoid. These errors are (and this should come as no surprise) the *acceptance error*, as a result of which ideas are accepted for reasons other than merit, and the *rejection error*, as a result of which ideas are rejected for reasons other than merit. Though these errors are endemic to both established and new enterprises, the rejection error is the more common of the two. Ideas for new products and services should be rejected because they are silly, stupid, impractical, too expensive to implement, too far ahead of their time, or for any number of good and sufficient reasons. The rejection error comes into play when such ideas are rejected because they conflict with old ideas (or company policy), because some corporate priest finds them offensive to his or her cherished beliefs, or for any of the reasons Tom Fitzgerald (1987) outlined. The power of negative thinking is strongly and destructively at work when the rejection error occurs.

The acceptance error is less recognized but still very much present. We also call it "the same old stuff" error. It occurs especially when ideas for programs, products, services, or plans are accepted because of the prestige, importance, and clout of the individual presenting them without particular regard for the merit of the ideas. This error is even more likely to occur in a new and emerging organizational venture because of the solo concept of the entrepreneur. Frequently, individuals with good new ideas work alone. When their ideas are attacked, they will often adopt a "mountain man" strategy (i.e., retreat to some high ground and fight off all of the opponents). Such a defensive, reactive approach has historically proved to be far less effective than an offensive, proactive one: moving into the environment and developing allies who can assist in overcoming negative thinking and who can help secure rejection of bad ideas and acceptance of good ones.

Erroneous Acceptance or Rejection

There are four possible outcomes to the presentation of new ideas: (1) correct acceptance, (2) erroneous acceptance, (3) erroneous rejection, and (4) correct rejection. These four outcomes are outlined in the following chart:

Idea or Proposal Outcomes

IDEA	**Good**	**Bad**
Accept	Correct Acceptance (1)	Erroneous Acceptance (2)
Reject	Erroneous Rejection (3)	Correct Rejection (4)

As can be seen, two elements are involved. The first is the quality of a new idea or proposal. For simplicity's sake, let us assume the quality can be a good quality or a bad quality. The second aspect is what the organization does with the idea or proposal. Here, once again, let us simplify so that the organization can either accept or reject the idea or proposal. Clearly, along the diagonal in the chart, the set of correct responses exists. If an idea is good, then the organization should accept it. We call that *correct acceptance*, and it is located in Cell 1 of the chart. Similarly, if an idea is bad, it should be rejected by the organization. That cell is identified as Cell 4 on the chart. Two other outcomes, however, are also possible. First, and probably the less dangerous of the two, is when a good idea is rejected. That occurs in Cell 2 on the chart, and is called *erroneous rejection*. Examples of erroneous rejection might be a drug that would be effective for a particular condition but is not accepted by the drug companies for whatever reason (faulty testing, inaccurate measurement, etc.). These are missed opportunities in organizational life. They are difficult to assess because we can never know what it would have been like had the opportunity been fully exploited. Only over a long period of time, as organizational vitality is sapped, competitiveness drained, and organizational fat builds up can we begin to sense that there may well have been a sequence of missed opportunities.

More immediately damaging to organizational activities, however, and an area that organizations try to avoid at all costs, is the outcome in Cell 2: the *erroneous acceptance* of an idea or a proposal that is truly rotten, and should have been rejected for a variety of reasons. But the idea is accepted and, what is worse, it is sometimes continued for years. For a drug company this might be the case where a harmful drug was introduced into general use. The horrors of Thalidomide, for example, represent one example.

CONCLUSION

There are many reasons why ideas destroy the current paradigms, even if they are small, local paradigms. These are problems of process. They are significant problems but not the only ones. Two other kinds of problems—corrosive concepts and dangerous decisions—also become important.

Chapter 5

Corrosive Concepts: Drilling Holes in the Boat

Corrosive concepts—drilling holes in the boat—are ways in which organizations and people in organizations destroy new ideas. Mostly, these are observations, suggestions, comments, or remarks that occur in team meetings when new ideas are being discussed. They can be formal team meetings, or the kinds of hallway conversation in which someone says, "What do you think of this?" You will recognize these common phrases and commentaries. What might be surprising is how noxious they are, how acidic, made even more harmful and poisonous by their apparent innocuous nature. When you hear these phrases, watch out.

NOT INVENTED HERE (NIH)

A seemingly simple expression of reliance on what and whom we know, NIH means that if someone else has thought of it, it cannot really be that good, or even any good. It is the exact opposite of "benchmarking." Often others do something, have some idea that is wonderful and, as you hear it, see it, and taste it, you feel that you would like to do that or could do that. Indeed, it often seems that it could be improved upon. Recipes are this way. A dish enjoyed at a neighbor's house is brought home and improved. That is progress.

What a different point of view it would be if we said, "Well, since we had that dish at the Jones's we cannot have it here. That is that!" How odd, and how limiting. But those are the kinds of things that go on in organizations all the time. "Our way" (read, the sacred way, the right way, the only way) also means "not their way." It is much easier if "their" is a minority organization, a country we hate, people whom we distrust, or the like.

Indeed, organizations that are "second to market" often improve the product over those who have been "first to market." But to take the view that if they did it, it is not only something we should not do, it is something we would be wrong to do or punished for doing, is the NIH perspective. NIH means that everyone has to reinvent the wheel. What a waste.

WE HAVE TRIED THIS BEFORE (WHTTB)

Who among us has not experienced this withering comment. An idea, however humble, is suggested at a team meeting. Someone with a lot of historical stature in the organization says, "We have tried this before," and lets his or her voice trail off. Unsaid, but understood, is the rest of the sentence: "And it did not work then and it will not work now and you are a fool for suggesting it and an even greater fool for not knowing that we tried this before and why we keep you around here is a mystery not only to me but to all of us at this table so why don't you just shut up and listen to your betters [me] and perhaps you will learn something if you are not summarily dismissed for making such a stupid suggestion." It is amazing how much can be said in such a few words. WHTTB is a code, really, for a perspective that is hostile to new ideas, even if they are from the past.

Clearly, as one looks from a distance, the fact that "something like what I am suggesting" has been tried before would not prevent a fresh look. After all, at the very least the times were different. Even if a strategy (or whatever) were exactly the same as something previous, in a different environment it could be successful. But the WHTTB perspective is not really thinking along those lines. It does not like the new, and will use whatever challenge might seem at the moment to be lethal.

WHAT ARE OTHERS DOING? (WAOD)

What Are Others Doing? sounds the death knell to innovation. Actually, when spoken, especially by a skilled idea saboteur, it sounds so very reasonable, so very prudent. Here is Peter Postit coming in with his idea to George Glutite, CEO of the fabulously successful (so far) Stikittoem, a coatings firm which makes all kinds of bonding and adhesives.

Peter: This idea has great potential, George. Folks could stick notes onto a page without doing so permanently.

George: Let's see, Peter . . . you have this idea of sticky papers, papers that would come off a page. (The sarcastic aside, uttered sotto voce: Of course you realize that we make our money producing things that actually stick, but I will not stress that point.) But seriously, Peter, what about paper clips?

Peter: Paper clips mean that you have to have clips with you; here we have the semisticky stuff right on the paper. Besides, we would make it in many sizes and colors so folks could pick exactly what they need—

George: (Interrupting) For God's sake Peter, where is your head? Do we want to undercut our own market? Besides (and here comes the unkindest cut of all), what are others doing? I have not heard a whisper of anything like this. I want to be the edge of the envelope. I want to make glue for the edge of the envelope. I do not want us to be at the bottom of the mailbox (here comes another snide comment), having fallen off!

Peter: But that is just the point—or a point—we could be first to market, we could corner the market.

George: Peter, you sound like those students who say what we loose on each unit we will make up in volume. Now I have work to do. If you hear of others doing this let me know. Perhaps then we can look into it.

Peter was crushed. He left the office, and shortly thereafter Stikittoem itself, and went with a small, innovative company called AAA (Alaska's Amazing Adhesives). He, and they, were quite successful. In a way, he stuckittoem!

TAKING NAMES AND KICKING ASS (TNKA)

TNKA is a favorite concept of my colleague Noel Tichy (1997), of the University of Michigan. He argues that employers usually return to it from whatever forays they have undertaken, as surely as the swallows return to Capistrano or, perhaps more apt, the vultures return to Findlay, Ohio. This approach looks to place blame on those who's ideas may not have been successful. It is a classic American ploy. We are so fault oriented as a country that when something goes wrong (much less often when something goes right), we seek to find out who was responsible (taking names) and fire them (kicking ass). Never mind that success has a thousand fathers—defeat has only one or two, and we will root them out and dismiss them. It is a perversion of Deming's (1986) idea that we find the root cause. For Deming, root causes were systems problems. For many executives, root causes are people to blame, and ax.

TNKA has three problems. It is not only a quick fix, it is a shallow fix. Most problems have precipitating and predisposing causes. (The predisposing cause is Aristotle's way of looking at the "root" cause.) TNKA looks only at the precipitating cause. Problem two is that it give the appearance of a solution. Hence, the "real" problem continues to fester away, developing into something more lethal.

Most important for our purposes, however, is problem three: the chilling effect. Nothing stifles the development and introduction of new ideas further than the pervasive fear that you will be singled out for some misstep and canned. Actually, it is worse than *only* being canned: You are embarrassed, ridiculed, and then canned! The boss wants not only to find a victim, but to blame the victim as well (then no blame can stick on him or her) (Ryan, 1971). TNKA turns employees into turtles.

IF I WANT AN IDEA FROM YOU I WILL GIVE YOU ONE, OR JUST SHUT UP (SU)

SU occurs when the boss does not want to be bothered with anything you have to say, or feels that he or she knows it all. Under these conditions, employees are understandably reluctant to voice observations and suggestions. Indeed, this reluctance can have disastrous consequences. Organizational sociologist Charles Perrow has pointed out in his study of marine accidents that many occur while everyone was on the bridge watching the boat head toward the rocks. Subalterns were fearful of saying to the captain, "Uh, Sir, there is a shore coming up port, and quickly!" Few things drive ideas out of the system more quickly than SU (Perrow, 1984).

ME BOSS AND LEADER; YOU SUBORDINATE AND FOLLOWER (MBYS)

A related problem with SU is that it reinforces superior–subordinate social distance. Superiors are "leaders"; subordinates are "followers." Leaders propose ideas; subordinates carry them out. It would seem somewhat bizarre from this perspective to talk about bosses following and subordinates leading. But that is exactly what needs to happen in the organization of the future.

EXIT AND LOYALTY, INSTEAD OF VOICE

Several years ago, the brilliant economist Albert O. Hirschman wrote a book called *Exit, Voice, and Loyalty: Responses to Decline in Firms, Organizations, and States* (1970). Hirschman argued that when things begin to go sour, there are really only three options. One is that you can leave (exit). A second is that you can speak up and try to make things better (voice). A third is that you can be quiet and go along (loyalty). Each type of enterprise—a firm, an organization, a state—has its own preferred culture. In firms, exit is preferred. If you do not like the softer side of Sears, shop elsewhere! For other kinds of organizations—such as churches and schools—you are supposed to use voice, and try to make them better. Sometimes, as with public utilities, exit is impossible anyway. With your country you are supposed to be committed and not point out the problems. Loyalty!

What Hirschman suggests is important for the idea-driven organization. First, his suggestion of exit as the first and preferred response systematically pushes out those who would like to stay and make things better. That is what happened to Peter Postit.

But if you do not leave, the least you can do is be loyal and not bring uncomfortable problems into the open. Thus, the concepts of exit and loyalty, both good up to a point, act to suppress voice. And voice expresses the very things that might be helpful.

CONCLUSION

These ideas are just a few of the many noxious notions that stifle ideas and corrode concepts within firms and organizations. They make it hard for firms to actually capture the new ideas that may be bubbling—are bubbling—just under the organization's surface. These new ideas are the crucial resources for the future. The problem is that organizations actively—though perhaps not realizing it—have cultures and styles that are self-destructive. Firms make it difficult or impossible for individuals with new ideas and approaches to take leadership. If these concepts are sneaking around your shop—and they usually strut around—take action to neutralize them. Recognizing them for what they are—augers of doom—is a helpful start.

Chapter 6

Dangerous Decisions: A Race to the Bottom

Pernicious procedures and corrosive concepts are categories of problems that are destructive to new ideas. That ought to be enough, but there is another category that is problematic as well: dangerous decisions. Sometimes firms actually take action in the sense of making a decision, but the actual decision is awful. Firms here have two problems. One is that the firm has done something very dumb. But dumb is not dangerous. Dumb decisions become dangerous when they not only fail to solve the problem in a positive way but actually accelerate the difficulty; these decisions really make things worse! That is part of the race to the bottom.

The second problem is that the firm thinks what it has done is good. It is bad enough to make a bad decision; it is even worse to not fix it. This is a recipe for disaster.

Considerable work has been done outlining and naming desperately dangerous types of decisions. And I have added a couple from my own work. But first, a word about decision quality.

HIGH-QUALITY DECISIONS

Decisions are an important organizational product. Firms tend not to think of them in that way, however, and thus there is never any system in place for evaluating the decisions that are made. Decision evaluation will be discussed in Chapter 20. Suffice it to say, for now, that the *idea* that decisions are a product and need to be evaluated is an uncommon one (except, of course, when something goes wrong, and then we shift to taking names and kicking ass). That process, however, is not to be confused with *evaluation*.

Decisions are the last step on the idea formalization ladder. After a decision, a new idea can go ahead or is set aside for the time being (and thus is available for a version of we tried this before called we already discussed this). If a good new idea cannot make it into the decision arena and emerge with a favorable result, it cannot help the organization prosper. Thus, the decision process is that one which sifts and sorts proposals and, hopefully, picks the best ones to go forward. Unfortunately, many organizations are characterized by the reverse—good ideas are rejected and bad ones accepted. This is the process of making low-quality decisions.

LOW-QUALITY DECISIONS

Low-quality decisions are those which have awful results—Janis (1983) calls them fiascoes—and accelerate the process of organizational collapse. While we all make poor decisions through the day, no doubt, organizations making them are of special interest because of the huge repercussions they can have.

Folly

One bad decision is *folly*. This idea is developed by Barbara Tuchman (1984) in her book, *The March of Folly*. Folly occurs when a firm does something really dumb, but it is more than just picking a bad direction. Tuchman insists it is folly when and only when some other criteria are met. Other alternatives must have been available. There has to have been a clear set of voices articulating these other options. Finally, it occurs over time (so it is not the result of one crazy person). A perfect example of folly was discussed in the *Newsweek* analysis of the history of Montgomery Ward, called "You Snooze, You Lose" (McCormack, 1997). The author asks, "How could corporate planning go so wrong?" The answer is not that Ward made a mistake. Companies do that all the time. The real problem was that Ward stuck with its mistake. That is folly.

Groupthink

Another kind of problem is the popular *groupthink* phenomenon developed by Irving Janis (1983). Groupthink points to decision making under conditions of high cohesion, where no one wants to "disturb the peace." Hence, everyone agrees because no one wants to be thought of as a wimp, or someone who "does not fit in." Janis gives many examples in his book, the Bay of Pigs being among the most famous. While he thinks of government decision making, we have all seen this at the corporate table as well.

How does groupthink work? Janis gives us seven points:

- First, the group's discussions are limited to a few alternative courses of action (often only two), without a survey of the full range of alternatives.
- Second, the group does not survey the objectives to be fulfilled and the values implicated by the choice.
- Third, the group fails to reexamine the course of action initially preferred by the majority of members from the standpoint of the nonobvious risks and drawbacks that had not been considered when it was originally evaluated.
- Fourth, the members neglect courses of action initially evaluated as unsatisfactory. They spend little or no time discussing whether they have overlooked nonobvious gain.
- Fifth, the members make little or no attempt to obtain information from experts who can supply sound estimates of gains and losses to be expected from alternative courses of action.
- Sixth, selective bias is shown in the way the group reacts to factual information and relevant judgments from experts. [Specifically, they like facts that support what they want to do and spend time discussing those facts; they tend to ignore evidence of a contrary nature.]
- Seventh, the members spend little time deliberating about how the chosen policy might be hindered by bureaucratic inertia or sabotaged by political opponents. Consequently, they fail to work out contingency plans that could endanger the overall success of the chosen cause of action" (Janis, 1983, 10).

In sum, the seven points are as follows:

1. Incomplete survey of alternatives.
2. Incomplete survey of objectives.
3. Failure to examine the risks of the preferred choice.
4. Failure to reappraise initially rejected alternatives.
5. Poor information search.
6. Selective bias in processing information at hand.
7. Failure to work out contingency plans.

Powerthink

Powerthink, a variation of groupthink, occurs when teams capitulate to the influence of powerful persons in the team meeting. It frequently occurs in a team meeting when an influential boss puts on heavy pressure to have a decision go a particular way. Other employee members of the group, fearful that they would be punished in some way, or who simply do not want to "take on" community influentials, acquiesce. This agreement is false. Even during the team meeting attendees are thinking, "This is crazy." The minute the team meeting ends, attendees are usually complaining among themselves about it. Usually—almost always in fact—the feeling and the actuality of coercion means that members, while agreeing in public, plan sabotage in private.

Abilene Paradox

A third kind of problem is called the *Abilene Paradox.* This is a misunderstanding discovered and discussed by Jerry Harvey (1988), and there is even a movie about it.

The story Harvey tells is one of a group of people sitting on a porch outside of Abilene on a very hot day. They do not have any air conditioning in their car. Somehow it is decided to go to Abilene for lunch. They go, and travel a long way in a very uncomfortable automobile sitting in blistering heat. The lunch is awful, and on the way back they discover that no one actually wanted to go to Abilene for lunch. Harvey calls it the mismanagement of agreement. The Abilene Paradox has come to refer to those kinds of organizational decisions where nobody really wanted to do it, but everyone somehow fell into it. Everyone, underneath, knew what they wanted. No one expressed their true opinions.

Brutethink

Brutethink is one of my contributions. It occurs when teams and task forces think they can bulldoze their way to a solution. Instead of engaging in "problem bracketing" (setting a problem component aside for a while and coming back to it), the team just keeps at it and at it and at it until team members will accept almost anything just to get out of the room. Sometimes, of course, keeping at it is what is needed. Often a break helps. It is the old problem of "knowing when to hold 'em and when to fold 'em." Frequently, such intense pressure causes new ideas to crumble.

The Garbage Can Model of Organizational Choice

In an influential paper, Cohen, March, and Olsen (1972), argued that firms and organizations have four kinds of people, or roles, in them.[1] One kind are *problem knowers*, those individuals who know the kinds of problems the organization is facing. A second kind are *problem solvers.* These are individuals with a creative bent, who know how to come up with ideas for solving problems and getting things done. We all know employees like this. But they may not know the problems the organization faces. A third group of employees are *resource controllers*, who control important firm resources—namely, people and money. They always need to be involved. Finally, there are *decision makers looking for work*, usually upper-level managers and executives who "bless" the decision. Cohen's point is that for high-quality decisions, communities need to have all these types involved in the process. That means all four types need to be in the same room at the same time. Most of the time these roles are assembled at random, as if thrown into a garbage can. Hence, a garbage can decision is a decision made almost at random with respect to the different kinds of decision makers who need to be involved.

Defensive Routines

Defensive routines is an idea developed by Harvard University decision analyst Chris Argyris (1985). Defensive routines refers to a situation in a group where (1) certain topics are undiscussable, and (2) the undiscussability is undiscussable. Such routines may come into play in an organizational decision-making setting, for example, when there are obvious problems but they cannot be mentioned. It is a sort of "Emperor's New Clothes." The guy is naked, but no one can say it; everyone pretends he is actually dressed. New ideas suffer this fate. There is never "time" to discuss them, and of course there is never "time" to discuss why there is never "time." Creative people and new idea champions leave in disgust.

Occam's Razor

William of Occam (a clergyman who lived in the early fourteenth century) formulated a rule for judging between competing mathematical proofs. William's idea, useful today in all organizations, was that simpler was better; the proof with the fewer steps was the winner. "We have an Occam problem here" usually means that the proposed decision is very involved, very complicated, and usually involves assuming that about ten things which have to go right will actually go right. New ideas, for example, are often burdened with complex testing and production requirements that almost guarantee failure. As the complexity of a decision compounds arithmetically, the problems of implementation compound arithmetically. Making a decision that is too complicated to work is the same as making no decision.

The Rube Goldberg Construction

Closely related to the Occam's Razor problem is the *Rube Goldberg Construction*. In this case, the decision is made in small parts at different times, almost as if one planned Sunday dinner an item at a time, Monday through Saturday, with each day's work having little or no connection to that of the previous day. One emerges with a decision cobbled together without any particular integrity (it is the decision version of the Jerry-built structure discussed in Chapter 15). New ideas often have this and that added to them until they are so fat that the original beauty of the concept is totally lost.

Zeno's Paradox

Zeno was a fifth-century B.C. Greek philosopher. He pointed out that if you are approaching a structure and at each step cover half the remaining distance, you will never actually reach that structure. This happens in firm decision making. You get closer, and closer, and closer, but never actually make the decision. It is one kind of decision avoidance psychosis (DAP).

One other contemporary application occurs in those offices which have a coffeepot with a sign over it which reads, "Will the person who uses the last cup please make a fresh pot." Here Zeno applies exactly. Users keep taking half of what is left until there is only a molecular sheen of coffee in the pot, but there is always "half" left so the drinker does not have to make a fresh pot. This is a kind of "Russian Defense" for new ideas. You meet and talk, meet and talk, meet and talk, until the idea champion says, "The hell with it."

The Non-Decision, or the Boiled Frog Phenomenon

The last decision-making problem is called the boiled frog problem, and it is sort of a non-decision. It occurs when organizations allow events to proceed without taking action to keep themselves current, and thus find themselves out of the race, in a sense, "dead." In the boiled frog metaphor, use the old high school science experiment: Take a frog, put it in a petrie dish, and slowly heat the frog in the water over a Bunsen burner. The frog eventually boils to death. Why doesn't the frog jump out? The answer lies in the concept of the "just noticeable difference" (Tichy & Devanna, 1986). Change is always going on. We are forced to react to fast change, but slow change can take us by surprise. Organizational leadership sometimes does not perceive the change occurring, and thus fails to come together and act. Workers—the problem knowers Cohen and colleagues (1972) mention—know about change but usually cannot get the decision makers looking for work to pay any attention. A lot of American firms have become boiled frogs. In this case, not to decide was, truly, to decide to die.

CONCLUSION

There are a lot of rotten decisions. The catalog here, impressive as it is, is not complete by a long shot. Notice there are a range of people who have been worried about this problem, from historians (Barbara Tuchman) to social psychologists (Irving Janis) to philosophers (Zeno) to religious thinkers (William of Occam) to political scientists (Michael Cohen) to "wild and crazy guys" (Rube Goldberg) to decision analysts themselves (Chris Argyris). That is an impressive array, so, clearly, bad decisions attract a lot of attention. What is surprising is that good decisions attract less. And decisions involving the development of new ideas attract even less than that. We need to move away from them and toward high-quality decisions, decisions that have a healthy admixture of the new and the innovative. Part III provides a range of ways that IdeaManagers and IdeaLeaders can be helpful to the many new ideas that are already in the organization, just waiting for a little help, a little blocking, and a bit of a boost.

NOTE

1. Cohen is a professor at the University of Michigan; March, a professor at Stanford, has written a book, *A Primer on Decision Making: How Decisions Happen* (1994).

PART III

Helping New Ideas Along through Leading and Managing

The three sets of problems—pernicious procedures, corrosive concepts, and dangerous decisions—are the bane of an organization's life and almost always fatal to the new and the different. In fact, these organizational defensive routines have evolved to protect the organization from the new and the different. They work, even as a cancer does, to destroy their very host.

New ideas need to feed into the organizational decision process. A significant number of these new ideas need to emerge as the programs of the future. But they must run the gauntlet of problematic procedures, corrosive concepts, and dangerous decisions. Ideas need to be helped along.

The first step, of course, is to look, generically so to speak, at issues of IdeaLeadership and IdeaManagement themselves. It is important to understand the differences. In a nutshell, leadership is a role, something everyone in the organization can play at one time or another. Management is a position. Both are crucial.

Second, we need to spend some time on issues of leading and managing in the idea creation process; followed by a chapter on what happens after there is a supply of ideas available. Here is where the Half-Baked Ideas Conference comes in.

The last chapter in this section deals with leadership and management in the idea development process. The Seven I idea outlines an idea development process, and details the stages ideas have to go through to get from art to part, from concept to customer.

Chapter 7

IdeaLeadership and IdeaManagement

So much has been written on these topics that one hesitates to get into the fray. On the other hand, most of it seems to be unread by current managers. Or, if read, unabsorbed. Problems of management are everywhere. It is rare that one goes into a restaurant, a cleaners, or a hospital and comes away with the feeling that it is even well managed. In the main, organizations seem starved for leadership and starved for management. These problems may even surface in more difficult ways in the next millennium, because of the focus on and the need for ideas as a central organizational resource. Managing and leading for action is one thing. Managing and leading for idea development is something different, and perhaps more difficult. There is greater ambiguity. Development time is slower. Results are less immediately clear. And, of course, there is always the issue of balance. While this book focuses on ideas as an organizational resource, people and money are also very important organizational resources, and continue to be so. Hence, there is a necessity on the part of the leaders and managers of the organization to look toward balance. Typically, leaders and managers provide what is not being provided in the organization. That is why the leadership and management of ideas becomes crucial. They are typically a desperately needed resource.

LEADERSHIP AND MANAGEMENT

Leadership and management are different, though they are often used as synonyms for each other. The best way to think about them is this way: Management is a position and is something to which you can be appointed in an office in which you reside. It begins at the lowest level of the organization, the administrator or program assistant, and rises through a variety of ranks and program descriptions to the CEO. I find a four-part classification of managers to be helpful: lower-level managers, middle managers, senior managers, and the CEO.

At all levels, the manager's job is efficiency—doing the right thing and creating high-performance organizations. Another way to look at this situation is that the manager's job is innovation: doing what you are doing better. Clearly, one kind of idea—the innovative idea, the improvement, what the Japanese call *kaizan*—is important here.

Leaders, on the other hand, play roles. Unlike managers, who occupy specific and focused positions within the organization and have job descriptions, leaders have scripts. Leaders can come from anywhere, and in fact the very best organizations cultivate a distributed leadership in which everyone in the organization takes or assumes leadership at one point or another. While managers have subordinates by "right" or hierarchical organization, leaders have followers because they earn them. No one is assigned to be a follower any more than one is assigned to be a leader. Leadership, being a role, is a gift which, though assumed, must also be earned. The job of leadership is effectiveness—doing the right thing. That implies environmental scanning, picking out the right thing, helping to decide what the right thing is, and so on. Doing the right thing often means (in fact, must always mean) reinventing, recreating, and reforming the organization from the old to the new. Hence, while management deals with stability, leadership deals with change. Management deals with doing things well; leadership deals with what things should be done. To some extent, management flows down, while leadership bubbles up. Leadership is lateral, but management is vertical.

Leadership involves the creation and sustaining of change without crisis. Obviously, the change part is crucial. But what does one really mean by "without crisis"? There are two aspects. One is that leadership initiates change without the prod of crisis. By the time crisis comes, the ability of leadership to actually lead is usually rather limited. What we call a crisis is really the node of a developing difficult situation which has reached public proportions. Sometimes crises even need to be created in order to overcome the inertia of the status quo. But leadership is able to ignite interest in the absence of overwhelming external pressures for change. And let us consider the downstream side of change. Leadership is able to keep change going and keep people interested in change without creating a crisis.

Obviously, positions have differential opportunities to express leadership. While all positions within an organization can and should express some leadership, the extent of position rigidity varies by its location in the hierarchy. That is, the lower down you are, the less opportunities you have proportionally. The lower-level manager may have a canned 15-percent opportunity to express leadership, whereas the CEO may have a 60-percent opportunity to express leadership.

Among the more serious problems in the organization is that people at the higher end of the scale fail to appreciate the need for leadership that their position empowers. They instead overmanage and underlead. Most organizations today, or at least a large number of them, are, according to Bob Quinn (1997) at the University of Michigan Business School, starved for leadership. Another way of putting this is expressed by the question, "Where have all the heroes gone?" Organizations need to have leadership, those individuals at the top of the organization who provide the kind of vision and stimulus through change that leadership embodies. Without leadership, the action is likely to become very conservative and very self-involved. Since leadership provides the direction that management uses to prioritize and make decisions through, with, and by, the absence of leadership is going to make the organization very conservative, as people try to CYA ("cover your ass") in the absence of effective guidance.

IDEALEADERSHIP IN THE IDEA-DRIVEN ORGANIZATION

Leadership in the idea-driven organization is about ideas. It involves encouragement at every step of the idea process, from interest to involvement and implementation. It involves creating a culture which welcomes and accepts new ideas, generates them, cherishes them, uses them, and offers them forth. A good metaphor for leadership is that of the orchestral or jazz conductor. The conductor typically is not playing an instrument—virtuosos are sometimes added for special effect—but organizes, orchestrates, and champions the new and the different. That, of course, does not mean that everything that is new and different is accepted. There is organizational processes of assessment that have to be undertaken. But it means that a broad net is created, and a climate in which that broad net can be used effectively. Hence, pumping through the idea-driven organization, driven by the pump of leadership, are new ideas and approaches such that the organization can be redefined, reinvented, recrafted, reorganized, refocused, and refreshed.

It is important for the people taking leadership roles to understand that they do not have to come up with the new ideas, though that is certainly not ruled out. And if no one is coming up with any new ideas, then that is a task that they might wish to undertake. As important is the support for new ideas. New ideas are vulnerable. Because they are new, they mostly do not have all their parts, they have not been thought completely through. Hence, it is easy to attack them. Leadership weighs in on the tolerance side, or one could say on the diversity side—in this case, the diversity of ideas. And leadership seeks to keep several balls of ideas in the air at the same time. Someone once defined leadership as the ability to drive a two-ton truck full of three tons of canaries. You assume that one ton of canaries is in the air at all times. As silly as that example is, it does convey the notion that a lot of fluttering around is going on, all of which will not necessarily result in a program. But, rather, out of that fluttering will come useful innovations, inventions, and new directions.

Leadership also takes risks. In the case of the idea-driven organization, risks come in several forms. One form is simply suggesting the weird, the strange, the counterintuitive. Consider the story of the electric fork:

The Electric Fork

My wife is Italian in background. As a result, she has made a lot of pasta over our wonderful thirty-plus years of marriage. The problem is, of course, that I have had so much pasta—spaghetti, linguine, spaghetti, spaghetti—that I have developed an illness of the wrist from twisting and twisting that fork. I call it Carpal Pasta Syndrome, and it hurts. One night while brushing my teeth an idea hit me: "Eureka," I thought, "The electric fork." The next day I took the electric toothbrush into the shop, changed the gears a bit, and inserted a plastic fork into the end. It worked great. That fork turned round and round—perfecto!

Until I ate with it. It went a little fast—very fast actually. There was a ring of sauce across my shirt, and not only my shirt. So it was back to the drawing board. I slowed the motor down, and then added an embellishment. At our house we eat quickly, often grazing off the plates of the other slower eaters. If you are not moving on that cutlet, someone will say, "You done with this?" as they spear the cutlet. I thought that if I could make the fork part extend in and out, then I could spear the cutlet from a greater, and safer, distance. It also worked like a charm. The fork shot out in harpoonlike fashion, speared the cutlet fragment, and retracted, all in a nanosecond. Magnificent. Except for one thing. The extending feature was only supposed to work in the down position, not the eating position. Another case of product liability.

Can you not imagine the derision such a suggestion would invite at, say, Sunbeam. A cacophony of condemnation. Yet perhaps such a fork could indeed be useful for those with certain kinds of neurological disorders who cannot use a conventional fork well. The point is that many products never see the light of day, products that would have improved our lives immeasurably had they not been squashed. IdeaManagement and IdeaLeadership suspends disbelief and structures a bit of exploration of the new and the different.

Leadership involves broadening the boundaries. Many organizations operate along an options path that runs from A to B. Naturally, if there is a narrow range of options, such as only two of them, much organizational energy will be spent fighting over A versus B instead of considering some others. Broadening the mix is a key leadership skill. A leader might say, "What about J?" Now there is where risk comes in. Obviously, J is "far out." And everybody might poke a little fun at the leader for suggesting J. But, of course, what the introduction of J has done is of vital importance. It has legitimized the possibility of C, D, E, F, G, and H. The mix is now a lot broader. And combinations among those are possible. The gift of leadership is that instead of the organization fighting over A versus B, the organization can now look at the range of options A through H (or even add J, for that matter), and see what might be made to work from that larger, richer constellation.

Leadership prods, pokes, pushes, promotes. Leaders are always asking, "How's it coming?" "What's new?" "How's this?" "Got anything new?" We might call it the prick of leadership: lots of tiny jabs, none of them fatal, but enough to keep you moving. Leadership praises, celebrates, and provides psychic income. Leaders tell others they have done a great job, they have made a good contribution, their work is valued and valuable. Leaders know you can almost never provide too much psychic income.

IDEAMANAGEMENT IN THE IDEA-DRIVEN ORGANIZATION

While the role of leaders is to engender confusion, to some extent, the role of managers is to set up systems and structures that create and produce regularity. For managers in the idea-driven organization, the concept "fit is it" is a pretty apt phrase. They try to insure that all the organizational parts and elements align together so that everything and everybody is working in the same direction.

There are a number of typical problems that everybody will recognize. A strategic plan is constructed. Lots of organizational energy and money is put into it. The best brains in the organization lay out areas of emphasis. Some months later, the plan is found, covered in dust, in the back room of the print shop. What happened? The organization has failed the alignment test. It has failed to do much more in many cases than send out a memo saying, "We hope everyone will pay attention to the new strategic plan." As my mother-in-law used to say, "Put hope in one hand and spit in the other, and see what you have more of."

Another kind of problem has to do with the misalignment of reward systems and organizational goals. The goals in the strategic plan may say X, but the reward system (reward systems often are the last things to change, if they ever change) may say Y. Hence, employees know that regardless of what the plans says ("We stress cooperation and service to the customer"), what they get paid and promoted on is something quite different. This is what Kerr (1995) calls "On the folly of rewarding A while hoping for B."

Managers are problem processors. This gives them an excellent opportunity to look at problem patterns. One problem can probably be solved and dealt with. A series of the same problem means something is wrong in the organization. Hence, what managers supply to leaders, in addition to orderly process, is disorderly information; or, put a different way, information about things disorderly which then become grist for the mill of the leader.

Regrettably, managers often fail here. James March and Herbert Simon talk about this problem as the "principle of uncertainty absorption" (March & Simon, 1958, 165). What it means is that as information passes up the organizational hierarchy there is a preference schedule: good news, bad news, ambiguous, or uncertain news. Simon's point is that ambiguous or uncertain news tends to be absorbed into either bad news or good news. Thus, people at the top of the organization get information that is "more certain" than it really is. Since uncertainty is the fertilizer of change, the process of uncertainty absorption robs senior managers, CEOs, and leadership throughout the organization of a vital piece of the perspective pie.

Management and leadership in the idea-driven organization is a lot like management and leadership of people and other resources. The management piece involves doing the job and improving the job. The leadership piece involves doing new jobs: thinking them up, figuring out how they ought to be constructed, involving relevant managers in them. Management also involves managing up (if you are on the bottom), managing down (if you are on the top), and managing across (making the kind of networks that allow for processes to operate smoothly). But in the idea-driven organization of the twenty-first century, managers will have much emphasis on the IdeaManagement process. That will more or less involve harvesting the hundreds of ideas that everybody who works in the organization has about ways that things could be improved, combining and packaging them, and putting them to work.

Let me give you an example:

The Airline Counter

Anyone who has flown out of the Detroit airport knows that the check-in line at one of the major airline's domestic counter is always very long. It seems that no matter what time of day one is there, it snakes back and forth to two or three layers at least. The counter is long—quite long. And the idea of the snake structure is quite sensibly that individuals will not be caught behind any one customer with a particularly difficult problem, but rather will be able to go quickly to "the next available attendant." The problem is that because the counter is so long, and the line ends more or less at one end of it, it is very difficult to see when an attendant is free. Many times attendants at the other end of the counter have to stand up on the scale and wave and shout, saying, "Next, please! Next, please!" When I was waiting there one time, I counted the number of minutes that were consumed in available attendants waiting for individuals to either notice them or come down once they had been shouted to attention. On the average, attendants at the far end of the area waited three to four minutes. I am not pretending it was a scientific survey, or that I am Frederick Taylor (Taylor, 1947), but it was easy for me to see that a considerable amount of time was lost in transit. When my turn came, I spoke to the attendant and said, "You guys should really have a green light or something above your stations, so that you don't have so much down time." The attendant said, "Tell me about it. We've told management over and over again ways to improve that. We're sensitive to the problem, and it upsets us. But you know management! Unless they think of it, nothing will ever happen. And besides, they never have to wait in these lines."

This situation reminded me a lot of the problems that the automobile executives had involving insensitivity to service situations. They never had to have their cars serviced at a local dealership, so local dealership issues and concerns, high on the minds of consumers, were more or less irrelevant to many of them.

The Greedy Hotel Case

Another example comes from my stay at a relatively high-end hotel in Santa Fe, New Mexico. As I was checking out, I looked at the bill and was appalled to find that they had charged me 75¢ per call for using the telephone. As readers may know, this is very common, and very irritating, but I was furious in this case because the hotel offered itself and marketed itself as high in the "amenities" department, and, indeed, charged appropriately. So here I was, in effect, being nickeled and dimed through using the phone. Since I had made about fifty calls, I had about $35 in charges for phone calls. I called the manager on duty and said, "I'm appalled by these charges. I'm a good customer, you're a high-end hotel. I can't imagine why you would want to put the screws on customers in this way." He looked at me and said, "Dr. Tropman, everybody says that." I thought to myself, "Everybody?" How long does it take before lust for the quick buck is not the dominant motif of discussion in the weekly staff team meeting of hotel managers?

These are two examples of ongoing problems that organizations face. There were a lot of opportunities for solutions that somehow were routinely rejected by management. Middle managers may have cost organizations a lot more than their combined salaries—they may have cost them a good piece of the future.

Leadership in the idea-driven organization is also heavily focused on capturing and using what is already there: inventions. The difference, of course, is that the managers are trying to better the things that they already do, while the leaders are trying to do different things from what they already do. It is the difference between change in the system and change of the system.

Let me give an example of leadership. Consider the case of "Joe," a former athletic director (AD) at the University of the Mind. Athletics at Mind is big business, and the athletic director has to contend with pressures from the press, problems with players and staff, incessant publicity, and fans who each want something different and feel passionately about what they want. The AD also has to contend with faculty who are, it is probably fair to say, somewhat suspicious about big-time athletics; the faculty has an approach–avoidance attitude. The AD has made a number of improvements in the athletic department, but the leadership act I want to call attention to is his sponsorship of the newly developed Athletic Institute at the University of the Mind. This is a scholarly institute designed to pull together sports research and sports teaching, and to more fully link the activities of the athletic department to those pedagogical and knowledge-generating activities at the university as a whole. It was a leadership act.

Or consider "Carl," CEO of Social Ministry Services (SMS), one of the most outstanding not-for-profit organizations in the country. SMS was concerned about the way it was preparing—or, as Carl felt, not preparing—its management for complexities of the future. Under Carl's direction, and with the help of "Dave," VP for Human Resources for SMS, and Dave's able staff, he created a program called Management On The Go. This program brought about thirty-five of the key managers together for a series of weekends of reflection, mutual teaching, and preparation for management and leadership in the future. This program is imbedded in a larger program, SMS–U, or Social Ministry Services–University, in which the organization is committing itself to a potentially large variety of training and developmental exercises, including the research and evaluation of those exercises. All these concepts are contained within the university idea. It is an attempt to bring the teaching function into the organization rather than rely on external teachers. One might call it the "found objects" theory of development, in which the organization begins with a large amount of talent it has and seeks to expand and empower that talent in a variety of ways. The university idea within organizations is not new, but it is new in the not-for-profit sector; and SMS is a perfect example of an organization which is trying to manage ideas and use them as a resource.

So management in the future—the management of ideas—is starting. How is it different? Well, ideas are more difficult to manage because they are more ambiguous. People and money come in teams and piles. One can see them, one can touch them. Ideas are more abstract, less tangible, and thus create greater potential difficulties. Managing people has a historical sense to it. Even bad managers can say, "Well, we tell them what to do, and they do it. That's management." You can direct money to be invested here, spent there, recalled from some other place, and so on. It is very difficult to tell ideas what to do, divide up the ideas and allocate a certain proportion of them to each of the divisions, or decide to have a 2-percent increase in ideas this year. So, ideas, given their more ephemeral nature, are more difficult to manage around and lead toward. It is more frustrating, less clear, and, thus, overall perhaps a greater challenge.

CONCLUSION

Leadership and management, then, will need to add for the twenty-first century an entirely new dimension to the activities that they have typically undertaken. Perhaps "new" is really not the right word; "conscious" is a better choice. Obviously, leadership of ideas has always been an important part of the leader's and the manager's role, but it has been buried or sequestered within money management and people management. Many if not most discussions about budgets are really discussions about ideas: which ideas to fund, which ideas to defund. If the context of the discussion being money suppresses the idea aspect, many discussions about people are similarly shadow discussions of ideas, except that the ideas remain in the shadows and people surface. Now we are simply going to need to be much more aware of the power of ideas.

Chapter 8

Leading and Managing Idea Generation and Storage: The Half-Baked Ideas Conference

Ideas, like cops, never seem to be around when you need them. Part of the problem is that firms wait until a problem comes up, and then look for a solution. That is not a bad approach, and it works well for the regular, ongoing activities. We can call that the problems-needing-solution approach. It is the tactical path, and it is characterized by innovations.

However, the problems-needing-solution approach does not work so well when bigger, more complex problems arise. Then, paradoxically, firms need to have the solutions before the problems arise. This perspective, the solutions-looking-for-problems approach, is the strategic path. It means that firms must have ideas in the bank, just like firms have fiscal reserves and bench strength in human resources.

There need to be ordinary and extraordinary mechanisms to bring them to fruition. Both processes—the regular and the irregular—are needed because they support and complement each other. Regular processes mean that employees feel comfortable about suggesting improvements on an ongoing basis; they do not have to wait from some "magic moment" when it is "time." On the other hand, special conferences which emphasize only new ideas provide showcasing, progress reporting, and encouragement. The Half-Baked Ideas Conference (HBIC) is such a special conference, designed to assess the idea bench strength and add to it. It is designed to produce inventions through liberation; to use some and store others.

THE HALF-BAKED IDEAS CONFERENCE: PREPARATORY PHASE

A Half-Baked Ideas Conference preparation begins with an assessment of the innovations quotient. An organizational team assesses the flow of regular new ideas (number of suggestions, number of implementations, number of processes under review, etc.) and assesses as well how the actual innovation rate relates to the expected innovation rate.

The team then moves to assess the inventions quotient. What really new things have happened (change of the system as opposed to change in the system), and how many potential inventions—ideas in the bank ready to be looked at in detail—there are. For an auto company, it could be smart cars, smart roads, cars you can dissemble and take with you, and, yes, the Gerontocar. These are new products treading water, waiting at the starting gate.

Typically there will be good news—things going right—and bad news—things going wrong. Perhaps wrong is not the right word here: lack of achievement might be better—innovations quotients that are too low, inventions that have not gotten off the ground, too few inventions in the bank, inventions in the bank that look like other inventions in the bank so that there is not the diversity of possibility present on the bench (it is not really "strength" to have a bench of twelve quarterbacks).

Meanwhile, everyone who will be attending has some assignments as well. Individually, or in pairs or small teams, they need to come up with some crazy new ideas that would be useful in the organization. The electric fork is that kind of idea. Or here is one that a medical technician told me: They needed new motors for the machine that tilts the vials of blood back and forth. She had the idea of attaching that machine to a gerbil wheel. The gerbil would run and run and accomplish the same thing as the motor.

Crazy? Sure, but it might just work. And even if it did not work it serves a liberating function. If we thought of them as fluids, most organizational cultures would be opaque and viscous. There is a lot there but most of it is stuck, or moving very slowly, and you cannot see it. The idea behind the HBIC is to act as a solution which clears up the dimness and reduces the viscosity. Then the ideas and concepts which are trapped within the organizational culture can come out.

In addition, participants are invited (or ordered, or expected) to bring a joke, a cartoon, and a newspaper clipping. Each one is targeted—it cannot be only funny or informative (in the case of the clipping). It must also contribute to the theme of the conference: jokes illustrating the problems with new ideas or a new idea itself, cartoons that show the difficulties of developing new ideas, clippings that reveal imaginative and new business approaches and their success or failures.

Cartoons are available from many places: magazines, newspapers, and the World Wide Web. Even word processing programs (e.g., Microsoft Office has something called ClipArt in it) have visuals available. They are posted on a cartoon board. The articles are posted on an article board, and, at random moments, members are asked for their joke.

There is a serious side to funniness that needs to be stressed here. For one thing, humor breaks tension. It keeps things on the lighter side, which means that criticism and attacking are lowered and receptivity is heightened. That is just what you want for the HBIC.

But there is something else about humor, something in the medium-is-the-message department, that is equally important. Things are funny because of reversals of expectations, abrupt shifts in the line of thought. Consider Groucho Marx's classic line, "You don't like my principles? I have others." By the end of the first sentence you have one set of expectations, expectations which are completely undone by the second sentence. Jokes are like geology, in the sense that there are fault lines where things abruptly shift. Those kinds of shifts, those changed assumptions, those altered expectations, are just what is helpful to the creative process. The whole idea is to loosen things up, emotionally and intellectually. Dress, of course, is very informal.

THE HALF-BAKED IDEAS CONFERENCE ITSELF

At the conference itself there are two sessions. In the morning, the team reports on the innovation quotient and the invention quotient. Small teams of attendees process this information within their teams and report back on how they see the problems and make suggestions for solutions. In particular, the concept book is reviewed to see if any of the solutions can be used for emerging problems. The group presentations are sprinkled with jokes, of course.

In the afternoon, individuals and teams report on their half-baked ideas. As in brainstorming, no criticism is allowed. Instead, the group is invited to expand the applications of the suggestion, to find other places where it—or variations of it—might be useful. These ideas are then added to the concept bank.

CONCLUSION

The HBIC is, first of all, a good time. It is a chance to approach the job from a fun perspective. However, the good time has an extra purpose: A certain mental attitude is needed for invention. It is not, in our experience, true that "necessity is the mother of invention." Necessity is often the mother of innovation, of doing the same thing better. Invention—the change of the system—can of course come from necessity, but usually necessity brings with it too much anxiety for one to feel free to invent. The quick fix is more likely. This conference is designed to be the occasional opportunity where the bigger, stranger, more fundamental ideas can be expressed, and where they can be given a chance to swim around a little, to be tested but not taunted. It is not a substitute for the regular implementation of innovations; rather, it acts as a support and a balance to that regularity.

Chapter 9

The Seven I Idea

Ideas do not just emerge. They go through a process, a series of phases. Once there is interest, ideas may come forward, and they have to be shepherded along. There are a number of problems in each of the phases. A major task is to keep the idea from becoming stalled or lost. There is every possibility that a stall can occur within the phase. On the other hand, once the work of a particular phase is complete, ideas have to be passed from one set of idea workers to another. There is always the possibility that ideas can fall between the cracks, or that someone drops the ball.

THE SEVEN I IDEA

The Seven I idea is a template to structure the idea development and application process. The Seven I idea consists of the following concepts: *interest, innovation, invention, ignition/incineration, involvement,* and *investment*. These ideas represent parts as well as processes. In one sense, they represent parts of the idea process. Obviously, there has to be interest in doing things differently. There has to be invention and innovation. There has to be involvement and investment. In this simple sense, they follow one after the other. Idea managers must keep this rough sequence in mind. Figure 9.1 illustrates this conception.

On the other hand, one might view them as partially overlapped. In this respect, instead of a bar one might see them as a stack, as in Figure 9.2, which illustrates the concept of partial simultaneity. At any given moment in time, a subset of the elements need to be engaged, but not all. As one can see, at T1

Figure 9.1
The Seven I Idea Line

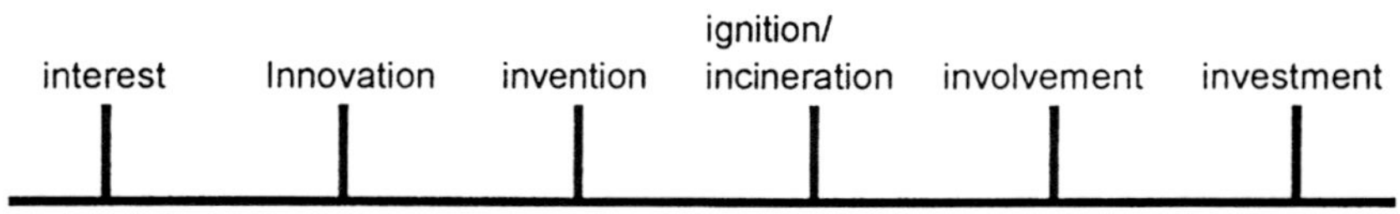

Figure 9.2
The Seven I Idea Stack

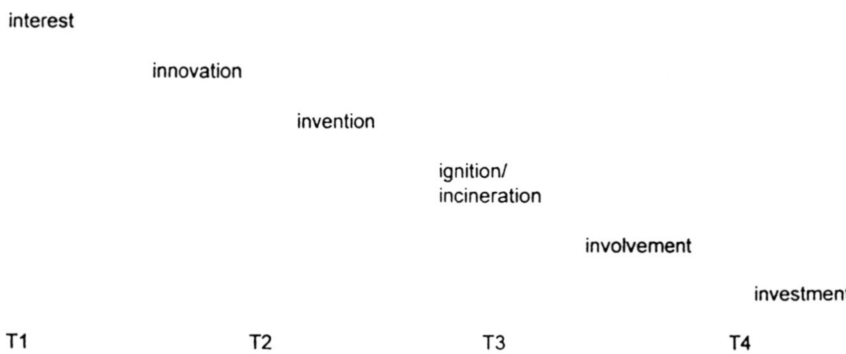

the first three elements are involved, at T3 the last three elements are involved, and in the middle all of the elements are involved. This is a different approach.

A third way to look at it is as total process rather than semiprocess. In this respect, the proper rendition is as a series of concentric circles, as shown in Figure 9.3. Here, the IdeaManager, taking any given slice, finds that all the Is must be engaged simultaneously.

The question is not which of these drawings or diagrams is right. Each in some respects is right in its own way. What is important, rather, is to keep in mind that both parts and process are involved, and that managing is required to select and order the different elements, depending on the situation at hand.

Interest

The first thing that is needed in the idea development process is interest. Interest is another way of talking about curiosity. It contains the questions, "I wonder why that is so?" "Is that really true?" or, "Can we do this a better way, a cheaper way, a faster way?" Being interested in things is the fundamental piece of the new idea process. The antithesis of interest, of course, is satisfaction. Satisfaction leads to stagnation, and stagnation—a sort of arterial sclerosis of the organization—leads to death. IdeaManagers, therefore, must find many ways and have ideas about ways to get ideas, so the organiza-

Figure 9.3
The Seven I Idea Circles

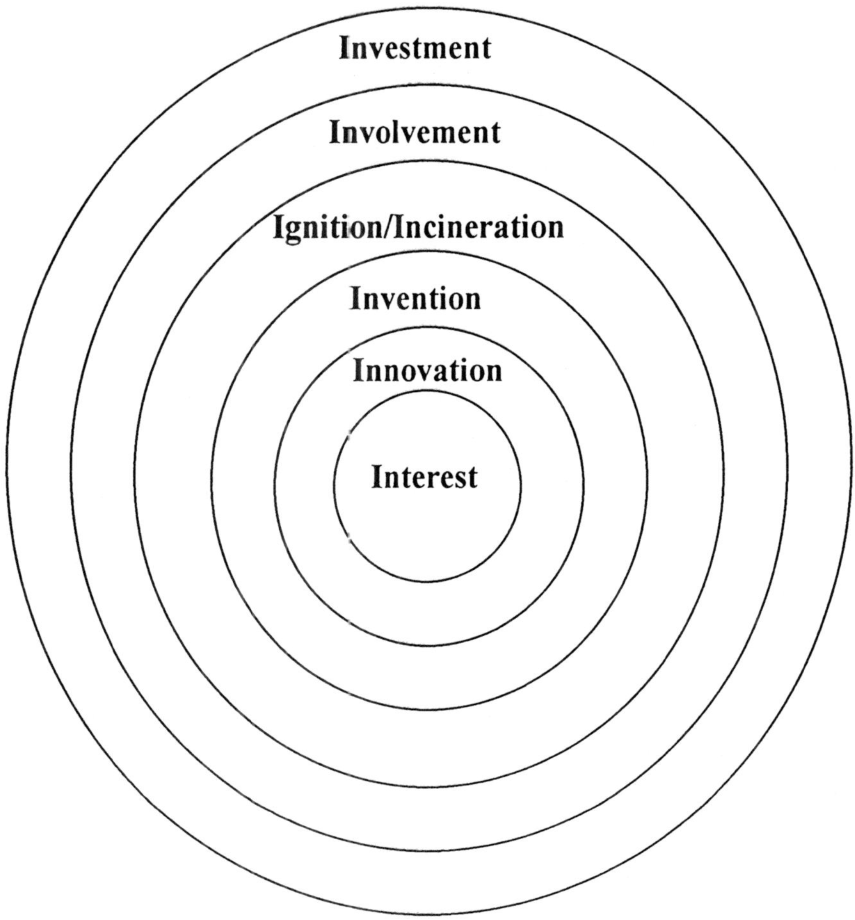

tion can continue to percolate. One IdeaManager I know has given himself the name CQO: Chief Query Officer. He feels that, fundamentally, questions are more important than answers. Answers tend to end things, whereas questions tend to keep things going. Interest, then, is interrogative, and, as such, it invigorates.

Innovation

Interest drives innovation. For our purposes, I would like us to think of innovation as change in the system, improvements in the things that we are already doing. Looked at in this way, innovation is an improvement in efficiency, but not necessarily an improvement in effectiveness. Innovation changes and simplifies how we do things, but does not necessarily address the issue of what we do. Innovations represent—indeed, are—the hundreds of small ways in which we constantly improve the job that we do. Naturally, this job can be at work, but innovation also applies to the home setting, church, or even one's personal life. Firms looking for "the big bang" or "the perfect niche" or "the big new market" may fail to appreciate the importance of innovation, of doing better what they now do, of making it less costly. Indeed, that should be an automatic process in many instances. After all, everything has a learning curve, and if one does begin to learn about how to do X or Y, then one ought to be able to do it more easily.

Take my case for an example. I have written a number of books. Certainly, this one is a little bit easier than the first one. I have been through the process, I know what to expect, I have got the lay of the land. My experience should not only help me do a better job within the same time, and also reduce the time somewhat, while still improving. It gives me the kind of detailed knowledge that allows for, and indeed invites, innovation.

It is hard to be innovative about a recipe that you have never cooked, or a suggestion of improvement on a fly pattern you have never fished or a car you have never driven. Innovation, then, is the constant but low-volume product of interest.

Invention

Invention—some might call it re-invention—deals with the really new things, the change "of the system." It represents a departure from either what was done before or the way things were done before. The development of the minivan was an invention. Fiber-optics, the television, and the telephone were inventions. Of course, the car itself was an invention. Actually, the line between innovation and invention is a difficult one to pinpoint specifically. Some might say, "If you say the car is an invention, then how can the minivan also be an invention? Wouldn't the minivan be an innovation within the car invention category?" And the answer would probably be yes. But the minivan also became a tremendously popular product within the car area, changed fundamental car-buying habits, and spawned a host of imitators, so on the profundity scale it would rank pretty high, though it would not rank as high as if it had a whole new engine (cold fusion, hot fusion, etc.). The point is not to argue about the difference between innovation and invention, but rather to recognize that the innovation cycle is very quick, the kinds of things are typically rather small, there are lots of them, and they are constantly being applied to the improvement of day-to-day operations. Inventions are fewer, much further between, more fundamental, and have more far-reaching impact.

The IdeaManager must walk both the invention and innovation sides of the street. On the one hand, he or she must pay attention to and celebrate the tiny improvements in day-to-day work. They add up. On the other hand, the

IdeaManager must stimulate people to get out of the box as well as make the inside of the box better.

Ignition/Incineration

Ideas, whether invention or innovation, need to "catch on." That is the ignition part. Individuals within the organization must be excited about the specific idea in question and its potential, but they must be excited as well about the idea process in general. I sat through hundreds of settings and situations in team meetings where apparently well-meaning members of the organization said, "I need to have all the information before I can go ahead with this." In one team meeting, in fact, a distinguished team participant, a member—named "Edison" by all—of the firm, got up and said, "We don't have all the information. By the time we have all the information, it will be too late. We need to make a decision now. And obviously, if it doesn't work out we're not going to go ahead with it. If we always fuss so much, no one will want to suggest anything new, and our firm will fail."

That comment was terrific. It was exactly right, very stern, and deadly accurate. In that room, as in so many rooms, the fear of change was almost palpable. You could taste it. Wise, old, gray heads—one gray-haired woman in particular—seemed to delight in playing devil's advocate. My translation: making everybody pay for new ideas. In tone, she should have been a banker: "I think it would be unwise to proceed without a fuller analysis." There were murmurs of agreement, solemn heads nodding throughout the room. That defeated the proposal; the man left, actually getting a better job, and the organization is experiencing a slow death.

Obviously, ignition did not occur. The idea, in fact, went down in flames. And this is one of the incineration problems that new ideas create. Sometimes, as you strike a match to light the way the only thing that burns up is yourself. Most IdeaManagers need to help in a couple of ways at the ignition phase. They need to help with ignition. They need to provide tinder, in the form of support and affirmative comments. They need to "work the shadow side," as Gerald Egan (1994) puts it, in order to build backroom support. "Edison," the man I mentioned, was literally hung out to dry. The president—who should have been named Pontius Pilate—washed his hands of the whole affair under the guise of letting the group make the decision. (I secretly knew he was not interested in this proposal anyway). The vice president spoke against it. He raised the resources red flag, thus driving the final nails into the proposal's coffin. The problem with new ideas is that the innovator or inventor cannot also be the sponsor. It looks too much like a conflict of interest. You thought up the idea; of course you would say it is a good idea. Even if it is the greatest idea since sliced bread, your credibility is problematic. Thus, IdeaManagers need to help in sponsorship. But they also need to prevent incineration. Shooting the messenger is bad enough. Immolating him or her is even worse.

Involvement

Let us assume for a moment that ignition occurs. People are excited about the new idea. They want to try it. That is where involvement occurs. It is necessary to get buy-in. Buy-in is now an engineered concept. I talk with a lot of executives who say, "We've worked out the plan; now all we need is buy-in." Translated, that means, "I have the idea fully formed; now I want you to rubber stamp it." They become incensed when firm employees begin asking about why this, why that, why can't we do something else, you are screwing us again this time, and so on. But herein lies the problem to which the IdeaManager needs to give careful thought. It is much better to bring new ideas in early rather than late. If they are brought in early, there is a greater chance for the assembled group to actually participate in elaborating them and creating parts of them. Thus, it is genuinely a group product, even thought the ignition point may have come from one member. The problem, of course, is that the earlier they are brought in, the more problems they have. Thus, the earlier they are brought in, the greater the peril of incineration. Involvement is a good antidote to incineration. I was involved in a similar "innovation introduction" situation to the one involving "Edison" that had a very different outcome. In this case, involvement was used as a kind of asbestos to both encourage ignition and prevent incineration. At a certain point, the same kinds of questions came up in this team meeting that came up in the previous one: resources, we do not really have the full picture, and so on. The forces of darkness were out. But the IdeaManager said to the group, "Folks, this is just at the beginning phase. What we'd like is an approval in principle so that we can go ahead and involve you in its fleshing out. Obviously we have the same questions that you do. On the other hand, if we don't have some support now, we can't get the resources we need to go ahead." He even asked the larger resources question: "We're sure that you all have a lot of good ideas that could help here. But we need to get started first."

In effect, the IdeaManager validated the resources concern, but used the carrot of involvement (which was totally authentic—the group always had a lot of good ideas) to generate a different tone in the room. That proposal got approved, a task force was put together, resource issues were dealt with, and it was a fabulously successful new venture for the company. What was the connection? Apart from an intellectual one, the person who proposed it was "Edison," the same guy who got dumped on in the story mentioned previously. He simply took his idea, went someplace else, worked it through there, and has the good fortune of knowing he has contributed a lot to his new employer's bottom line. So much so, in fact, that within a few months his new employer would acquire his old employer—Pontius Pilate and the IRS lady were furloughed. Their ability to deny runs high, however. When I talked with them later, they denied it was the same proposal, and denied that their team meeting and the subsequent departure of the new star had anything to do with their demise. They are bitter, and blame market forces "over which we had no control." They have long lunches together, a lot.

Employees thus need the opportunity for authentic participation. If that is what buy-in means—and I stress the concept of authentic—their ideas have to be part of the total package. Then it will be great. If it is inauthentic, and rubber stamped, then it simply is not buy-in.

Investment

Investment is implementation time. Once people are ignited and the process of involvement has fleshed out the skeletal new process or product, then people have to get on board and implement. Why didn't I use the word "implement" for this section? I chose investment because of the emotional quality of attachment that it conveys, against the somewhat neutral "implementation." Implementation has an automatic sound, almost as if "that's all we need to do," when "all" is exactly the wrong word. This is a key stage, and people have to be committed to the implementation. Hence the word investment. As I use it here, investment implies committed implementation. Commitment is likely to be higher, because part of my idea is in the total payload. IdeaManagers have to help design investment plans and keep encouraging, prodding, and pushing so that premature death does not occur at this phase.

A couple of things are typical. One is that the people who thought up the idea are often not those who are too interested in implementing it. And they may be tired, or have run on to something else. So the driver may be lost. That is where the IdeaManager comes in. The IdeaManager is a full-game ball carrier. Obviously, if somebody else is carrying the ball, you do not have to wrestle it away. But, very frequently, individuals are skilled and interested in different phases of the process. Some are really good at the front end: innovation and invention. They come up with new stuff every twenty minutes. In fact, they come up with so much that people say, "Damn! Another new idea from Leonardo! Will he ever stop?"

The second thing that can happen is that the system may become tired. Working through new ideas, getting investment and involvement, and working out the whole pattern is tiring, and sometimes people feel very much like a doctoral student who has passed his or her prelims: "I've pretty much done it; now 'all' that's left is the thesis." Again, the word "investment" tells an important story. It produces the energy needed for the final push. If one believes, as I do, that success is always at the margin, then this is a very important margin. It is necessary to go up to this point, but having gone to this point is not enough. One has to push the ball over the goal line.

A third problem that can occur comes from the fact that in the investment implementation phase, one is dealing with the place where "the rubber hits the road." There may have been pilots, there may have been trials, but now is the time for roll-out. There are certain to be glitches, things we did not think of, problems that were unanticipated. Frustration rises. The IdeaManager has to acknowledge and validate the frustration and work through it. Frustration is normal. It can be expected and accepted. Quitting is not. Paradoxically, complaints about something which, if validated, could provide energy for renewed investment are often taken as reasons for quitting.

I was in an organization not too long ago where a new computer program was being implemented. It involved new protocols, new hardware, and people had to learn new software—there were, indeed, complexities and problems. I was in the office of the Chief Information Officer (CIO) when a couple of people came in and said, "Everybody's complaining about this system. I think we made a mistake. We better back off. Let's make it optional." They had a deep discussion of this, and it was decided to make it optional. Before they announced it, they asked me what I thought. "Bad mistake," I said. Of course, it is difficult; of course people want to complain. And of course you do not like to hear those complaints. What you need to do, however, is to accept the complaints, accept the fact that it is tough, accept the fact that people are going to have a difficult time. And provide them support in doing that. It is very much like teaching a child to ride a bike. The child tries, and falls over. He tries again, and falls over again. He is complaining to you constantly—the bike was not designed right, it is not made for human beings, the seat hurts his crotch, normal people do not do this kind of thing, and so on. You have got two choices. One choice is to say as you have just said, "Well, let's make it optional. You can stick with the trike." On a quick-fix, short-term basis, he may like that solution. On the other hand, he is going to look a little bit odd on a tricycle when he is thirteen. Or you can say, "It's tough, it's difficult, I've been through that, I know you are having a difficult time, and I want to support you and encourage your courage in proceeding. Why don't you take a break and we will come back in a few minutes? But one thing we know is, you have got to learn to ride the bike, because that is the next echelon you need to get to."

A couple of the people in the room said, "That really puts the thing in a whole new light. I think maybe you're right. Maybe we are about to act a little hastily." One person said, "Well! I don't think that's right at all. You're talking about employees as if they were children. Employees aren't children. I find that offensive!" I turned to him and said, "You know it was an example, and I know it was an example. I know you know it was an example. And assuming that it's something more than just an example, and arguing about the example instead of the real issue, is a way of avoiding the real issue. You know that, I know that, and I know you know that. The principle is true." He huffed and puffed. "Well, you're just a consultant!" I replied, "Yes, and perhaps an ex-consultant. But as my friend Bob Quinn says, I have to practice care-frontation. You folks have got to get through this thing. You don't like it. You think getting rid of the cause at the moment of complaints will solve your problem. It won't. It'll just make your problem worse. Paradoxically, accepting the criticisms, accepting the complaints, assuming a nondefensive posture, will have a much better effect, and will help you move forward as well."

To my great relief, that is what they decided to do. They decided to have a team meeting and invite me to speak at it (they were still a little hesitant). I learned a lot from that experience. I learned that there is going to be a cacophony of complaints during the implementation phase. I also learned that these come across to managers and senior managers a lot like blame, and if there is anything senior managers hate more than a padded expense account, it is being blamed. They will do anything to avoid it. They will bob, weave, turn, squirm, even sell out the company. They do not think of it this way, of course, but we should. Accept the responsibility, support the problems, validate the feelings, and keep going toward the objectives. That is an important role for the IdeaManager to play.

CONCLUSION

In today's organizations, ideas are going to be the change vessels of the future. They will be the baskets of values. Organizations which continually come up with new ideas, can process them, and can actually implement them with excitement and enthusiasm will be success stories we will be reading about in the headlines of tomorrow. IdeaManagers help explain the ideation process to the organization, help structure and organize, and help nourish. They can, if necessary, be ball carriers, but they are better as coaches, helping others to be the carriers.

PART IV

Helping Ideas Along through Team and Decision Leadership and Management

In the idea-driven organization of the twenty-first century, team-based, group-based activity is key. This means American society has to move from the "mountain man" concept, as celebrated in the Old West, to the "team as hero" concept, also celebrated in the Old West, but not recognized for the vital force it was (*Trailblazers*, 1973, 73).

> Beyond the routine problems of survival in rugged countryside and brutal weather, mountain men were confronted with a great variety of special ones endemic to their work. Jim Bridger, for example, once went about for three years with a long, barbed Blackfoot arrowhead buried in the muscles of his back. Finally Bridger ran into the missionary-physician Marcus Whitman, who dug out the arrowhead, presumably without any anesthetic except, perhaps, a bottle of whiskey. (*Pioneers*, 1974, 89)

Of course, that was not all the Old West had to offer. While the mountain man was the hero, the wagon train did much of the work. "With their wagons loaded and their animals assembled, all that remained for the pioneers to do at the jump-off point was to organize themselves. Here the American town–team meeting tradition proved useful. As if by reflex, they would nominate candidates, hold elections and set up temporary governments. . . . Alonzo Delano heard of one [wagon train trail government] that contained a court of appeals, an executive branch and a legislative body, all set forth in a written constitution" (*Pioneers*, 1974, 89).

In sports, the team concept is more accepted. An important perspective is expressed by Coach John Wooden (1986) in a little piece he wrote called "On Staying Power," published in the *New York Times Magazine* as an essay paid for by the Panhandle Eastern Corporation. In a paragraph called "The Main Ingredient Of Stardom," Wooden says the following:

> I always taught players that the main ingredient of stardom is the rest of the team. It is amazing how much can be accomplished if no one cares who gets the credit. That's why I was as concerned with the player's character as I was with his ability. While it may be possible to reach the top of one's profession on sheer ability it is impossible to stay there without hard work. . . . I look for young men who would play the game hard but clean but who would always be trying to improve themselves to help the team. (p. 60)

Indeed, as DeVries (1985) points out, the very energy that is characterized by an entrepreneur—what Wooden calls "ability"—may well have a negative impact on an organization if it cannot be channeled and used. This "one man band" theory of management and leadership needs to be modified to involve others.

The group, the team, the wagon train, was—is—an important part of our history, one we need to reclaim and refurbish for the future. Michael Crichton (1987) puts it this way:

> Similarly, group dynamics was perceived as old fashioned, a field that had seen its heyday in the gestalt encounter teams and corporate brainstorming procedures of the early 1970s, but now is dated and passé.
>
> Norman, himself, could not comprehend this. It seemed to him that American society was one in which people worked in teams, not alone; rugged individualism was not replaced by endless corporate team meetings and group decisions. In this new society, group behavior seemed to him more important, not less. (p. 12)

In short, teams were a things of the past—they were important in the past but we did not recognize them. They are important in sports today, and perhaps that is why so many of us spend so many hours watching sports teams play every day. We wish that things could be that way at work. As Crichton has suggested, teams will be the linchpin of the idea-driven organization.

In Part IV, three areas of attention for the IdeaManager and IdeaLeader are discussed. One is some simple rules that will help team meetings go better. The second is a review of the scripts we "play out" in team meetings. The third involves leading and managing the deep structure of team meetings—decision rules. This material comes from the "Team Meeting Masters Research Project" at the University of Michigan. I have spent many years looking at "team meeting masters," individuals who run "excellent" team meetings. The people I have studied run team meetings where three things always happen—decisions get made or action happens, the decisions or actions are of high quality, and people in the team meeting have fun. The next chapters share their wisdom, which is crucial if ideas are not going to go down the drain at the weekly staff meeting or the process improvement team meeting.

Chapter 10

Leading and Managing the Team Meeting Process

In 1976, Anthony Jay published "How to Run a Team Meeting" in the *Harvard Business Review*. That article is now regarded as something of a classic, but a bit of an anomaly. It became the basis for a couple of wonderful British training films starring John Cleese: *Team Meetings, Bloody Team Meetings*, and *More Bloody Team Meetings*. Each of them is about a half hour long, about all the time individualistic Americans care to devote to developing team-based skills in the workplace.

Team meetings are a sort of resented, necessary evil of organizational life. This chapter explores some of the reasons why things go wrong in team meetings.

WHY THINGS GO WRONG IN TEAM MEETINGS

To prescribe a suitable remedy, we must first have a proper diagnosis. We begin with a series of questions: Why are team meetings generally viewed with such negativity? Why do team meetings not accomplish what they should accomplish? Why do so many view team meetings as a waste of time? In short, why do things go wrong? There are many answers. Here are some of the most important.

Individualistic American Values

Group decision making—most group activity, in fact—runs counter to the popular view most entrepreneurs hold of themselves as fierce individualists.

We believe that things run better if we do them ourselves, on our own, without having to rely on others: "I can't get any work done if I have to be in team meetings all the time." The implicit assumption here is that team meetings are the antithesis of work, that work is something we do alone in our offices.

Not only is work viewed as best done alone, but credit for work is seen as an individual reward. In our arts and in our industry we glorify the individual and deprecate the group. Every day must be a replay of *High Noon*. Things go wrong in team meetings because, too often, the team room is a coliseum of conflict instead of a center of cooperation.

Hidden Functions

Hidden agendas often come from hidden functions. Team meetings and teams perform a number of hidden functions on behalf of society. These can confound and confuse decision making. Social purpose, for example, is embedded in the team meeting process that is related to American traditions of representative democracy and pluralism. In our society we recognize that individuals have both a need and a right to have their say on important issues. This has extended itself into the political system of American business, where the team has become a way in which diverse factions are allowed to argue their various points of view. It gives those who would lose out in a simple majority vote a chance to be heard.

Lack of Training

Playing the team meetings game effectively requires a certain amount of skill that can only be achieved through expert training. Though we provide ample opportunities for practice (everyone participates in team meetings), such practice is without guidance and focus. As important as the group decision-making process is to every aspect of business life, our society devotes little time and almost none of its resources to teaching the rules of the team meetings game and training individuals in the application of those rules. Things go wrong in team meetings because the participants simply have no idea how to make them go right.

The Self-Fulfilling Prophecy

Because we have no good team meeting referent, much of our experience with team meetings is negative. Out of that experience base have come strong negative expectations about team meetings and the effectiveness of the group decision-making process. We expect team meetings to be time wasters, and we engage in behavior that proves them to be time wasters. Things go wrong in team meetings, in part, because we expect them to go wrong.

HOW TO MAKE THINGS GO RIGHT: SIX GENERAL PRINCIPLES OF THE TEAM MEETINGS GAME

Team meetings and group decision making can be improved. Learning and then applying a few simple rules (prescriptions, if you will, for curing the ailing team meeting process) will quickly yield dramatic improvements in both the quality of team meetings and the quality of the decisions that emerge from them. Six broad principles form the basis for these rules. Examining those principles will help to place the twelve rules in proper perspective.

An important caveat must precede that examination. Principles and rules go only part of the way toward improving business team meetings and the decisions that come from them. People are people. Potential conflict between us and among us exists whenever and wherever two or more of us gather. Yet there are places—a courtroom, a ball game, a play, an orchestra performance—where the very existence of rules makes for better performance possibilities. Still, rules (and the principles that underlie them) do not of themselves guarantee outstanding performance in team meetings. (Neither do they guarantee it in courts, ball games, plays, or orchestra performances.) What they do accomplish is to give teams more of a fighting chance by preventing some bad things from happening. There are many principles involved in the team meetings game. The list that follows is not exhaustive. These six, however, are seen by team meeting masters as most important (Tropman & Morningstar, 1984).

The Orchestra Principle

In considering the dynamics of the group, consider how an orchestra works—there are a lot of similarities. The orchestra has a score to perform (something like an agenda). There are the rehearsals before the performance (as there is some degree of preparation for any well-planned team meeting). There is a conductor to lead the orchestra through the performance (as there is a team captain to guide the team meeting). The musicians, each with his or her own contribution to make to the totality, come together as a body on a preplanned basis to make music, just as team meeting participants should always be brought together on a preplanned basis to make decisions.

We would find it surpassingly odd if we attended an orchestra concert at the outset of which the oboe player stepped forward and played all of his notes in a Beethoven symphony and then left with the explanation, "I'm feeling a little pressed, and I've got to duck out early." That this kind of behavior happens routinely in team meetings sheds still further light on why the team meeting experience is so frequently unsatisfying. The orchestra provides a metaphor of things which mostly go right. We can apply it in team meetings.

The Content Principle

This principle is closely related to the Orchestra Principle. Excellent team meetings are organized by content. Poor team meetings are structured by person ("We will now have Bill's report"). In poor team meetings, individual participants are allowed (encouraged, required) to present all of the material specifically related to them, all at one time, without regard to the possibility that this material might be of many different kinds and relate to many different items with which the team meeting is concerned. Thus, when Bill gets up to give the report the team captain has just called for, it is just like our oboe player giving us all of his notes at once. At best, team meetings organized by person result in a great deal of repetition that fosters inefficiency and lengthens team meetings unnecessarily. At worst, such organization reinforces the focus on personalities and works to the detriment of good team meetings.

The Three-Characters Principle

Matters before decision teams have one of three characters or are one of three kinds: they involve information sharing, decision making (or building), or brainstorming. Each is distinctly different. In the well-played team meetings game, these are separated before the team meeting begins and organized together so that the group can deal with all the information items at once, all of the decision items at once, and all of the brainstorming items at once. This is what we mean when we talk about organizing team meetings by content. This kind of organization leads to dramatic increases in the efficient use of team meeting time and resources. More important, it leads to better work by the team. Why? Because it focuses all the team's energy on the same kind of work at the same time. Decision building requires, for example, closure. Brainstorming requires openness. If teams jerk back and forth between these two types of items, the team members get lost.

Such organization may (and usually does) require some individuals to appear more than once on the agenda. This is no more odd than our peripatetic oboe player doing his or her thing as the score requires throughout the symphony.

The No-More-Reports Principle

Reports are a major enemy of team meetings. This is true for two reasons. First, they involve one individual heavily and all others only passively. That is not the reason the group was brought together. Second, they tend to be organized by persons rather than by content (again, the ever-popular "Bill's report" or any other case where individuals get up and report on all matters pertaining to their departments, regardless of the character of the information presented). Reports make it difficult for teams to cope with their expected tasks, because reports generally require team members to move rapidly back and forth among items of different character, that have differing requisites, and that make differing demands. The informational content of Bill's report should, in fact, be allocated across the agenda items and presented whenever, wherever, and only to the extent that it is relevant. The information contained in any individual's report should emerge as a natural part of the decision or discussion processes.

The No-New-Business Principle

The introduction and discussion of new business is a team meeting enemy even more formidable than reports. It achieves this status not because there is no need for new business. Rather, introducing new business at the team meeting disrupts the orderly flow of the team meeting process.

New business is, by definition, that about which little is known. The ability of the group to process new business is severely limited. Neither the quality of any discussion about it nor any decisions made concerning it are likely to be of high quality. Injecting new business into a team meeting is roughly equivalent to a football coach introducing a new play into a critical situation of a football game, a play that not only has never been practiced but is one with which the players are not even familiar. New business not only has team members dealing with the unfamiliar, leading to awkward performance; it derails teams from doing what they came to do in the first place. In the well-played team meetings game, what might be called new business is introduced at the end of the team meeting, without much discussion, as a kind of preview of some subsequent team meeting.

The Proactivity Principle

Most teams spend most of their time reacting to issues. This fosters the appearance of items on an agenda that are already at some crisis point. The reactive position is always structurally weaker than the proactive one. It is therefore in the interests of a good team meeting process to reach out for issues and to garner them before they require crisis management. Small problems are easier to solve than big ones. Small decisions requiring minimal discomfort are easier to make than large decisions involving great pain. Team meeting masters reach ahead—downstream, as it were—and take items earlier in the decision stream. It gives team members a chance to think about things, increases participation, and hence increases the quality of decisions.

TWELVE RULES FOR HIGH-QUALITY DECISIONS

The goal of the team meetings game is high-quality decisions. Well-played team meetings games have nothing to do with making people happier in teams (though that will happen, because some of the problematic activities will no longer be present or will have changed). For the most part, the feelings of the players are of only minimal concern. The real focus of the game is on the output of the group over time. That output needs to be assessed on a constant basis to provide effective feedback to the players on how well they are playing the game. What follows are twelve rules for making things go right in team meetings. The last of these rules provides one possible mechanism for conducting this ongoing assessment.

These rules need to become a part of the operating strategies for every IdeaManager and IdeaLeader. As you will discover, when you apply them things will go right in team meetings. When you ignore them, things will go wrong. These rules focus on both the substance of information and on the procedures for presenting it. They are concerned both with team meeting items and with the kinds of considerations that are desired from those items. The latter is particularly important, because it is from such consideration that team members come to know the kinds of things expected of them as they go into the team meeting.

Some of these rules deal with the team meeting itself. Others deal with the preplanning and preparation that go into the team meetings. It is extremely important to keep in mind that the rules apply whether you meet once a year or twice a day, and they apply regardless of the kind of team meeting you think you are calling: morning staff team meeting, sales team meeting, directors' team meeting, whatever.

The Rule of Halves

Identify the halfway point that lies between the end of the last team meeting and the beginning of the next. During the first half of that period, gather information about the kinds of items that are to be considered at the upcoming team meeting. End the item gathering at the halfway point. At that point, examine all of the items that have been gathered. Remove all of those that can be handled on a one-to-one basis in people's offices. If something does not need group attention, do not put it on the agenda. The team meeting masters made clear to me that about 25 to 40 percent of all items that generally come before team meetings should never be there. That does not mean they are not important items, they are just not important for this particular team meeting. Removing such nongroup items permits more intensive focus on the remaining items.

For each potential team meeting item, assess what people, information, and/or resources are needed and arrange for their presence at the upcoming team meeting. If the appropriate information, individuals, or resources are not available, eliminate the item from the team meeting. It makes very little sense to waste the group's valuable time discussing them. Sort the candidate items into the three kinds mentioned: information items, decision items, and brainstorming items. Team meeting participants not only want substantive information about what they are discussing, they want that information given to them in a procedural context: Are we just hearing about this? Are we deciding it? Or are we just noodling around? Information that once would have been presented in a single report should be examined for each of its informational, decisional, and brainstorming components and scheduled appropriately.

The Rule of Sixths

As the final agenda is taking form, inspect the team meeting items and seek to find those that flow in about the following proportions: (1) About one-sixth should be items from the past, historical items that have not yet been completed; (2) about four-sixths should be, relatively speaking, here-and-now-type items; and (3) about one-sixth should be future-oriented, "blue-sky"-type items about which the team meeting participants can do some proactive, plan-ahead-type thinking (the blue-sky items are where the proactivity principal really works).

The virtue of this system is not only that good ideas are generated, but a certain amount of positive affect, especially around controversial items, is allowed to be expressed in a nonthreatening situation. Individuals are allowed to express their creativity in a context where creativity may be expected to have some impact. This becomes psychic income that team meeting planners can provide for the group. It is likely to keep individuals pleased, happier, and willing to return for additional team meetings. This is a side benefit of proactivity that reaps great rewards.

The Two Team Meeting Rule

As this system gets underway, in the team meeting planning phase look for controversial items and seek to schedule them according to the Rule of Sixths. At the very least, controversial items should be discussed at least twice; in other words, in at least two different team meetings. The first discussion should be just that: a discussion. This process allows for affect to be expressed and for new ideas to be introduced about how the difficult items might be approached. The next time such issues come up, it can be for decision.

For very controversial items, three or even four periods of discussion may be appropriate before a decision is taken. All too frequently, our hesitancy to deal with controversial matters encourages us to delay them, raking them up only at the last possible moment under severe constraints of pressure and time. Separating the discussion process from the decision process for such items greatly reduces equivocation and enhances action. And it actually takes less time, because there is prework instead of rework.

The Rule of Three-Fourths

By the three-fourths point in the time period between team meetings, the agenda should be in its final form. Send it to the individuals attending the team meeting so that they have time to review it and to read any accompanying materials. Usually, the team meeting packet contains three items: the agenda, minutes of the last team meeting, and reports of various kinds. Each of these will require some specific attention before the team meeting takes place.

The Rule of the Agenda

The physical appearance of a team meeting agenda is important. Agendas should look like a menu. Most agendas, unfortunately, are simply lists of topics that regularly pass up opportunities for structuring the decision-making context in a helpful fashion. With a menu-type agenda, items are segregated into their information, decision, and discussion teams. Instead of simply "The PDQ Report," for example, the agenda might say something like "Information about the PDQ Report" or "Decisions concerning the PDQ Report" or "Discuss the PDQ Report."

Below each agenda item—the "dish" on the menu—provide a one or two sentence summary of the key elements of the item so that individuals scanning the agenda can have a full sense of what is involved. As part of the item itself or in parentheses next to it, use one of the three key words (information, decision, or brainstorming). This allows the team meeting participants to understand the context of the item. Finally, on the right-hand side of the agenda, where the price might be on a menu, put a running clock with differential amounts of time allocated to the different items. This tells the team meeting participants when the team meeting will start, when it will end, and how much time in the team meeting is roughly being allocated for each item. The following presents an example of how a well-constructed agenda might look:

A Sample Administrative Team Meeting Agenda[1]

Information/Announcement Items

1. Previous Meeting Notes — 8:30–8:35
   scan record of previous team meeting
2. Announcements — 8:35–8:45
   Team Bowling Night: October 7th is it!
   Team Jackets: They will be here early in September

Decision Items

3. Approval of New Meeting Schedule (decision) — 8:45–8:50
   per discussion, Monday @ 8:30 AM–10 AM
4. Holiday Schedules for Summer Staffing (decision) — 8:50–9:05
   flextime approval 6 AM–6 PM is the flextime range
   for May–August

5. New Team Pay Schedule 9:05–9:30
   team pay bonus to be distributed equally to all teams
   members throughout the plant . . .
   though all teams will not have the same bonus $ . . .
   that depends on target completion (budget, quality, speed)

Brainstorming Items

6. Initial Discussion of the New Flex Benefits Plan 9:30–10:00
7. Adjourn

The Record (Minutes) Rule

Provide content-focused minutes that give brief summaries of the main points of discussion. Skip a line and, in capital letters, put in the decision or action. It is good to put it in a box. It is here that names are mentioned, times are given, and responsibilities are assigned. This cures the frequent problem of team meeting attendees being unable to recall from one team meeting to the next precisely what was decided. It also tends to prevent descriptions of decisions that are so vague no one later knows what they meant (e.g., "Take appropriate action").

Team meeting records are frequently taken in the wrong way. They get set down as descriptions of the team meeting process, with long litanies of "he said" and "she said." These, not surprisingly, are called process records or minutes. Not only do they fail to fully convey the extent of team meeting work that went on, they focus on individuals (which you now know is absolutely the wrong thing to do). When such individuals perceive the minutes as placing them in a bad light, it is not uncommon to engage in protracted discussions of the minutes in order to improve their positions retrospectively. Content minutes will cure this problem.

The Rule of Reports

Use the executive summary technique and the option memo technique for all reports to be presented at a team meeting. Most team meeting planners send out too much information. Too much information often becomes disinformation: the potential team meeting participant looks at the huge packet of material sent to him or her as preparation for the next team meeting and puts it aside. "I'll look at this when I can really devote the appropriate amount of time to it." That time never comes, the packet of preparatory material was worthless, and the team meeting participant attends the team meeting completely unprepared—and invariably concludes, "Boy, are these team meetings a waste of time." The executive summary technique is the answer. Reduce all reports to no more than two pages. If an attendee wants or needs more information, it is available on request.

Options memos go hand in glove with executive summaries. Option memos are designed to enhance discussion and to prevent it from getting off the track, one of the most common problems in teams. This technique presents all reports, written or oral, in four steps: (1) a problem statement, (2) a set of options that reasonable people might consider to handle the problem, (3) a set of recommendations for action based on a selection from the option set, and (4) some brief discussion of upsides and downsides of the recommendation.

Options memos encourage the work of the group and discourage rubber stamping the work of a single individual or subteam (the "Okay, here's the problem and here's what I think should be done about it" presentation). It virtually eliminates the problem of the group focusing on whether to accept or reject a proffered solution. Instead, it leads the group into looking at the proposal itself as a basis for discussion and improvement. Options memos present information that the group wants and needs. They answer latent questions and stimulate the process of discussion to begin. The act of discussing options often leads to the discovery of still other alternatives and may also uncover hidden difficulties. The final result is a decision on which the full force of the group has been focused. That decision is almost always a good one, with difficulties removed or diminished and positive features added.

The Rule of Two-Thirds

All team meetings are divided into three parts: (1) a "git-go" part at the beginning, (2) a heavy work part in the middle, and (3) a decompression part at the end. Allocate information items and simple decisions to the first third of the team meeting. Process difficult items in the middle third. Deal with discussion items in the last third. Teams need a little time to get going. Key items, therefore, do not belong at the beginning of a team meeting. Toward the middle of the team meeting, maximum attendance has been achieved. Energy, both physical and psychological, is at its high point. This is the time to handle the toughest items.

The decision making that occurs in the group under this model does tear at the fabric of group cohesion. This cohesion needs to be rebuilt whether the group is a group of strangers or is made up of people who work together on a daily basis. Discussion provides a way to continue group work on the one hand, while allowing for group rebonding on the other.

The Rule of the Agenda Bell

Orchestrate team meetings so that the emotional component follows a bell-shaped curve. Figure 10.1 demonstrates how this might be done.

Item 1 is always the Record Review/Minutes. If your team approves the record and there are not enough team members there to do it "officially," act anyway and they can be reapproved at a later point. It is essential to begin on time.

Figure 10.1
The Agenda Bell

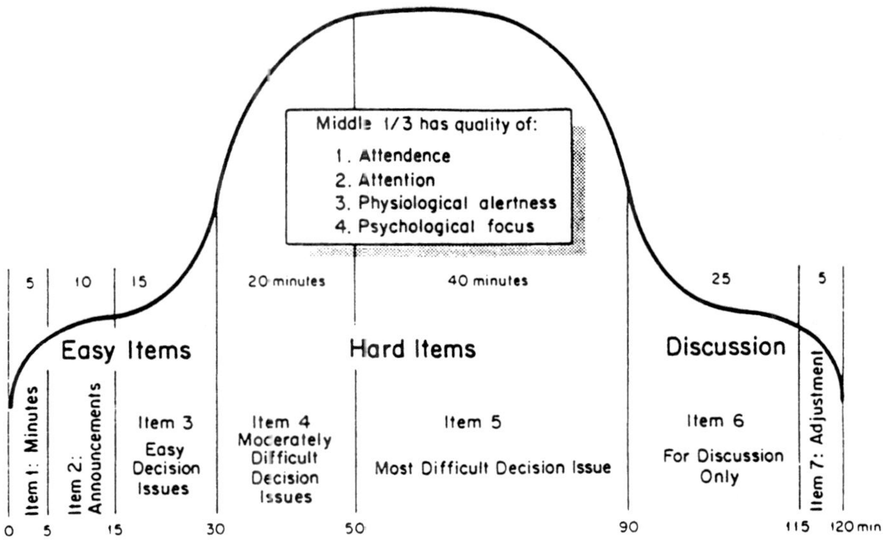

Item 2 is always made up of information items. These may take no more than about 10 percent of the total team meeting time. This will prevent the team meeting from becoming simply an oral newsletter.

Item 3 (and there can be a, b, c, etc.) contains decision items of only modest difficulty. Short, easy decision items allow the group to get going.

Item 4 (a, b, c, etc.) covers the more difficult decision items. These and the Item-3 items represent a moderate and then strenuous warm-up for what is to follow.

Item 5 is always the single most difficult item on the agenda for that particular team meeting. It should occupy space between the 40- and 60-percent points, allowing for optimum group attention and energy. Because of its difficulty, this item will almost always follow the Two Team Meeting Rule. That means that this will be at least the second time in the history of the group that this item is being considered.

By the completion of Item 5, with one minor exception, all of the decision items have been handled. Item 6 (a, b, c, etc.) is composed of discussion items. These are items where thought is needed but where final resolution is not yet appropriate or is not yet in the purview of this particular group.

Item 7 is a short, easy decision item on which all can agree. Usually this will be adjournment! Such an item allows the team meeting to end on time and on a psychological note of management and accomplishment ("Well, at least we got *something* done").

The Rule of Temporal Integrity

Start on time. End on time. Keep to the rough internal time order. Carefully planned team meetings combined with properly prepared team meeting attendees should almost never require more than an hour and a half.

The Rule of Agenda Integrity

Deal with all of the items on the agenda. Do not deal with any items not on the agenda. Individuals make attendance decisions based in part on what they are informed will be covered. They invest time in reviewing team meeting materials. Maintaining the integrity of the agenda reinforces the decision to attend and provides a substantial return on the time investment. Nothing short of an act of God justifies changing the agenda at the last moment. Nothing whatsoever justifies wandering from the agenda during the team meeting.

The Rule of Decision Audit and Decision Autopsy

For important teams, go back on a year to a year-and-a-half basis and look at some of the key decisions made by the teams. Any evaluation can be used. Here is one that has proven effective.

Take a sample of past decisions. For each decision, rate it "A" if it was an all-win situation; everyone benefited, though not necessarily equally. Rate it "B" if the decision had some winners and some losers, but on balance had a positive result. Give it a "C" if a decision was made but nothing happened. A "D" rating is the inverse of "B"; both winners and losers, but on balance the result was negative. An "F," also known as the "Nuclear War Decision," is an all-lose decision.[2] Calculate a grade point average for the sample and feed it back to the teams. Whatever rating mechanism is used is purely a matter of choice. What is crucial is going back and looking at decisions in an effort to assess where strengths and weaknesses lie in the decision-making process.

This assessment leads to the autopsy. In any such review, take the very best decisions and the very worst ones and take them apart. Answer, to the extent possible, the questions, what went right and why, and what went wrong and why. It is imperative that both good and bad decisions be linked together in the autopsy process. Using only bad decisions in the autopsy generates group defensiveness and fault-avoidance behavior.

CONCLUSION

The mechanics of team meeting orchestration provide one of the most important areas of influence for the IdeaManager and IdeaLeader. Though an actual invention or innovation may not be thought up right there in the team meeting (though many are), team meetings are crucial to creating the climate in which ideas flourish. They are the forum in which ideas are shared (or not shared). Team meetings act as the mechanism through which ideas can be improved and linked with other ideas to make a total innovation package. Finally, team meetings are the decision gate through which ideas must pass. For these reasons, organizational management or idea management pays special attention to team meetings and always seeks to come to high-quality decisions.

NOTES

1. Microsoft Word has an Agenda Wizard which can be used as well.
2. IBM's system for "Process Quality Management" uses a grading system as well (Hardacer & White, 1987, 188).

Chapter 11

Leading and Managing the Team Decision Process: Players on the Team / Actors in the Drama

> Team captain: Will you please shut up!
> Team member: Why should I shut up? I've had this meeting up to here!
> Team captain: Because I'm the Chair captain, and I told you to shut up.
>
> Upon discussing this incident later, the Chair says, "Well, I stayed in charge," and a commentator says, "Yes but what you were in charge *of* was a non-meeting."
>
> —*More Bloody Team Meetings*

In the game of football, it is not enough to know the rules to play the game well. It is also important to understand what is required of each position on the team: what the quarterback does, what the center does, what the line-backer does, and so on. The same is true of the team meetings game. To play it well, it is important to understand what is required of the various positions on the team meeting team, because over the course of time we will each play all of the positions. Work in team meetings is very much like the management and leadership discussion. The management part involves positions: team captain, team member, and so on. The leadership part involves "roles"—and roles shift among team participants throughout the meeting.

THE TEAM CAPTAIN POSITION

The team captain is a key position. IdeaLeaders and IdeaManagers captain team meetings, but most of us have never learned to captain a team meeting properly. For most people, indeed, the decision to accept the responsibilities of a team meeting captain is a fairly casual matter. Employees make the decision without regard to much more than whether they have the extra time available that is always assumed to go with captaining. Though that assumption is usually correct, the time involved in captaining a team meeting does not have to be appreciably more than that of any other team meeting role. Everything depends on the team meeting being conducted properly—at the very least, according to the rules we have outlined for you.

Five Basic Questions for Team Captains

Being an effective team captain requires you to make certain of several things. First, the group that will be team meeting must have necessary and sufficient resources to do the kinds of things that it is being asked to do: the necessary money, if money is required; the necessary staff, if extra staff is required; and so on. If this condition is not met, you should decline to captain the team; you are being set up!

Second, to be an effective team captain you should have a feel for the politics of the team. Are they something you can work with, and, if so, how? A careful political assessment done in advance can save many future problems. If you cannot figure out what is going on, or if you sense that there are murky hidden agendas on the part of some or all of the members, you might consider declining.

Third, if you really want to get good at the team meetings game—and you should, for it can place enormous power and capabilities for accomplishment in your hands—it will be necessary for you to engage in a certain amount of self-assessment in connection with captaining a team meeting. You must ask yourself questions like the following: What does it mean for me to be team captain of this group? What kinds of signals does my reputation in the business convey? How will others react? Others will be reacting to you on the basis of these signals. If you are aware of what you symbolize, you can avoid being trapped by the perceptions of others.

Fourth, you must thoroughly understand the purpose of the group you are expected to captain. If the team captain is to be the custodian of this purpose, it should be written down and provided to the other participants. This is true even for the simplest staff team meetings held on a frequent, regular basis. If someone else is the custodian of the mandate, then that individual should be asked for it in writing. During the crafting period, negotiations about the nature of the mandate, the scope, and the resources can be undertaken.

Fifth, and perhaps most important, in undertaking the role of the team captain you need to ask yourself whether it is possible for you to move from the role of partisan to the role of statesman. Many team captains feel that once they assume the team captainship, they will be able to get their own way. Unfortunately, as Anthony Jay (1976) pointed out, self-indulgence is one of the great problems teams face. It is necessary to assume the posture of a statesman if the team meeting process is to be successful at facilitating the product of the group rather than promoting one's own wishes and desires.

The Captain's Chair: Some Requisites

The position of team captain has certain things that are required. The captain is responsible for the mechanics of the meeting: getting agendas prepared (recall the rules in Chapter 10) and getting input from team participants—getting, in other words, the information and people needed (recall the garbage can model in Chapter 6) together in the same room at the same time. It is, indeed, much like an orchestra conductor.

Then the captain helps keep the group on the agenda. Anthony Jay (1976) points out that there is a sequence to the discussion process that facilitates that process, if it is followed. First, there is the discussion of the problem. Second, there is discussion of evidence and points of view about the problem. Third, there is an agreement about what the evidence and perspectives mean. Fourth, there is a decision. Fifth, there is action.

As far as possible, it is your job as the team captain to keep the discussion moving through these stages, seeing that each one is resolved before the next one is begun. Throughout, the team captain maintains equality for persons but equity for issues; people are all treated equally but issues are not. More attention is lavished on some issues than on others in order to achieve the appropriate and necessary group results. Throughout, you as the team captain have overall responsibility for the group product, not for getting your own way. The team captain exercises influence by asking questions, by directing the discussion, by structuring and shaping the agenda, and through the preparation and supervision of options memos. Then there is follow-up, based on what has been agreed to. While the captain is not the only one to follow-up, he or she follows-up the follow-up.

THE TEAM PARTICIPANT POSITION

A popular view is that the member's role is a passive one, with nothing to do and nothing special to know: "There's nothing to it. All I have to do is show up and doze off." Like so many popular views relative to team meetings, this one is wrong.

To begin with, there is the matter of preparation. No procedural problems loom larger in poor team meeting practice than those caused by the unprepared participant. Without proper preparation, discussion becomes driven and participation turns to prattle. The unprepared participant presents the worst example for other participants. Unprepared participants will often attempt to cover their lack of preparation with bluster, rancor, sarcasm, and general negativity. So, preparation is the first responsibility of the participant.

Knowledge of how the team meetings game is played is a second team participant responsibility. This not only means a thorough understanding of good team meeting procedures in general (such as the team meeting rules presented here), but a complete knowledge of the specific rules of that participant's team (though the rules of some teams are more formal than of others, all group decision-making bodies have specific rules of their own). It is the member's responsibility throughout the life of the group to cooperate in the enforcement of team rules. At the very least, this includes such things as coming on time, coming prepared, and requiring the team meeting planners to provide a straightforward agenda.

Third, the team participant needs to constantly monitor his or her level of participation in the team meeting, contributing at a level that is appropriate for this particular group decision-making activity. Some teams are high-participation teams; others, low participation. Within either context, it is the participant's responsibility to both contribute at the appropriate level and aid the team captain in seeing to it that all other participants likewise contribute appropriately.

Fourth, though issue crystallization and decision focus are generally the team captain's responsibility, it does not always have to be the team captain's actions that accomplish them. The team participant should be constantly alert for opportunities to provide summative reflections at various points and to assist in the crystallization of ideas.

The team participant should be equally alert to other members who have a tendency to dump on the group; those who raise problems then sit back with arms folded as if to defy the group to provide solutions. It is both correct and useful when one has a problem with a particular proposal or line of thinking to share that perspective, provided such sharing is accompanied by good faith attempts to seek solutions. It is incorrect, unfair, and harmful for a team participant to raise an issue without making it clear to the other members where one is at with respect to that issue. It forces the group to shift its focus away from the issue and into a mode where it must probe to see what the recalcitrant team member thinks. Finally, members owe loyalty to the group outside of the group. This means supporting group decisions that one opposed. It also means not knocking the group, its members, or its team captain in other team meetings, at cocktail parties, or anywhere else.

THE RECORDER POSITION

The recorder is the individual who is taking the team meeting record (using the Recording Rule, of course). The recorder is also responsible for getting copies to team participants in a timely fashion. Recorder roles should be shared. Do not only ask women in the group to do it!

THE CONSULTANT POSITION

A consultant is an individual who is paid or assigned to assist a team in carrying out its functions. He or she can be an internal consultant—from corporate or another division—or an external consultant brought in from an outside firm. This individual is different from other participants because the consultant is typically not a team member. This point is extremely important. All teams know who are members and who are not, even if everyone is well acquainted with one another, as is the case for most businesses.

The consultant performs five kinds of functions for most teams. First, the consultant is a researcher, providing various types of information for the team (political, historical, economic, scientific, items of program history, and so on).

Second, the consultant is a knowledge synthesizer. It is not enough to simply present a range of information to a group (though some use it as a procedure for dumping on the group). Rather, the information should be organized, synthesized, and integrated. This function is an important one for the consultant to perform. For a team considering executive compensation, for example, the consultant might say something like the following: "Here is a list of other companies and the compensation packages they provide their executives. They seem to fall into the following teams, based on what appear to me to be the following kinds of criteria and linked in the following ways to corporate income, and so forth."

Third, the consultant is a writer and a documentor. The role may involve recording. It usually involves the preparation of reports, preparing executive summaries, and generally doing the "leg work" of the team.

Fourth, the consultant is an aide to the team captain. In team meetings, this usually involves sitting close by the team captain in a kind of dead zone that diminishes the physical position of the consultant and emphasizes his or her "assisting" rather than "membering" function. The consultant does not participate directly in discussions or decision making in the sense of giving his or her opinion on this or that matter.

Fifth, the consultant is an administrator. In part, this relates to the function of aiding the team captain, and this may involve many things. The consultant may distribute the minutes, may assist in preparing the agenda, may review team meeting strategy with the team captain, may arrange for the team meeting room, and so on. This "stage manager" activity is not especially dramatic, but it needs to be done if the setting for the team meeting is to facilitate the team meeting process rather than hamper it.

OTHER POSITIONS

Teams have other people who join them. There are customers, suppliers, and individuals from upstream and downstream in the production process.

Some of these are time limited, and some are there "for the duration." Some are "formal," others are "informal." Again, much like specialists in an orchestra brought in for a special series or special performances, these others are coordinated through the captain. The reason mission and agenda are so important is that they allow the captain to schedule appropriately and keep the permanent team to a reasonable size—usually, the smaller the better. Without mission and agenda, team participants are added "in case they are needed," which is costly to the firm, the persons involved, and the integrity of the team itself, and, hence, its accomplishments (or lack thereof).

ROLES

Positions are locations we have with duties attached. Roles are actions we undertake to help the team function, and are, in a sense, group properties. By that I mean that roles such as facilitating discussion or helping achieve closure are not assigned like job descriptions—they bounce from participant to participant. It is through roles that much leadership is exercised, and it is important that, in a successful team, everyone has the opportunity for leadership and the experience of enacting leadership.

The Blender

Intellectually, the team needs to blend the ideas of those in the team meeting. Blending involve showing connections between the ideas of various participants.

The Question Mark

In blending, and in many other contributions, asking rather than stating is helpful. Instead of saying, "That's a dumb idea," or "That's a terrific idea," the participant raises questions of a "what if" nature. This is especially true of weak or bad ideas. The individual who offers a poor concept might well be the genius who provides the key to the solution of the next problem. Squelching that individual may cause him or her to retreat and contribute no further. The idea is to guide the contributing process in a way that invites the individual to confront some of the problems of the poor idea, yet still receive support for the basic effort of suggesting and trying. (See also pp. 126–127.)

Protect the Weak and Temper the Strong

With respect to interpersonal activities, the team must try to protect the weak participants and temper the strong in order to allow for an evenness of group participation. Those individuals who do not participate need to be invited to share their views (they are often the ones who will protest most vocally in the restaurant after the team meeting). Feelings and affect need to be diffused. This is best accomplished by direct recognition: "Jim, you seem to feel strongly about this." We deal with Jim directly instead of watching him glower in the corner.

Clash Is Good, Up to a Point

The team supports the clash and conflict of ideas. At the same time, participants seek to find aspects from different types of suggestions that may become part of an overall solution.

CONCLUSION

Team meetings can be improved. Therefore, team meetings should be improved. Improvement means that the output of team meetings—decisions—should be of the highest possible quality. In moving toward high-quality decisions, we have presented procedures that shorten time, focus discussion, and generally make team meetings less painful. But it is important for you to understand that it is not removing pain from the team meeting that is our goal. Rather, it is making the pain pay off. As individuals experience team meetings that are productive and invite and involve their participation, a process of reinforcement will begin that will ultimately reverse the negative aspects of the self-fulfilling prophecy and use that mechanism for improvement and achievement.

Chapter 12

Leading and Managing the Team Decision Process: Decision Rules

There are many times when ideas, concepts, and actions simply get stalled in team meetings. Preparation has been accomplished, participants are knowledgeable about their positions and roles, but something else is going on. That something else is what results in dangerous decisions. In this chapter, you can learn what to do about that possibility, and help to keep them away from your organization.

THE DECISION MOSAIC

The first thing that it is important to know is that the word "decision" is a collective noun, like "deer" and "fish." The best way to think about a decision is in a group or collection of things. One of my favorite metaphors is that of a mosaic. A mosaic gives the impression of being a single thing, but it is really a collection of small things seen, as it were, from a distance. Decisions are like this. They are assemblages of things—smaller decisions, actually—which give the appearance of a whole. Those smaller decisions are called *decision elements*.

DECISION ELEMENTS

A decision element is the smallest piece of the decision mosaic. The specific elements will vary, of course, from decision mosaic to decision mosaic, but I can give you an idea of what to look for. Consider the decision my wife and I make every day, and you probably do too. It is called the "What Shall We Have for

Dinner Tonight, Dear?" decision. Now, that looks like a whole decision, but it is really a collection of elements—including small decisions like "in or out," "time," "who cooks," "what is in the fridge," and so on. There are probably twelve or so elements which have to be brought together into a coherent package. It is in this sense that decisions are built, one element at a time, until they are complete. When a decision has been built, it goes through a process of *decision sculpting*. I call the process of building one of *decision crystallization*.

DECISION CRYSTALLIZATION

Decision crystallization is the process of crystallizing or precipitating a decision out of the viscous fluid of discussion. In my research, I learned a good bit about how groups actually come to decisions. It was a slow process, but clearly some of the meeting masters knew something that others did not. In some cases, individuals in a group would propose an action. For example, "Let's do X." They would be roundly criticized and faulted, and it was very clear that exactly what the group did not want to do was X. It was also strongly implied that the individual was a fool for mentioning it. But other times, most common among the meeting masters, they would listen to a discussion for a while and then go through a little bit of a review process and suggest a course of action. With astonishing frequency, group members would say, "Exactly, right on the head, you've understood clearly what we are saying." This ability to hone in on exactly the key issue or problem was sometimes even shocking, because the cacophony of group participation, the disparity of views, the strongly held and apparently implacably opposed positions seemed to allow for no possible resolution. And suddenly a resolution would be stated that seemed to satisfy most of the people in the room. How did this happen? It involves knowledge about decision rules, and knowledge about the process of decision crystallization. Let us begin with decision rules.

DECISION RULES

Decision rules—norms from our society—are legitimizing rules, and I accept them as authoritative. In most groups, there are multiple decision rules (about five of them), and they conflict. By conflict, I mean to suggest that the operation of any rule alone would yield a different set of results than the simultaneous operation of all five. One of the secrets of the meeting masters was that they were aware of the decision rules and orchestrated solutions such that they could be shown to meet several of the rules simultaneously.

The Extensive Decision Rule The extensive decision rule is perhaps our most popular rule, or at least our most public one. It refers to "one person, one vote," and it tests the breadth of preference. Each team member gets the same weight of say, and the fact that some individuals feel very strongly and others really do not care is irrelevant in the application of the extensive decision rule. We have used this rule since kindergarten. "How many want to have hot dogs? Hands up. The ayes have it." When teams do a round-robin and each member gets to vote on an idea the team is considering, it is an example of the extensive rule in action. But most groups of any sophistication recognize that there are other bases on which a decision needs to be tested, and therefore the extensive decision rule, most often represented through voting, is really inadequate unless it is the sense of the group that some of the other decision rules and the results that the application of these rules would have generated have been addressed.

The Intensive Decision Rule People have feelings. Some team members feel more strongly about some things than others. Depth of preference is something never addressed by the extensive decision rule, as it has no way to deal with it (though sometimes team participants—when they do vote—put up two hands to show they really feel strongly; it is a humorous way to indicate depth of preference). Teams try to find ways to discover who feels strongly, and how strongly they feel, so that they can take their strength of preference into account in coming to a discussion.

The Involvement Rule Most decisions have implementation actions that follow, and frequently team participants will be involved in the implementation. Implementors often have preferences about how the implementation is to be carried out, and participants involved in the implementation usually have more say in the decision than those who are not. Consider a simple family example. In most of our households, a simple example of this rule is the statement, "The one who has to make dinner gets to pick dinner." In teams, there is always implicit, and frequently explicit, attention to the question of who will follow up, and then attention to what their view on the matter is.

The Expert Rule In many areas of team decision and discussion there are questions of expertise involved—legal, scientific, and so on. And there are things that experts know, for which it is not a matter of voting. It is not always clear whether an issue needs an expert opinion or not, and how certain that expert opinion might be, but groups would at least like to be aware of what experts are saying. They might not go along, as in the phrase, "Defense policy is too important to be left to the generals," but they still want to know what the generals (the lawyers, the doctors, the professors) have to say on the matter.

The Power Rule In a business organization, this rule is often expressed in the question, "What does the boss think?" In teams, there is the same question, but there may be several bosses. In a matrixed organization there are at least two. And then there is the team captain, whose views carry a bit more weight. That is on the formal, positional side; informally, teams have *influentials*, people without formal power but with relationship power. Teams spend a lot of time finding out what the powerful think and feel, and blending those elements into the mix we call a decision.

In blending the rules, what seems to happen, based on observing the meeting masters, is that successful decision making involves crafting, building, and developing alternatives that can be shown to address three or more of these decision rules. Because they would create a different distribution of outcomes if each is applied alone, successful alternatives need to address issues of power, expertise, depth, breadth, and implementing concern. From my perspective, this amounts to a working definition of consensus in a team situation. It is my observation that when groups talk about consensus, their operational definition is actually a proposed solution that needs all five of these. They can get a broad base of support, from those deeply concerned, that has powerful and expert people on its side and that is certainly not opposed by and may even be endorsed by the people who have to carry it out. There is no question that if one can come up with options that meet these criteria, there is a winner in store. The difficulty, of course, is that this often has to be done on the spot, so knowledge of the decision rules is not enough. It is how they are used that becomes a key skill. This is the process of decision crystallization.

Crystallizing a Decision

Crystallization involves acting on behalf of the group, not on behalf of one's own interests. It involves taking risks: of being opposed, of stepping back, of actually engaging with the group in a give-and-take construction process. Crystallization goes through phases:

1. round of discussion
2. team sweep
3. summative reflection
4. action hypothesis
5. action legitimization
6. discussion refocus

Based on what I saw team meeting masters do, here is the way it works. Often the team captain performs the function of going through this process, but really anyone can do it, and in the best teams, everyone should do it. I will use the term *item manager* for someone on a team who is responsible for a particular item. Let us go into a little more detail.

An item manager who is responsible for a particular decision initiates the discussion on a particular topic. Using the interrogative technique, he or she can ask questions, but not really contribute too much of his or her own view. He or she might express a small view here and a preference there, but it is important to do more listening at this point. That is because it is important not to "sway" the early discussion (through the power rule) with the preferences of the item manager (because everyone wants to know about what the item manager thinks), and because the item manager is working on securing, sorting, and conceptualizing the team's expressed ideas. Item managers are listening and organizing with the rules in mind: What is the breadth of preference, what are the depths of preference, what do the implementors have to say, what is the expertise, and what does, or might, the boss (or bosses) want?

Rounds of Discussion Item managers are sensitive to rounds of discussion. A round of discussion occurs when each person has said one thing or when everyone who wants to make a contribution to that particular round has done so. There is usually a small pause in the group process at this point, and it is vital that item managers begin the process of crystallization here, at the end of the round, lest individuals go into a second, repetitive round. (For a second round to be helpful, it has to be based on some degree of closure being achieved during the first round; that is, a second round has to be built upon some initial team agreement in the first round.)

Team Sweep At the end of a round, the item manager engages in something I call team sweep. He or she has been noting who spoke and, to some extent, how often. The team sweep process involves asking those who have not participated or who have had very unclear participation to express a view (unclear participation means that a participant has said words, but no one can be sure where the person actually is on the issue at hand). At the end of team sweep, the next step—summative reflection—begins.

Summative Reflection A summative reflection is a simple, straightforward, yet organized summary: "Here's where we are. What I've heard is . . ." This allows the group to hear back what it actually has been saying, but in an organized, coherent fashion; it comes as a surprise to many individuals that, in the heat of discussion, not everybody remembers what everybody else has said. And no one is really taking time to organize and present in a structured way what, indeed, has been said. As the item manager is listening, though, he or she is organizing—sometimes on paper, sometimes with notes, sometimes in his or her head—and feeding it back in the process of summative reflection. This last point is an important one: Summative reflection is an organized approach to the discussion, not just "he said, she said." Flowing out of summative reflection is an action hypothesis.

Action Hypothesis When the reflection has been completed, the action hypothesis phase begins. The item manager should say, "And so it seems like the following is a reasonable course of action." This is why the Abilene Paradox is avoided. Somebody has taken it upon themselves to actually vocalize an alternative. The hope is, of course, that the alternative will be presented and legitimized in such a way as to make it palatable and stimulate agreement. However, it is also known and always known that vocalization is a test. It is a trial balloon, a floater, and it is an interaction between the person who vocalizes, working on behalf of the group, and the various group members, with their differing interests, extensiveness, depth, involvement, expertise, and power, that a decision is actually shaped.

Action Legitimization At the end of the action hypothesis there needs to be a "because" statement: "This seems like a reasonable course of action because . . ." The because statement is where the decision rules come in. For a team to accept a proposed action, that action has to meet, and be shown to meet, at least three and preferable all five of the decision rules. This is why item managing toward a decision is such hard work: it requires the item manager to absorb the discussion and reshape it; come up with an idea about how to go; suggest that idea and then legitimize it in terms of the breadth of preferences expressed, the depth of preferences expressed, and the implementive concerns expressed; and address questions of expertise and power as well. It is a formidable job, and it is done in ordinary language. Here is a small case example.

Where Shall We Go for Lunch?

A team captain may say, "It seems that McDonald's would be a good place to have lunch [the action hypothesis] because [the legitimization] most people seem to find that acceptable [extensive decision rule addressed], it has a salad bar for those who don't want to eat meat [intensive decision rule addressed], John doesn't care where he drives us for lunch [involvement rule addressed], they've been using the new low-fat burger [expert rule addressed], and the boss doesn't care where I spend our lunch money [power rule addressed]." It is almost a certainty that at that point people will reply with, "Yes, sounds like a great idea. Fine with me. Hits it right on the nose."

Discussion Refocus At that point—the decision point—the item manager refocuses the group on the next issue, helping the team move on to the next step in its business. He or she points the group at the next item to deal with on the agenda or in the decision package. Rather than using phrases like, "Well, what's next?" the item manager suggests that the team can now move to X.

This process is a subtle one. Lights do not go off and bells do not ring, but, upon reflection, I think readers will see groups in a new light. The risk, of course, is that individuals will receive criticism for suggesting an action hypothesis. On the other hand, risks taken on behalf of group advancement is recognized by the group (as long as it is not a cover for individual interests being advanced), and is rewarded in group influence. The process goes on, element after element, until the entire decision is constructed. This is how leadership is used build decisions.

Things do not always go smoothly, though. What if participants do not agree when an action hypothesis is suggested? That is actually rather typical, because, for many teams, hearing an actual alternative is somewhat shocking. It is a lot like listening to someone complain and complain about their spouse. You say, "Well, perhaps you should consider separation." They draw back, astonished at your words. What they have failed to realize is the impact their words have on others, an impact different from the impact their own words have on themselves. So item managers need to be prepared for problems as a routine matter. When the problem comes within the element, item managers can go to a second round. When problems come between elements, or involve the linking of several elements, item managers can use decision sculpting.

When a Second Round Is Needed

Sometimes, after the initial advancement of an action hypothesis, the reaction of the group is negative. It was useful to advance, because people clearly understood they did not want to do that. In that case, the item manager suggests a second round of discussion, but asks people to express preferences different from those they have already expressed. If this request is not made, the second round of discussion will simply be a repeat of the first round. Participants will say, "I think this, I think that," which they have already shared. In the second round of discussion, therefore, they need to be invited to stretch their preferences and to think of new things, new approaches, new opportunities. Then, after the second round of discussion, the same process—summative reflection, action hypothesis, action, legitimation—is repeated, except this time it is more complicated because the item manager needs to keep the array of ideas from round one and round two together, and is synthesizing opinions from round one and round two. For difficult items that require three, four, or five rounds of discussion, it becomes a daunting task, doable but tough. It is in this way, however, that discussion progresses toward a decision rather than simply spins wheels.

Decision Sculpting

Once a group has agreed to all the elements—that is, the small decisions have been reconstructed into a larger one (e.g., decisions on each meal item have been combined into a "menu")—the item manager engages in the final step in the process: decision sculpting. Decision sculpting involves looking at the entire package of decisions, small decisions, or the decision construction that has been assembled, and assessing whether anything has been left out, whether the way it has been assembled has created problems, and whether adjustments and alterations are needed. Once the team is satisfied that the total menu looks balanced, appeals to a variety of interests, and is sensible, they move ahead. If groups can do this, they will feel successful because they are successful.

CONCLUSION

IdeaManagers and IdeaLeaders need to be accomplished at the process of decision facilitation in a team context. Teams are becoming more and more popular in organizations, and will be a central, if not the central, organizational vehicle in the twenty-first century. Teams can make ideas better, or, more commonly, destroy them through pernicious procedures, corrosive concepts, and dangerous decisions. It is in the team meeting, or series of meetings, that the competitive edge of the organization will be honed or blunted. Team management skills are not only interpersonal ones (these have been the subject of lots of courses for "facilitators" and "conflict processors") but also intellectual ones. Intellectual and interpersonal issues are different ones, and the idea of a team as a group that shapes ideas and puts them into action has been ignored somewhat. IdeaManagers and IdeaLeaders need to at the forefront of team decision management in the twenty-first century.

PART V

The Power of 11: From Art to Part—From Concept to Customer

Several years ago the Seven-S System was introduced in some popular business books (Peters & Waterman, 1982; Pascale & Athos, 1982). The design is relatively simple. Each S represents an important area for management attention. Three of the Ss are so-called hard Ss: strategy, structure, and systems. These were widely thought of as being favored by American-style management orientations. Three of the Ss are soft Ss: style, staff, and skills. These were widely thought to be favored by Japanese-style managers. One S—superordinate values—was seen as an integrating feature of the other Ss.

In 1989, Gersh Morningstar and I expanded the Seven-S System to the Ten-S System (Tropman & Morningstar, 1989), including three areas that had, we felt, been omitted from the original seven: self, superordinate structure, and superordinate culture. The individual person was not in the original list; neither, it turned out, was context. Because "the world outside the organization" is so complex, we divided it into superordinate structure (the physical environment, population changes, legal changes, inflation rates, etc.) and culture (changes in national and international values, reconfiguration and reweighting of values, blending and melding of cultures, etc.). Because an organization's "values" are a sort of subculture within a dominant culture, we renamed superordinate culture, which referred to the organization's culture, subculture.

This volume adds yet another S, shift. Shift refers to the changes in the other ten Ss which is constantly going on. It seems, in the fast-paced world of the twenty-first century, that any model which does not include a dynamic element would be seriously flawed.

These Ss—now eleven—nest inside the Five Cs in the following way:

Characteristics	Competencies	Conditions	Context	Change
Self	Skills	Systems	Superordinate	Shift
Style	Structure	Culture		
	Staff	Structure		
	Strategy			
	Subculture			

In addition, our focus is on the management of ideas, innovations, new products, and new services. This Eleven-S System is best visualized as a rotating plate with a two-circle center cut into six equal sizes and with a very thick crust. It is displayed in Figure V.1.

Self is at the center. The elements here include the characteristics thought to be key for IdeaLeaders and IdeaManagers. Characteristics are important. They define the "us" that others know, and that we think we know. Two points need emphasis. First, relative "fixed" characteristics here are not things that can never be changed. If you are not as tolerant of ambiguity as you would like, that tolerance can be increased. Changing characteristics is perhaps not as quick as acquiring new skills or shifting a style a bit, but it can be done, is done, and sometimes needs to be done. The second point is that we should not overly rely on characteristics as a "determiner" of IdeaLeadership and IdeaManagership success. "Natural" occurrences of IdeaLeadership and IdeaManagement may occur, just as individuals have athletic and musical talent. But, in each case, practice (skills) and style (doing things well) are needed.

Surrounding the self are skills and style. Both of these elements are personal, in the sense that they are in the possession of the person and can be used by the IdeaManager and IdeaLeader. Skill is having a competency at doing something; style involves doing it exceptionally well, and points to certain forms of skill expression.

Beyond skills, style, and self lie four organizational elements: strategy, structure, staff, and systems. These are the elements on which skills, style, and self work and focus. A fifth organizational element, subculture, is described here as a ring that integrates person and organization and links them to the external—superordinate—environment.

The third major ring is superordinate culture and structure. These elements represent the environment, the external conditions of markets, regulations, public opinion, values, and attitudes that can be responded to and occasionally shaped.

Figure V.1
The Tropman Eleven-S System

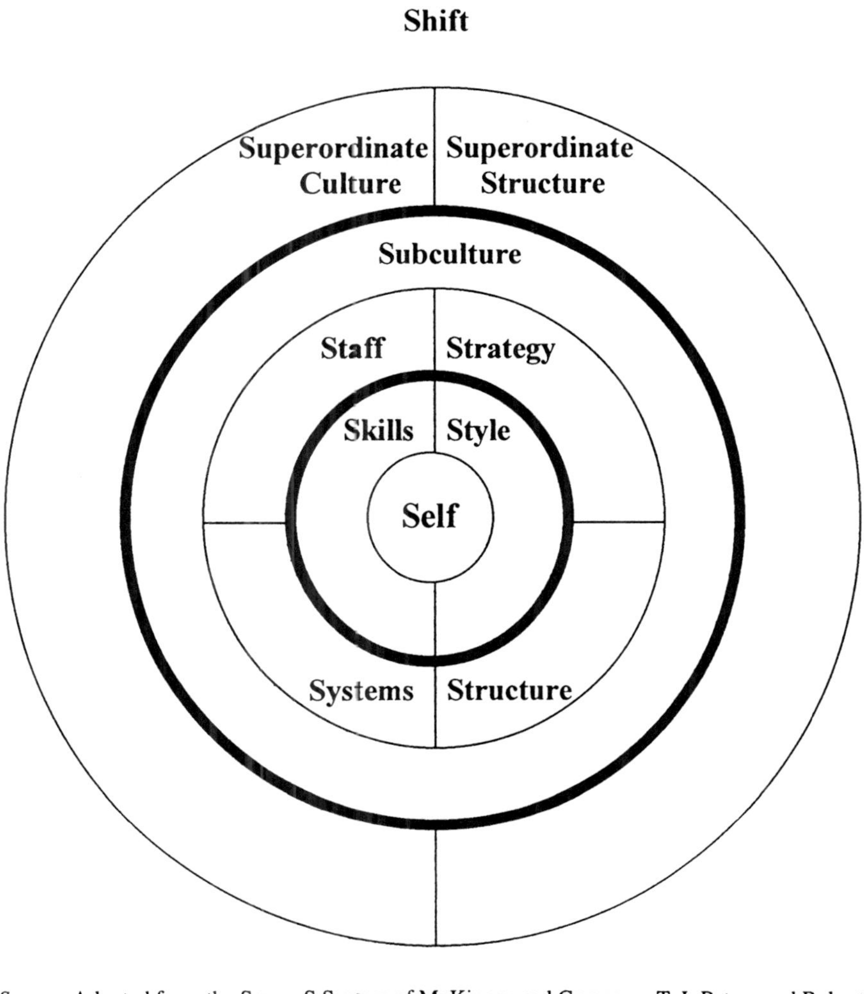

Source: Adapted from the Seven-S System of McKinsey and Company, T. J. Peters and Robert Waterman, Jr., *In Search of Excellence* (New York: Harper & Row, 1982).

Finally there is shift—or, in the model here, one might call it spin. Consider that the plate of ten Ss is rotating, constantly in motion, or consider a sort of solar system with eleven planets rotating in elliptical orbits. There is a constant dynamic quality. That was missing from the Ten-S rendition.

IdeaManagers and IdeaLeaders need to attend to each of these eleven areas. The chapters in this section take them up, one by one. Each chapter title begins with the word "creating," and the purpose of that structure is to emphasize that the perspective here is driven by the book's mission—to help individuals approach each area with the idea component foremost. That stress is in turn driven by the conviction that ideas—generating them, structuring them, and using them—will be the competitive edge in the twenty-first century. That being so, the person with the plan for comprehending and capitalizing conceptual resources wins.

Chapter 13

Creating the Idea-Driven Self

How does one create the idea-driven self? A good start is to ask about the characteristics of people who are the idea-driven "kind." Having had the opportunity to observe people like this in consulting and at the university (and also to observe people not idea driven in consulting and at the university), I think I can share some of their features. Research has made it easier, as scholars working in different fields are coming up with concepts useful here.

The term "characteristics" needs to be carefully understood in this context. One way it can be used is to refer to permanent kinds of things, like race or gender. That is not my meaning. Rather, I refer to things typically associated with the IdeaManager or IdeaLeader. The attributes—organizationally driven, having ensemble and emotional intelligence, and possessing the question mark—are not ingrown, but rather acquired. I call them characteristics rather than skills, not because they cannot be acquired, but because they are more associated with the presentation of self of the IdeaManager or IdeaLeader than skills. In fact, I think it is the high degree of integration between characteristics and self (where, in some senses, characteristics become self) that leads me to conclude that the person "always" was this way, and thus success can be explained by traits of some kind. Nothing could be further from the approach I wish to encourage. The executives I observed "constructed" themselves and their characteristics. They were not born with them.

The IdeaLeader and the IdeaManager is, in many respects, like the entrepreneur—a combination of a thinker and a doer. In fact, Morningstar and I began moving in this direction when we defined an entrepreneur as a person who develops and implements new ideas (Tropman & Morningstar, 1989).

Hence, skills at thinking up ideas are part of IdeaManagement and IdeaLeadership, but skills at implementing them are vital as well. The magnificent dozen—twelve traits that we found kept coming up over and over again as possessed by our "Idepreneur"—can continue to serve us well here. But there is more. Schelling's (1978) idea of the two-self model is important to consider, as the IdeaManager and IdeaLeader are always working both in the here and now and the then and there (Thaler & Shefrin, 1981).

Crucial as well is Gardner's (1983) list of seven "intelligences." His work vastly increased our idea of what intelligence really is. He introduced the concept—as one of the intelligences—of "self-awareness," something followed up by Daniel Goleman (1995) in his work on emotional intelligence.

ORGANIZATIONALLY ENERGIZED

In *Entrepreneurial Systems for the 1990s*, Morningstar and I identified twelve traits that seemed to characterized IdeaManagers and IdeaLeaders. These were as follows:

1. *Risk taking*: The entrepreneur is an individual who takes risks—who is characterized by risk-taking behavior. The entrepreneur is, therefore, one in a new business, operating outside of established organizations.
2. *Independent*: The entrepreneur is an independent individual who does not like to work for others, who would rather work for himself or herself.
3. *"Internal locus of control"*: This concept, developed by psychologist Julian Rotter (1966), differentiates people along the dimension of how they perceive life's events to be controlled. Those who believe they have a great influence on what happens to them are characterized as having internal locus of control. Those who believe that what happens to them is the result of luck, fate, chance, or forces "out there" have an external locus of control. People who begin new ventures are more likely to be internally rather than externally oriented.
4. *Thriving on discomfort*: Though some individuals seek the tranquil life, others are excitement and action oriented. IdeaManagers and IdeaLeaders fit the latter category, because they like the excitement of the new and the different.
5. *Self-starting*: IdeaManagers and IdeaLeaders begin things on their own authority, using their own ideas and energy as justification. "If you wait around for new ideas to be introduced, you often have a long wait."
6. *Self-confident*: Entrepreneurs have abundant self-confidence, a strong belief that the new product, service, idea, or approach they are proposing has merit. This confidence is necessary, because others are less likely to be supportive of new ideas. Hence, one not only needs to believe in the new idea but must have sufficient self-belief to overcome hostility and criticism.
7. *Flexibility*: IdeaManagers and IdeaLeaders are flexible. Markets and systems change, and businesses must change with them. One's own ideas may need to be adjusted either over time or overnight.

8. *Persistent*: IdeaManagers and IdeaLeaders are persistent. They are individuals who can keep at things in spite of setbacks. Sometimes persistence may be the opposite of flexibility and, indeed, one may be flexible in change when one should be persistent and persist when its time to hex. How does one know?
9. *Ambiguity*: IdeaManagers and IdeaLeaders can tolerate the ambiguity of choice that confronts them. Some individuals find uncertain situations difficult to deal with, threatening, and psychologically problematic. Not so for the entrepreneur: IdeaManagers and IdeaLeaders are not only less affected by ambiguity, but are capable of exploiting it and turning it to their own advantage. Indeed, ambiguity may enhance their excitement.
10. *Pattern recognition*: IdeaManagers and IdeaLeaders are capable of resolving conflicts through pattern recognition. They are capable of seeing how everything fits together, and catching a glimpse of the forest while others are struggling with the trees.
11. *Low need for support*: This is closely related to self-confidence, but IdeaManagers and IdeaLeaders are more than confident. They have a low need for the support of others, which allows them to take action that others might consider risky. With new ideas, however, the validation from others is low. Because of this lacunae, one not only needs confidence in ideas but also needs the ability to proceed without a lot of encouragement and backing.
12. *The right stuff*: Tom Wolfe's phrase (1984) sums up the psychological view of IdeaManagers and IdeaLeaders. It is having the whole package.

These dynamic dozen are really the kinds of things IdeaManagers and IdeaLeaders need. That is not surprising, because there is a lot of similarity between the entrepreneur and the IdeaLeader and IdeaManager. Each needs to be appropriately risky; each can tolerate ambiguity, has a low need for support, and needs to be persistent. In some respects, the IdeaManager and IdeaLeader might be what Pinchot (1983) has called the "intrepreneur."

DUAL TIME FOCUS

The IdeaManager and IdeaLeader requires a dual time focus. This concept points to the ability to look at time along two dimensions: the present and the future. Harvard economist Thomas Schelling (1978) discusses this concept in a piece called "Egonomics, or the Art of Self-Management." What you want in the "here and now" (a cigarette, some consumption good) may be bad for you in the "then and there." Social psychologists also talk about this skill—the ability to be a planner (think about the future) while also being a doer (acting today) (Thaler & Shefrin, 1981). IdeaManagers and IdeaLeaders are continually balancing the present with the future; what is needed now with what will be needed then.

ENSEMBLE INTELLIGENCE

IdeaManagers and IdeaLeaders have a broad range of intelligences. Howard Gardner (1983) calls this "multiple intelligences." Gardner proposes that there are more than the two areas we often think of as intelligence. Most of us are familiar with the verbal definition of intelligence—words, words, and more words. Then, too, there is the math kind—often linked to music, with music being seen as a kind of subset of math. Gardner sees seven, not two and a half: linguistic (verbal), logical/math, and musical are the first three. Musical is separated out into its own sphere. To these he adds spatial, bodily–kinesthetic, and the personal intelligences (interpersonal and intrapersonal). What do these mean?

Musical intelligence involves attention to sounds and their combinations, beat/rhythm, and aural attention. Verbal involves raw vocabulary knowledge, the ability to make combinations of and with words, a general facility with language, and a precision with language. Logical/mathematical intelligence involves performing logical operations and engaging in analogic thinking. One example of this kind of thinking would be the following type of question:

Napoleon is to brandy as Caesar is to

» salad

» Rubicon

» palace

Spatial intelligence involves locating yourself in space, a sense of proportion in spatial terms, and a sense of spatial magnitudes. Ideas about office design, office location, and distribution of field offices would be involved here, as well as finding your way around spaces. Also included here are visual and artistic elements, such as a sense of proportion, a sense of color, a sense of wholes and parts, and an ability to work in multidimensional configurations. Such multidimensionality involves things like light, flow, and the packaging of elements like these together.

Bodily–kinesthetic intelligence refers to the skilled use of one's body. It involves physical grace and control, and an awareness of the body as subject and object. Dancers, athletes, and actors have this skill, but it is important in other kinds of performances: oral presentations, "executive presence," and so on. We are perhaps most aware of the negative demonstrations of this element—the "klutz" who can never seem to avoid stumbling, falling, tripping, and generally being a walking calamity.

Interpersonal intelligence is that piece that allows us to know how we relate to others. It involves awareness of impact on others, the ability to move among different groups smoothly and easily, and "street smarts," or the ability to read new situations involving people and figure out what needs to be done.

The personal intelligences have two elements. Intrapersonal intelligence means possessing a knowledge of your own knowledge of motives and desires and an ability to be aware of and understand your own feelings. This element is so important that it is the subject of the next section, and I will discuss some of the work of Daniel Goleman (1995) on the subject of emotional intelligence. The other personal intelligence is interpersonal. It involves "the ability to make distinctions among other individuals, and, in particular, among their moods, temperaments, motivations and intentions" (Gardner, 1983, 239).

I call the possession of several of these kinds of intelligence *ensemble intelligence*. IdeaManagers and IdeaLeaders need to have ensemble intelligence because the material they work with—ideas—has a complex nature. IdeaManagers and IdeaLeaders I observed all seemed to me to have intrapersonal awareness and several of the others, but they did not have the same others. What they did do (intuitively, it now seems, because Gardner's [1983] work was not yet out), was to create their team around the multiple intelligences conceptual framework. There were logical strengths, there were verbal strengths, and there were all the others. IdeaManagers and IdeaLeaders have a few, and build around the rest.

EMOTIONAL CONTROL

Emotional intelligence involves understanding your own feelings. Many of us do not have a clue, or much of a clue, about why we do what we do, what drives us, and what we really need and want. I work on a one-to-one basis with many executives, assisting them in "coaching." Coaching involves providing them with cues and clues about their career; suggestions about what to do in this situation, in that situation, with this board group, and that staff group; when to stay and when to look around; and the like. What they do not realize is that under the guise of coaching a lot of counseling goes on.[1] Counseling in this context involves dealing with feelings—envy, anger, hate, revenge, bewilderment—and developing skills so that the emotional energy involved can be focused on career advancement, not career destruction. In *Emotional Intelligence*, Daniel Goleman (1995) pulls together some work going on in the fields of psychology and sociology of emotions, and involves his own thinking as well. As with Gardner (1983), Goleman crystallized and gave vocabulary to something that I had observed but could not quite express.

For Goleman, emotional intelligence involves five factors: self-awareness, motivation, empathy, social skill, and the management of feelings. Some detail is displayed in the following list.

Emotional Intelligence

Self-Awareness	knowing what you feel; using gut sense to make decisions you can live with; emotional intelligence
Management of Feelings	controlling impulses; soothing your anxiety; having appropriate anger

Motivation	zeal, persistence, and optimism in the face of setbacks
Empathy	reading and responding to unspoken feelings
Social Skill	handling emotional reactions in others; interacting smoothly; managing relationships effectively

Why is emotional intelligence so important? Well, for one thing, you can see that some themes are being repeated among the three lists. Persistence appears at least twice, understanding yourself appears twice. Social skills and interpersonal awareness could be much the same kind of thing. So we begin to get confirmation that these traits or attributes are important ones. No doubt they are important in all kinds of successes. However, I stress them especially for IdeaManagers and IdeaLeaders because ideas have more than just intellectual or technical content, they also have emotional content. New ideas destroy old ideas. Think, for example, about the destruction Darwin wrought. People who had very different ideas about how humans came to be and the role of God in that process must have been—indeed were—stunned, turned upside down, inside out, and emotionally crushed.[2] Successful IdeaManagers need to be able to handle not only the technical, intellectual, and operational elements new ideas involve but, just as important, the emotional elements of ideas, the destructive parts, and the feelings people have about those destructive parts.

THE QUESTION MARK

There is one last feature (trait, attribute, or characteristic) of the IdeaManager and IdeaLeader that is important. I call it the question mark. IdeaManagers and IdeaLeaders are interrogative in nature. Questioning is a part of their persona. They are relentless in their interest in things, and seem to be always asking questions. Questions such as "Is this really true?" and "How do we know that?" and "I wonder why that is?" just keep coming. This can naturally be, under some conditions, pleasant. At first you think you have found someone who is really interested in the process you have developed, who really wants to understand what you are doing here, and who is also interested in you, how you are holding up, and the stress you are under. And it is true. IdeaManagers and IdeaLeaders are interested in these things. It is pleasant to have someone who is interested.

But sometimes employees feel that their integrity is questioned. If you have just finished a technical report and the boss says, "Are you really right?" it is hard not to feel criticized. Typically, IdeaManagers are driven more by their curiosity then by any "picky sense." But employees do not always see it that way (and IdeaManagers and IdeaLeaders are not always that way, either). Hence, they can get under your skin.

Nonetheless, relentless questioning has many more advantages than disadvantages, and by relentless I do not mean hostile. It can expose weak spots, uncertainties, and assumptions that, upon examination, are not warranted. Just as important, if done correctly, an interrogative approach keeps the dialogue going. Questions require answers and responses, something that statements do not.

For this reason, IdeaManagers and IdeaLeaders are not only good at getting information because of the actual questions they ask, they are also good at getting information because of the dialogue they engender. In these two ways, curiosity saves the cat.

CONCLUSION

The IdeaManager and IdeaLeader has a self with characteristics that aid him or her in the many elements of the idea generating and implementing process. These characteristics are personal, in the sense that they have come to be integrated into the presentation of self, and, in that way, seem natural as opposed to learned. But they are learned. Energy, a dual time focus, an ensemble of intelligences, and emotional intelligence are able to be developed and honed.

NOTES

1. For a discussion of coaching and counseling, see Whetten and Cameron (1998).
2. For an dramatic illustration of the practical results and problems this particular new idea presented, I recommend reading or, better yet, seeing the play *Inherit the Wind* (1955).

Chapter 14

Creating Idea-Driven Skills

The skills successful IdeaManagers and IdeaLeaders must have fall into three major categories: intellectual skills, interpersonal skills, and organizational skills. Intellectual skills are those that involve essentially cognitive elements; that is, knowledge or awareness of ideas and a comfort in working with them. The creator sums up many of the skills in this area. Interpersonal skills involve the heart rather than the mind. Interpersonal skills require the ability to deal primarily with people and with their feelings and emotions. Here the advocate captures the important elements; advocacy involves bringing people and ideas together. Organizational skills involve creating organizational forms. These are forms that foster the generation of new ideas. Organizational skills involve sculpting—shaping ideas to fit environments that they can succeed in—and jazz—improvisational skills that allow one to take advantage of the emerging elements in an idea-rich situation.

INTELLECTUAL SKILLS

Intellectual skills involve dealing with ideas—their structure, their parts, their wholes.

Securing New Ideas: Scour the Environment

We have already mentioned the innovation inventory and techniques to increase creativity. It is vitally important to make sure that your own supply of new ideas is, itself, adequate. It is very difficult to introduce new ideas into other systems if you have none yourself. We are not speaking necessarily of earthshaking, Nobel Prize–winning technologies and ideas, though these certainly may be possible. Rather, we are referring to the regular, ongoing set of procedures and processes that each person must engage in if he or she is to be reasonably current. Inventory techniques, assumption audit techniques, or creativity techniques will not help if there is not a sufficient body of information to use them on. IdeaManagers and IdeaLeaders, therefore, need to be information gatherers and gardeners.

Read the Paper The procedures for doing this are not terribly difficult. As an IdeaManager and IdeaLeader, you already know a lot. You must simply add to your existing knowledge base. Begin with newspaper reading. Read—or skim—at least three newspapers daily: one national newspaper, one local newspaper, and one trade or professional journal. Keep current on new books. If there is not time available to read the whole book, then subscribe to a service that provides summaries or listen to them on tapes. It is not necessary to become a scholar, but it is necessary to be aware of and alert to the different topics that are capturing the attention of writers and readers, not only the substantive material, but the number of times it is mentioned, the depth of coverage, and the scope of reader interests. These things will alert you to new trends, new possibilities to be explored, and problems to avoid.

This injunction seems very simple and yet it is among the hardest to follow. As we all know, "daily routine drives out planning." There tends to be little time in most people's busy day for anything more than the most cursory look at semirelevant or not yet relevant materials. But that is the whole point. You do not yet know the relevance until you expose yourself to the printed materials available to you.

Ask Others for Information The printed word is not the only place where new ideas come from. You also get them from other people. IdeaManagers and IdeaLeaders should spend a good bit of time just listening to people. That is taking advantage of the situation. We all meet people throughout the course of our day: colleagues, people on planes, people in airports, family members, and so on. We should seek to use these opportunities both as sources of new ideas and as testing grounds and reaction points for new approaches, new products, and new services. One IdeaManager I know of claimed he got all his information from people in airplanes. He felt that they were completely neutral, knew nothing about him or his enterprise, and could thus give a completely unbiased view of the kind of problem and the potential solution that might be helpful.

Get Out of the Office Another IdeaLeader I know of used to fly out to places and get a firsthand look at new or competing modes of production and marketing. All these people said approximately the same thing: Without a great deal of input from diverse sources, they were not confident they would obtain important information about changes that might affect them.

Approach Your Staff with Caution Can your staff get information? Of course. Most IdeaManagers and IdeaLeaders have staffs who can do these things, but March and Simon (1958), in their concept called "Principles of Uncertainty Absorption," state, "Uncertainty absorption takes place when inferences are drawn from a body of evidence; and the inferences, instead of the evidence itself, are then communicated" (p. 165). Editing removes precisely the "uncertain ties" and "ambiguities" that might be relevant to the development of new products and markets. To a considerable extent, then, some part of the environmental scanning must be done by you personally.

Securing New Ideas: Creative Conditioning and Practice

Top-level intellectual performance, like top-level physical performance, requires conditioning and practice. You cannot wait around until new ideas strike (see Argyris, 1982). Rather, you must actively seek them, beginning with yourself in day-to-day work. The IdeaManager and IdeaLeader can engage in, and encourage others to engage in, innovation assessment. Considering family life, work life, and relationships with colleagues and children, ask yourself, "What is new? What is different that I am doing in the approach to the problems and concerns that I have? Have I tried different approaches?" If you are unlikely to introduce anything new into your own household, you are similarly unlikely to introduce anything new into your own workplace. A pattern of innovation receptivity and awareness of the risks associated with innovation needs to be established and cultivated. Set specific goals in the various sectors important to you. Set goals aimed at the introduction of new approaches, new perspectives, and, in the workplace, new products, services, plans, and programs.

Seek to improve your own thought processes and your own creative approaches. To do this, consider following the example of James Rumsey, "the most original" inventor in American history. Edwin T. Leyton, Jr. (1987) describes Rumsey as "a remarkable American inventor," whose role lay in "changing the very process of invention" itself (p. 50). Leyton comments

> Rumsey's methods have been incorporated into modern engineering design technique, usually as aids in creativity. First, he would gain an abstract understanding of the elements of the machine; then he would manipulate these elements by mental operations similar to those employed by scientists in considering the spatial relations of geometric figures or the interactions of material bodies. That is, *he would combine mechanical elements, separate them, reverse their roles, change their spatial relationships* (e.g., move an object from vertical to horizontal, turn it upside down, etc., reverse the direction of motion or flow, or reverse the motion of an entire machine; that is, imagine it running backwards). Reversibility has proved an especially powerful analytical tool for technologists, and Rumsey was one of the first to use it systematically. He apparently realized that just about any machine, if reversed, will result in another machine. (p. 54, emphasis original)

The essential techniques of personal creativity are neither new nor impossible to achieve. We have deliberately sought an example from a historical figure to illustrate that the principles of thinking about new ideas, making new combinations, and introducing new approaches is not something that depends on new technologies, microcomputers, laser beams, or pies in the sky. Rather, it depends on the mental work of combination, recombination, inversion, and taking an overall fresh look. Rumsey's approaches are as valid today as they were years ago. Rumsey was an entrepreneur. He failed because he lacked certain competencies involved in negotiating the system within which his inventions would take place and from which they (and he) could prosper. But as we think today about how we can introduce creativity and new approaches into our lives or into our own firms, his kinds of questions are as sensible now as they were then. If a product has been sold routinely to the customer, consider involving the customer in the product innovation process. If a product has been aimed at a youth-oriented market, consider aiming it at an older market as well.

The point of all this is to systematically engage in explorations that challenge conventional assumptions and postulates. You might decide that those conventional assumptions and postulates retain their vitality. Such a decision will have validity only if it comes after rigorous investigation and testing rather than being based on easy agreement. The kinds of things that Rumsey speaks of are sometimes called *assumptions audits*. The point of an assumptions audit is not to necessarily change anything but to have a systematic practice through which questions about traditional, usual, regular approaches can be asked. This audit can be part of the other audits already undertaken in the Five-C's Conference and the Concert of Components Conference. The technique is intellectual and requires certain interpersonal skills and organizational structures, but you must begin with your own self.

Securing New Ideas: Failure Analysis

Other people and one's own creativity are good sources of new ideas. A third vital source is one's failures. An interesting example of failure analysis comes from the wine industry.

For many years, French wines were the undisputed "king of the hill." California wines were not worthy of consideration. However, English wine merchant Steven Spurrier and his partner, Patricia Gallagher, who operated a wine shop in Paris, felt that some California wines were actually of exceptional quality. In 1975 and 1976, he brought some California wines back to Paris and organized a blind tasting, with the Californias set against the very best of the French reds and whites. The blind tasting was performed by the crème de la crème of the French wine industry. Members of the jury knew only that some of the wines were French and some were from California. The Californias snagged the two top spots for whites and the first spot for reds. The initial reaction was, of course denial. "Sophisticated arguments were put forward to explain away the choices." But that did not last. "The tasting gave

California a shot of confidence. . . . But it also gave the French a valuable incentive to review traditions that were sometimes mere accumulations of habit and expediency, and to reexamine convictions that were little more than myths taken on trust" (Asher, 1997, 97).

America's preoccupation with success often leaves us less able to learn from our failures. Consider a comment made by the successful restauranteurs, the D'Amico brothers. They are frequently sought out because of their innovation and creativity in helping flagging, sagging restaurants, but in spite of the trouble these restaurants are in, and the premier talent they recruit to help them, they really do not want to change: "People would hire us based on our innovation and creativity, and when you get there they don't want your innovation and creativity. They decide what they really need is a gourmet hot dog" (Lessen, 1996, 36).

All too frequently, though, we do not really analyze what went wrong. Instead, we seek the quick fix, or more accurately, the quick pseudo-fix. We like to blame it on some individual and get rid of that person, or we paper the whole thing over and forget it ever happened. Both of these approaches are means of denial. They do not really come to grips with the fact that the failure occurred. In fact, for many IdeaManagers and IdeaLeaders, "failure" is not a concept they use a lot. It is too bogus; too general. They tend to dwell on particular deals that fell through rather than examining the strategies and tactics that led to the failure and finding in such examination lessons for future success. If one establishes the climate where failure—at least some failure—is both acceptable and expected, then individuals will be much less uptight about looking at it. When people go bowling, after all (or golfing or playing tennis or engaging in any popular game or sport), they spend endless hours discussing their game, what went wrong, where the problems were, and so on. It is perfectly all right to make mistakes in these areas, to discuss those mistakes, and to learn from them. But it is not generally all right in most organizations. It must become so. Some level of mistake, some level of error, must be tolerable in an effective IdeaManagement system.

Once acceptability of at least some mistakes is established, regular failure analysis sessions need to be set up. There is no particular format for such a session. What is important and crucial is the scheduling of it and the doing of it.

Introducing New Ideas

Having new ideas—whether you think them up or get them from the environment or from failure analysis—is not enough. You have to introduce them. Though almost everyone would agree that the introduction of new ideas is important and worthwhile, the actual process of introducing new ideas—the actual things one might do and points one might consider—becomes substantially more vague. New ideas require work, and the IdeaManager and IdeaLeader needs to feel comfortable enough with ideas to put new ones on the table. The problem is not a new one, as an article in *Scientific American* points out in a March 1987 review of its own history:

Inventors often complain of the experience in inducing capitalists in joining them in their enterprises. Not infrequently the blame rests as much with the inventor as with the man with money. The capitalist is often blamed for not seeing out the advantages of an enterprise when the fact is it has never been presented to him in the right light. Every man, therefore, who would seek the aid of capital in furthering his plans for introducing an invention should first be prepared to show the whole state of the art covered by such an invention and wherein the improvement lies. Second, he should, if possible, show what particular market needs to be supplied by such an improvement, and something approximating, too, the returns which reasonably may be expected. Third, he should have some well settled plan of introducing a new product or furthering the new scheme. If his invention is worth pushing, in nine cases out of ten there will be little trouble in procuring financial help if the proper methods be employed. (p. 10)

Stealthtech Stealthtech is the skill at making new ideas seem like older ones. Successful IdeaManagers and IdeaLeaders frequently incorporate a protective coat of history as a new idea is introduced. Minimizing "newness" under the guise of "oldness" can often be an effective technique.

Shedability Budget planners have used this technique for years. In doing a budget, they "plump it up," including some items which they know will be cut. In budget meetings there is sort of a norm: You can cut more than X percent. Budgeteers craft a budget with X plus 2 or 3 percent. When the "night of the long knives" arrives, the "cutters" trim X percent, the budgeteer looks suitably chastened, and "life goes on." Of course, the "cut" budget was already the plump budget, so the cutter and the budgeteer can both save face.

IdeaManagers and IdeaLeaders do the same thing. In a proposal involving a new idea, they will often include an even newer, more outrageous idea. That is the nightcrawler. The "large mouth bass" (opposition talkers) grab at the nightcrawler and force its expulsion from the proposal. The proposer agrees, reluctantly of course, and with suitable protest and anguish. The truth, of course, is that cutters and opposer have sway, but only so much sway, in firm councils. Once they have cut, or opposed, they have used their influence, and used it up. If they have not used it on the right things (from their perspective), that is too bad. The proposer sheds the unneeded proposals, and the really important ones can slip through. If you think this technique is impractical, think of the Trojan Horse.

Blessings Sometimes the IdeaManager or IdeaLeader needs to come into the scene with approval from the organization's "archbishops," "cardinals," or (occasionally), the "pope" himself or herself. Involved here is the process of checking our the idea with the higher-ups, and getting them to be supportive of something tentative, such as a pilot or a trial. When discussion begins, it can be mentioned that Cardinal so-and-so was very supportive. This technique is often a winner.

The Blended-Idea Technique IdeaManagers and IdeaLeaders often find the blended-idea technique useful. In this approach, an idea is asserted to be blended from the ideas of several to many others. At the very least, the "others" are quite a few of those in the room. Names of those who thought up relevant parts of the idea are specifically mentioned, so that credit moves away from the presenter (who presents himself or herself as a mere vocalizer). Not only does credit flow away from the speaker, which makes the idea a bit harder to oppose, but the generous recognition of the contribution of others diffuses credit, thus creating a sort of group product. From a timing point of view, this technique works best at the end of a round of discussion (see Chapter 6 on meeting management; it is something like a summative reflection but explicitly includes a lot of names with the ideas). Sometimes, of course, vocalizers will "overattribute" an idea to a member, giving more credit to the participant than the participant really deserves. Participants who have gone to sleep during discussions are very useful for this purpose. If anyone questions the attribution, vocalizers can say it was "implicit" in their contribution. Readers will also recognize a variation of this technique as one used by politicians in speaking. At every appearance they usually manage to mention at least the names of prominent people in the room, and oftentimes many others as well. The difference between the IdeaLeader and most politicians is that for the IdeaLeader there is a mix of names and ideas. The politician usually gets the name part and drops the ideas part. (This comment is not as cynical as it may sound. Politicians, living in the public view as they do, cannot afford to have each thought on the front page.)

The In-Principle Technique Often those opposed to new ideas will pick some tiny point and gnaw away at it, not infrequently endangering the whole proposal. Because new ideas are vulnerable, it is often hard to answer questions like, "Exactly how much will this cost?" or "Specifically when do you expect to go on-line?" From a distance, one can see that those questions are attacks; if you knew all the answers the idea would not be new. But incomplete or inconclusive responses often sound like waffling, an interpretation encouraged by opposers. Unless IdeaManagers and IdeaLeaders act, they are almost certain to lose. Acting often involves the in-principle technique. This technique means that you say something like the following:

> That is an excellent point; in fact, I have been asking the same questions myself [you steal their position here]. However the issue before us now [you are telling the group that the opposer is asking an inappropriate question for purposes here] is to see whether, in principle [i.e., in general, overall, assuming all will go well, etc.], we would like to move in this direction. The question you ask [a genuflection toward them again] and others yet to be asked of a vital nature [you are good, but not that good] will take time to address properly [no quick fixes here] and it seems like a waste of time if this is not a direction in which we, as a group [you are now drawing opposers into your web] wish to move.

Opposers are about done for now. Then you can say (the coup de grâce), "And my sense of this group is that, in principle, it is strongly supportive." You have ensnared the opposers into agreeing with the new idea: a fine day for innovation! You say this because there is no point in waiting for someone else to say it—they might say the wrong thing.

Verbal Customization: Technical Business Knowledge It is imperative for the IdeaManager and IdeaLeader to have the standard business knowledge that is required of all business persons. Marketing, financial analysis, business planning, and so on are simply taken for granted. In addition, specific knowledge about the product, service, or area—substantive knowledge—is also important. Knowledge of the product or service without technical business knowledge leads to as much trouble as general business knowledge does when a person has no knowledge of the particular product or service area.

The reason this knowledge is vital is that technical business knowledge is the "vessel" that often makes new ideas acceptable. In other words, it is words and how you use them. They have to be the right words. Listeners are more accepting if proposals for the new are presented in language that they understand and accept.

There is an old story about the difference between the religious and the nonreligious university that illustrates this point well. Two people were discussing what the differences were. One commented, "I'll tell you: At the nonreligious university, two plus two equals four; at the religious university, two plus two, with God's help, equals four!"

This example may seem a bit frivolous, but it really is not. The "with God's help" phrase is a proxy for all the specific languages, phrases, localisms, and whatevers that are characteristic of specific subcultures. To the extent that IdeaManagers and IdeaLeaders can customize their language to that of the hearer, it makes a positive difference in downstream acceptance.

Writing, Presenting, and Speaking IdeaManagers and IdeaLeaders need to be capable of presenting new ideas in written, presentation, and oral form. While linked, these are three separate skill packages.

Preparing written memos and reports that get ideas moving throughout the organization is an important skill. The memo is an especially important document, yet it is one that most of us spend little time on and frequently do badly.[1] Achieving a simplicity of expression in terms of new ideas is difficult, as proposers tend to overinclude material about the idea, thus losing the key thoughts in a sea of text. A useful outline to follow is one like the following:

The Basic Memo

The Problem (1 paragraph)

The Options

1

2

3 (Always give 3 or more options to prevent polarization)

The Recommendation (IN CAPS, SO NO ONE CAN MISS IT)

Upsides and Downsides of the Recommendation

Recall that this format was mentioned before as the options memo technique in preparing agendas (see pp. 94–95). I am stressing the format here of the written presentation, and the organization of it. In introducing new ideas, the "medium is truly the message." Simple, declarative sentences within an options memo organizational structure will add greatly to your chance of successful new idea introduction.

The presentation is an intermediate form, involving both writing and speaking. In the presentation, the key points of the memo have been reduced to overheads or talking points. A very good method to use here is PowerPoint Presentation Software by Microsoft. It forces you to organize your ideas in slides, with a header and a body. The outline for the memo is more or less what a slide might look like. PowerPoint places the bullets in the correct font so audiences can see, and allows you to customize your presentation as well. You can print out "thumbnails" (small versions of your slides, two per page) so that readers and listeners can follow along. Remember that whenever you make a presentation about new ideas your audience should have a copy of your memo and a copy of your slides. This makes it easy for them to understand what you are saying.

IdeaLeaders need to be persuasive. The very idea of innovation and invention means working uphill, against time, and needing to convince and persuade. Sometimes you can persuade through written presentation. There are other times when you let the "target" persuade himself or herself through creative listening. But there are times, too, when you must go to a venture capitalist or a boss or a CEO or someone in a special power relationship with you and sell an idea. Sam Zell told me about this process in his own shop (Equity Financial Management of Chicago) as crucial: "If my staff can't sell me on an idea," he says, "it will never go anywhere." Speaking in public—and these kinds of presentations are public speaking—is frightening for most of us. We fumble. We are inarticulate. We speak with all of the involvement and excitement of a wax dummy. We make fools of ourselves.[2] Professional speech teachers and public speaking coaches, in fact, often compare the fear of public speaking to the fear of death.[3] There is only one way to conquer the fear: practice in front of an audience. That practice comes easiest in a supportive environment such as that provided by speech courses offered by community colleges, university extension services organizations such as Toastmasters, or any of the excellent specialty seminars offered by publicly funded institutions or privately operated business education companies. However you go about gaining the necessary experience, take heart in the knowledge that the fear does diminish with practice. Of all business skills, the one without which success may be the most difficult may well be the ability to behave as though you were reasonably comfortable in any sort of public speaking situation (even though your stomach may be churning). It is far better to gain the poise you require in such situations in less crucial situations (as in a public speaking course) than in the actual give and take of everyday business, where oral clumsiness can destroy you.

A special key to business speaking, though, is to speak from a presentation. By that I mean, as mentioned, that you have a set of slides and you are elaborating on them to an audience. There are a couple of general things to keep in mind. One is to recognize the importance of time. Try to work in small blocks—fifteen minutes is good—and divide that two-thirds to one-third. The two-thirds time (ten minutes) is for presentation; the one-third is for questions and discussion. If anything, extend the questions and discussions. The second point is to never forget the importance of questions. For new ideas, listeners have a lot of questions. It is not even important that you provide definitive answers to all the questions—they need a chance to get that question out. If they cannot do it with you, they will do it with less supportive people later, in the hall.

INTERPERSONAL SKILLS

Introducing new ideas into an organization requires that you have them in the first place. And there are better ways to get ideas introduced. I have just mentioned some techniques. The IdeaManager and IdeaLeader has to get others to accept them. New idea acceptance is as much an emotional and diplomatic game—a people game—as an intellectual game. For this reason, skills for dealing with people are as important as skills for dealing with ideas. Step number one is acquiring a *role repertoire*.

Acquire a Role Repertoire

In his book *The Presentation of Self in Everyday Life*, Irving Goffman (1959) talks about this very point. He asks us to think of life as a theatrical play and to think of the roles we play as similar to theatrical roles. Our presentation of self to family, to colleagues, to coworkers, then, can be thought of as a series of roles. That total constellation of roles that we have available to pick from can be called a role repertoire. Any given role performance involving one or more of our roles with the roles of others can be called a *role ensemble*. Most of us are aware of the fact that the performance of others is affected by our own performance, and that the roles of others are dependent in part on the roles we play. Most of us, however, fail to exploit this general knowledge in any immediate personal or practical way. We occupy ourselves with pointing out to ourselves what others are doing wrong. Implicitly, this approach suggests that if "they" would change things would be better. Because the IdeaManager and IdeaLeader is in a business of influencing people, the place to start is with himself or herself. No one has greater control over you than you do. One way to produce the desired behaviors in others, therefore, is to change your own presentation of self; that is, vary your own role repertoire. Change may be too strong a word. What we have in mind is adding a variety of personal styles so that you can enhance the likelihood that the new ideas you wish to introduce will be accepted and that the system within which you are working will be productive and creative of new ideas.

What would some of these roles be? There is the creator, the one who thinks up new ideas. There is the partisan, which comes in two styles: One is the critic, often called the devil's advocate. But it is equally important to be the angel's advocate, one who supports new ideas. (It is very interesting that we have a phrase which has come to be used for a critic, but no phrase that is common for the role of supporting new ideas; I had to think one up!) More dispassionate is the analyst. The analyst is one who looks dispassionately at the numbers and sees if the new idea makes sense in practical terms. There is the sculptor, the one who shapes an idea out of a mass of varying contributions. There is the orchestrator, who blends diverse contributions into a seamless performance. And there is the coach, who encourages the performance of others and gives hints and helps. These are not the only roles, but they are some of the available new idea enhancing ones. What is key for the IdeaManager and IdeaLeader is that he or she vary among the roles. It is vital not to get "stuck" in one role. No matter how good you are, colleagues apply a discount rate to your contributions if you overdo them in any one directions. We did not like people who had all the answers in the first grade and we do not like them today ("Can you believe it; another idea from Leonardo. Why doesn't he just shut up?"). Success increases as you vary your presentation of self in everyday workplace situations. In this case, variety is the spice of ideas.

Observing Ego

Self-awareness is the first step in understanding and then expanding your role repertoire. You need to develop what counselors and therapists sometimes call an *observing ego*. An observing ego is that portion of us that allows us to observe our own behavior. It allows us to comment on it to ourselves, to modify it, to moderate it, or to adjust it, depending on the nature of the situation.

An observing ego is a fairly objective, fairly external observer of ourselves. Naturally, none of us can be completely independent or completely objective. But some individuals are able to see themselves almost as well as others see them, to place themselves outside their own interaction and watch themselves perform. Most of us become so involved, so enmeshed in our own needs and wants that we lose all objectivity. Goffman (1959) concluded that your role performance will be better if you understand that it is a role. Overinvolvement leads to role malperformance. The development of an observing ego will give you greater role flexibility. It will help you to develop greater skill in using self-deferentially in interactions to achieve the kinds of deals that you wish to make.

The development of an observing ego will lessen the impact of personal ego on deals. Sam Zell told me that personal ego gets in the way of more deals than anything else he knows about. By personal ego he is referring, in this case, to the relative uncontrollability some have for displaying all of their assets, wealth, power, influence, and so on in particular situations. Others have to display their intellectual poweress—they always have to be right. Others can never admit they do not know anything.

How can one develop an observing ego? There are several techniques. One is to work with an executive coach who can provide some of the needed reflection. Another is to do some reading. There is an excellent self-awareness assay instrument in a popular college management book, *Developing Management Skills*, 4th edition (Whetten & Cameron, 1998, Chapter 1). Other personal assays, such as a Myers Briggs Type Inventory or an Enneagram are helpful as well (Keirsey & Bates, 1984; Palmer, 1995).

Modeling

Modeling is another important interpersonal skill. IdeaManagers and IdeaLeaders need to show others in the organization—and outside of it—that they are willing to place themselves at risk in the area of new idea introduction. Paradoxically, the fact that an IdeaManager or IdeaLeader has a history of some failures as well as some successes strengthens, rather than weakens, his or her value as a model. Nobody is right all the time. Those who have failed, who have not done well in some instances but have done well in others, have learned how to deal with rejection and how to cope with lack of success. One's own lack of success makes it possible for others to be successful. You can model learning from failure as well as learning from success.

Cooling Out

I have talked about pushing new ideas. And much of the time that will be important. But there is another side to keep in mind. It is important, as the song has it, "to know when to fold 'em." IdeaManagers and IdeaLeaders are often talented and imaginative individuals who like to be right. When the desire to be right becomes displaced by a need to be right, the scene is set for potential disaster. When the need to be right becomes a need to be right all the time, ultimate failure is almost a foregone conclusion. Rather than energizing the system, it is not uncommon for this presentation to destroy it. The very energy that can be creative can also be destructive. Hence, the IdeaManager and IdeaLeader needs, in some instances, to reverse or invert the techniques in order to "cool out" or "cool down" a situation. Not infrequently, the "coolee" is you yourself. We all get so excited about the new ideas—the gerontocar, the electric fork—that we lose perspective. That is why one of the intelligences, the intrapersonal one, is so important. Other times, though, it is important to cool out others. This is a vital process, because the ideas remain a part of the organizational resource, to be brought up in another week, month, or year when they can be appropriately processed. Sometimes the time is not right. Sometimes the organization is too occupied—"otherwise engaged"—

to attend to something new. And, of course, everyone does not have the excitement of the challenge of new ideas that the IdeaManagers and IdeaLeaders do. The skill at cooling out means that the integrity and "self" of the new idea generator is protected and enhanced while, at the same time, the actual idea is set aside for a moment. This can be handled in a variety of ways. Among these are sending the new idea person on assignment, focusing on some particular project away from the others, separating development activities from operating ones, and so on. At the same time, verbal validation of the person's creativity, importance, and imagination must go on. None of these techniques are terribly difficult to implement. The problem is recognizing that an individual who contributes can also harm. The harm that such an individual does is not lessened by the value of earlier contributions.

MIXED SKILLS

Mixed skills are those that involve both the mind and the heart—intellectual and interpersonal elements. Network building, for example, involves both recognizing in someone else conceptual similarities to what you are doing and being able to effect a link that creates a sharing atmosphere. Orchestrating, negotiating, and coaching and counseling are among those areas where this kind of mixture is useful.

Network Building

One mixed skill that an IdeaManager and IdeaLeader needs is that of network building. None of us is an island. Each of us, and therefore all of us, need others to accomplish our goals. A role repertoire is fine—necessary—but there is only so much you can do as one person. Success is almost always a collective game. Networking is a planned way to involve others in assisting you, while you are also assisting them. Because networking means building relationships with people, it requires interpersonal skills. Because networking involves assembling particular people for particular projects, it involves selection and judgment. These are intellectual skills.

Wayne Baker (1993), in his book *Networking Smart: How to Build Relationships for Personal and Business Success*, talks about the skills and approaches that successful networking involves. His approach involves three elements. First is a networking perspective, a recognition of interdependency. The second is a set of approaches for managing networks inside your organization. The third involves managing relationships outside the organization.

Networks are informal collections of people helping each other. Here is what Marilyn Ferguson (1983) says:

> The network is the institution of our time: an open system, a dissapative structure so richly coherent it is in constant flux. The organic model of social organization is more

biologically adaptive, more efficient and more "conscious" than the hierarchical structure of modern civilization. The network is plastic, flexible. In effect, each member is the center of the network. . . . Networks are cooperative, not competitive. They are true grass roots: self-generating, self organizing and sometimes even self-destructing. They represent a process, a journey, not a frozen structure. (p. 213)

Building networks means having connections in the bank. There are two basic kinds of connections. Catagoric networks are collections of and connections with people like you. Interdependent networks are collections of people unlike you. Network building involves constantly being alert to those others individuals, within and without the organization, whom you feel could be of assistance to you, and establishing and maintaining connections with them. Network building is an important resource for orchestrating people and information.

We think of network as new, but they have always been important. Consider this set of relationships, described by Lucy Cross (1997), among musicians in Germany:

The network of colleagueships, apprenticeships and marriages among the great musical families in Germany was surely a cohesive element. Franz Danzi's father, an Italian cellist and the highest paid member of the famous Mannheim orchestra, was an acquaintance of Wolfgang Amadeus Mozart; Mozart's father, Leopold, had been the violin teacher of Danzi's wife. Mozart's wife Constanze (as well as her famous sister the singer Aloisia Weber) was a cousin of Carl Maria von Weber's father, and Weber himself was Danzi's protégé and friend.

Orchestrating People, Information, and Skills: Forming Teams from Networks

IdeaLeaders and IdeaManagers are continually bringing people together around problems, concerns, and issues. In a sense, the loosely coupled system is crystallized from the network into a team at points in time, like a pick-up game or a jam session. Teams are formalized points on the spiderweb of the network. Team managers or team leaders frequently do not have all the authority needed for the responsibility they have been asked to assume (Sayles & Chandler, 1971). That is why such managers and leaders might be better thought of as IdeaManagers and IdeaLeaders. These individuals need to be able to work with people and information. Orchestration here means getting the right information to the right people and the right people to the right information sources. Working it out involves team building and the shaping of assignments to fit teams. And it involves the construction of teams to fit assignment needs. IdeaManagers and IdeaLeaders are individuals in organizations who always can put a team together with the "right" people—right for the task at hand, right for each other. Teams are configured, created, and constantly recreated from the larger network of people, both inside and outside of the organization. They are, as it were, required to configure new developments from old organizational parts.

One way to think about these kinds of teams is a series of concentric circles. You begin with the standing or regular members of the team. They are often few in number. Then come the temporary members. They join for a little while, usually around special functions, much like a string quartet may add a temporary member to play some of the quintet literature. In most organizations, there are informal/semiformal insiders. These are often individuals with whom you have to link or create liaison. Or they may be people who are excited about what you are doing and want to help, but are not assigned to the team at the moment. On a parallel basis, there are informal/semiformal outsiders. In the days of the boundaryless organization, where individuals like customers and suppliers become part of the organization, there is an even greater likelihood that individuals such as these will be a part of the picture. Finally, there are informal/semiformal personal resources. These are individuals the team leader knows (or team members know) who have been helpful and vital to him or her in the past. They are people you can draw upon for advice and counsel and who can come in and help you out. Whatever the collection of these you use, you can see that rather than a fixed plate or menu of people, you have something more like a cupboard or a buffet full of a lot of options which are brought together for a particular purpose, but which keeps changing as parts of the overall purpose (subpurposes) are completed and new subpurposes emerge. The team is constantly being constructed, deconstructed, and reconstructed as people flow in from the network, spend a bit of time (from a little to a lot), and flow back out again.

This virtualness means that bossing does not work for the IdeaManager. Individuals filling these roles are frequently in a position that involves orchestrating rather than bossing. For one thing, because of the wide range of sources of membership in network-based teams, you simply do not have the authority you might once have had. Since you still have the responsibility, however, you have to find skills to get things done that have current effectiveness (in that they produce results now) and future effectiveness (in that you do not create significant downstream downsides, and continue to enjoy commitment to and connection with network members). This is where mixed skills—intellectual and interpersonal combinations—come in very handy.

Orchestrating People, Information, and Skills: Coaching

Once a team is crystallized, it needs to be directed into productive activity. It needs to be coached, not bossed. In this context, coaching refers to providing the mix of attention to ideas (giving information about what to do) and attention to people (helping people want to do what they need to do anyway) that creates team accomplishment.[4] But what is a coach to do, actually? Sayles and Chandler (1971) provide some useful suggestion skill sets for this kind of situation (1–6), as does McCaskey (1982) (7–12):

1. Give problems their proper weight and context: Teams face many problems in their work. IdeaManagers and IdeaLeaders "set" the problems for the team, identifying what parts of problems are key, what can be set aside, which ones are of greatest interest to the boss, and so on.
2. Establish and shift decision criteria: Teams work along multiple dimensions. For example, in the marketplace of the twenty-first century (and no doubt in all marketplaces at all times), there is a competition among the criteria of faster, better, and cheaper. Products need to be delivered at anytime and also anywhere. One cannot do all these things all the time. Thus, setting initial criteria weights and changing the mix of these weights is a crucial task.
3. Take problems at the right time: For a variety of reasons, problems may be appropriately worked on at some times and not at others. "Okay folks, Itzhak is here—let's go over the violin concerto before he has to leave." Now, you might be thinking, "What a dumb example; of course, if Perlman were here we would do the violin concerto!" Not always. We have all seen teams squander resources on problem A when they should have been working on problem B because the resources for dealing with problem B were at hand. IdeaManagers and IdeaLeaders provide this kind of guidance, no less crucial because it appears obvious.
4. Take problems in the right sequence: Sequence is another problem that needs to be managed. Using A and B again, it is important to first take those problems for which the solution drives all other downstream work. Let me give you a simple example from daily life. You say to your significant other, "What shall we do for dinner tonight?" Some answers proceed others, in that, having been answered, they establish very different paths. One such question is "in or out." If we eat in, then we proceed to deal with one set of issues. If we decide to eat out, another set of activities is engaged. It is foolish, but common, to fail to deal with A, move to B, and deal with B, only to discover that not having decided A made our work on B useless. IdeaManagers and IdeaLeaders try to get the sequence straight.
5. Act as a metronome for the team "orchestra": Pace is an important element in team work. (Recall the "quicker" element that has been mentioned.) IdeaManagers and IdeaLeaders set the pace for the particular "symphony." On the one hand, a sense of urgency is needed; on the other hand, too fast can spoil many efforts. Getting the pace right so that there can be ongoing production and exhaustion can be avoided is essential.
6. Manage the sprint/pause cycle: Teams work hard at some times and ease off at others. Helping to create a balance, not only within work activities but between them, is an important task of the IdeaManger and IdeaLeader.
7. Find the problem: IdeaManagers and IdeaLeaders need to be able to help teams key in on the right problem, through the use of judgment, emotional tone (gut), and logic.
8. Help in map building: IdeaManagers and IdeaLeaders need to be able to conceptualize the problem with ideas which include "a way out of the room"; this skill often involves building alternative maps to the organizational destination.

9. Use Janusian thinking: Similar to map building, Janusian thinking (named after the Roman God Janus, who had two faces, one on each side of his head) means that the IdeaManager and IdeaLeader is comfortable with contradictions (see the section on values conflict in Chapter 16) and specifically can look at problems from at least two sides.
10. Controlling and not controlling: Two conflicting adages apply here: "Go with the flow," and/or "Only dead fish go with the flow." Knowing when to "hold them" and knowing when to "fold them" is a key skill.
11. Use problem bracketing: All problems cannot be handled when they come up. Trying to do so is brutethink. Problem bracketing is the skill of knowing when to suggest that it might be better to put the problem that you are working on now (and are not solving and are becoming angry about) aside and return to it later.
12. Use channel switching: In channel switching, the IdeaManager and IdeaLeader is able to personally move completely from one problem to the next, like switching a channel on television. He or she does not linger over the previous problem, but moves ahead. It is very useful when linked to problem bracketing. The IdeaManager and IdeaLeader also help the team to do the same.

ORGANIZATIONAL SKILLS

Intellectual and interpersonal competencies are needed if ideas are to be successfully introduced and maintained over time, and if teams working on projects like this are to work well. But certain organizational competencies are also needed. Features of the organization need to be structured so that the energy of thought can be released. In the new venture, these kinds of organizational features can be (and should be) built in. In the mature venture, they need to be introduced so that they can contribute to organizational renewals. IdeaManagers and IdeaLeaders need to consider developing the culture and structure that captures the energy of thought.

Manage and Lead Culture: Permissive Atmosphere/Accomplishment Driven

Discussions with IdeaManagers and IdeaLeaders focus heavily on the ideas of risk. Implicitly and explicitly, these risk discussions center mainly on financial risk. Substantially less attention has been given to "emotional" risk; that is, the willingness of individuals to come up with crazy ideas and to say to others (who are certainly likely to be suspicious), "Hey, what about this?" The successful organization of the twenty-first century has to have a climate where emotional risk is permitted and encouraged. However, it has to lead somewhere. There also needs to be results. Results do not always have to be a new product today, but a step along the way. For example, teenagers need to go to high school. There are different ways you can go to high school, from home schooling, to private schools, to public schools, and so on. Flexibility of mode is fine; what is firm, however, is the expectation that one actually achieve graduation (notch achievement). No one expects that high school graduation is the "complete package." But it is an achievement, and something to be celebrated; it is a firm result. That is the kind of accomplishment I am supporting.

IdeaManagers and IdeaLeaders need to create a climate of emotional and intellectual excitement and permission in which it is okay to advance new and fresh ideas and in which it is recognized that most of these new and fresh ideas will be crazy and will not work. The problem with new ideas is that you never know in advance which ones will be the most productive. Hence, one has to have a tolerant, permissive atmosphere in order to get as many ideas as possible out on the table for examination. If people who suggest new ideas are going to be subject to derision or made fun of or kicked around emotionally, they will just keep their mouths shut. This is a loss, because you never know what it would have been like if they had made the suggestion the environment discouraged them from making.

At the same time, IdeaManagers and IdeaLeaders need to ask about accomplishments. "How are you coming on your graduation requirements?" is a needed question. But it is a balance. Too much permissiveness can be fun but unproductive; too many accomplishment questions has a chilling effect on the idea supply. It might be called "managing the flow." But first expectations have to be articulated.

Manage and Lead Expectations: Everybody into the Pool

A congenial atmosphere is not just for the few; it is for everyone. What "everyone" means as a practical matter is that all employees are tasked with the innovation job. This means that part of each person's job is, at the very least, to improve their own job. Innovation expectation is built into the job description, asked about at performance appraisal time, and rewarded at bonus time. A good guideline is to write job descriptions so that from 5 to 10 percent of the job expectation is innovation. This nails the expectation into the day-to-day operation.

This is not to say that some people will not be better at it than others, or that some will not have slam-bang ideas while others will slam into the wall. The point is that to have innovation you have to do innovation; that means everybody, from the janitor to the secretary to the research scientist. Big products (the gerontocar) are celebrated along with little improvements (the foam rubber pad on the assembly line), because all of them add yeast to the mix.

Manage and Lead Resource Availability

For employees to develop innovations, there needs to be more than atmosphere and expectation. There needs to be resources of money and place. Most organizations budget up to the edge and beyond. It is part of the budget game. When someone comes along with an idea—the electric fork, the gerontocar—boss after boss says, "Well, it's a great idea but we are very tight right now." I once knew an executive who said to the staff, ever year for ten years, "Things are very pressed this year." Sometimes they were, sometimes they were not; it was a control technique. And it worked. He "controlled" innovative ideas to zero. An organization that had been known for the new and the edge of the envelope became run of the mill. What IdeaManagers and IdeaLeaders need to do is to have "pots" of resources around the organization so that when someone needs a few bucks to try something there are a few bucks available. This is in addition to the 5 to 10 percent available through the job description.

Create Skunkworks

Organizations need places where people can get together to work on projects. It is a kind of "workshop out back." In organizations, these are often called *skunkworks*. Skunkworks has come to mean small protected areas in organizations where new things can have the freedom to develop. They might be back offices somewhere, or some spare time. Whatever they are, IdeaLeaders and IdeaManagers need to work to create skunkworks and help them develop.

Think of these as unusual kinds of organizational forms. Typical of such unusual forms is the Crazy Idea Group. The Crazy Idea Group specializes in introducing weird or half-baked ideas for further consideration. The group's circle acts as the legitimizing factor, giving permission for people to bring ideas that are not fully formulated. That is the whole idea: to get ideas in the early, developmental stage before the system has the chance to reject them. One particularly useful norm for the Crazy Idea Group is to prohibit negative comments (the same rule that is applied to brainstorming sessions). People do not need to begin defending their idea at the same time they are trying to get it out. The idea is simply presented to the group by anyone, and it may not be criticized.

A second organizational form is the Weird Idea Board. This is a bulletin board on which individuals are invited to post crazy, unusual, surprising, weird, or striking clippings from papers, magazines, personal letters, or any other source. These would be items that might be amusing, interesting, or shocking to others in their organization or work station area. Their purpose is to act as a constant source of stimulus to people and involve them in looking for things to post themselves.

These are not the only kinds of skunkworks. They are just some examples of things that IdeaManagers and IdeaLeaders have developed to "prime the pump."

Manage and Lead the Flow: Balancing Challenge, Skill, and Complexity

How do all these things fit together? It is called, as I mentioned, "managing the flow." In a book called *Flow: The Psychology of Optimal Experience*, Mihaly Csikszentmihalyi (1990) looked at the enigma of peak performance. He felt that people were at their current peak when they were at the intersection of challenge and skill. Too much challenge for current skill and people became anxious. Too much skill for current challenge and people became bored. Figures 14.1 and 14.2, based on his idea, lay this out.

Notice in Figure 14.1 that though there is a "point" of high performance, one cannot stay there. One has to always move up the flow channel, or drift to one side or the other. This movement upward is the development of increasing complexity. IdeaManagement means keeping people "on point" (managing the balance at any intersection and getting employees back to balance); IdeaLeadership sets strategic objectives (if an employee or an organization is at 3/3, IdeaLeaders propose and generate excitement around 5/5 or 7/7). Notice, as well, in Figure 14.2, that it is easy to drift away. This is a constant danger, especially in turbulent environments (permanent white water).

Where do you start? Is it better to start with challenge and provide skill, or begin with skill and invite challenge? The answer is either, as long as it fits the person and the situation. Some individuals and situations respond to challenge, and will then seek skills to rise to the challenge. Other persons and situations are the reverse, requiring skills first and then, with skills up, challenges are sought.

Manage and Lead by Developing These Skills: The External Coach

How can you develop these competencies? First, recognize that they are needed and that they require work. Recognize, too, that the high degree of self-involvement in what is being corrected makes it extremely difficult to do this entirely by yourself. As someone once said to me, "If I want to play the violin I can go to music school; I can also hire a violin teacher."

I recommend the violin teacher approach, often called an executive coach. It is for this reason that the development of a trial mentor relationship is very important. Identify and seek out some individual who is not associated with your firm, your family, or your daily life routine. This should be an individual with whom you meet on a regular basis—once a week, once a month, once a quarter, but regularly. The purpose of such team meetings is to review your current situation. Invite this external observer to comment both on your own performance and on the kinds of dynamics and problems that might be developing within that organization.

Some may argue that such an outside person cannot be helpful because he or she does not know enough about the details of what is going on inside. My experience, and that of a great many successful individuals, argues quite the contrary. First, it is precisely because of this independence that your coach's views will be useful. Second, organizational situations and problems are much more common than one might think. To be sure, there are individual details that are unique to this or that situation. But, in general, an experienced organizational consultant or coach has heard it before and is able to ask the kinds of questions that you might

Figure 14.1
Going with the Flow

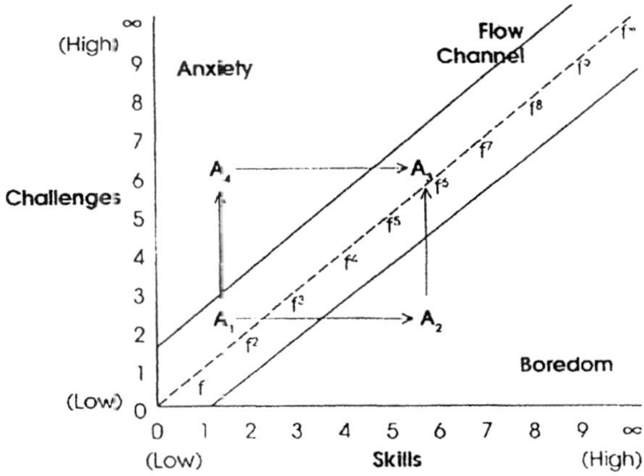

Why the complexity of consciousness increases as a result of flow experiences

Figure 14.2
Permanent White Water

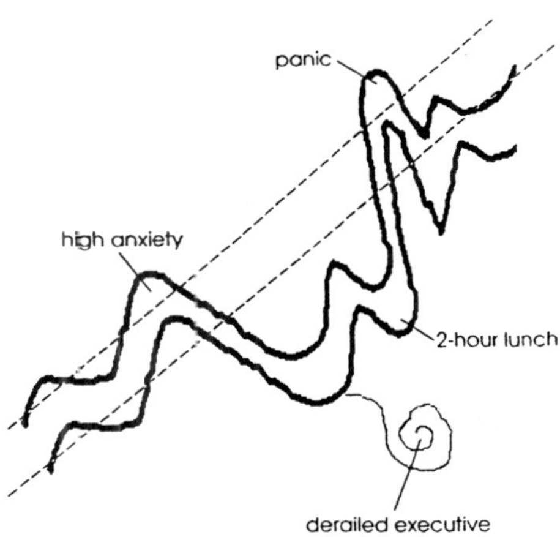

Source: "Permanent White Water," is a phrase used by Peter Vaill.

not think of. This beginning step in the development of observing ego, then, suggests that you start from the outside. After a period of regular meetings and discussions with this individual, you will be able. As that begins to occur, you must be careful not to delude yourself into believing that your external coach is no longer needed. Other issues, other perspectives, and other problems will come up on which conversation will be helpful.

The coach concept I am introducing here is different from the traditional mentor role. In the traditional approach, the mentor is someone within the organization who will sponsor a new or younger individual. It assumes that the older, more experienced individual does not need a mentor. Too often, inherent in the concept is the notion that an organizational individual who is working in a small group or alone does not need a coach to help find his or her way around the garage. One who accepts such a proposition is like the tennis player who agrees to take on all comers with his hands tied behind his back.

CONCLUSION

Competencies needed by IdeaManagers and IdeaLeaders are not a great deal different from the competencies that every manager needs. There is a special focus on the aspect of idea generation, on the exploring of new ideas, and on the problems and difficulties of getting new ideas implemented. There is also a special focus—as in failure analysis—on looking very carefully at ideas that did not make it so that we can learn as much as possible from them. Finally, there is an emphasis on the intellectual, interpersonal, and organizational competencies. None of these is sufficient by itself.

NOTES

1. One of the best sources available for memo writing is the book *Send Me a Memo: A Handbook of Model Memos* by Dianna Booher (1984). She not only goes through a range of ways to develop memos but also provides a whole series of strong and weak examples.
2. Mark McCormack (1986) speaks of making a presentation to John Z. DeLorean, then of GM's Pontiac Division, about some creative advertising that could be done with the Pontiac Chieftain symbol. At the end, DeLorean pointed out that Pontiac had just spent several million dollars to get rid of the symbol.
3. Someone said, in fact, that the fear of public speaking was greater than the fear of death. So, given the choice of presenting a eulogy or being in the casket, most people would choose the casket!
4. For an example of this, see Tracy Kidder (1981), *The Soul of a New Machine*.

Chapter 15

Creating Idea-Driven Styles

When managers get together, a lot of time is spent discussing the issue of management style: what styles are preferred, what styles are disliked, what is positive style, what is negative style. It is also true that employees in more informal settings talk a great deal about the style of their bosses. Yet few concepts are as elusive and hard to pin down in any concrete way as this matter of style.

Style seems to be the way an individual goes about doing the job rather than the specific techniques used. Style is best thought of as the distinctive pattern of behaviors and actions that characterize a particular manager, a group of managers, or a particular organization. For that reason, I am discussing personal style here; organizational style will be considered as a part of organizational culture and subculture.

PERSONAL STYLE

Reams of material have been written on style.[1] There have been discussions beyond counting of people-oriented managers and product-oriented managers, Theory-X managers and Theory-Y managers, and now, of course, Theory-Z managers.[2] Tests are available to find out if individuals have "organizational style" or fit the organizational mode. Individuals agonize over whether they have the right style or the wrong style.

The first thing that needs to be said about these ruminations is that there does not appear to be one style that is always effective and always leads to success. You might just as well relax a bit in the pursuit of the perfect style. There is not one. Several factors account for this fact.

To begin with, conditions differ. A style that might be successful under one set of circumstances might fail in another. Second, there are antecedent and consequent conditions to a particular episode of managing with a particular style that cause it to be successful or not. Third, people differ in their response to particular styles. An open style that emphasizes closeness and intimacy may work well with some employees and be rejected as inappropriate by others.

The main conclusion we can draw from all of this has good news and bad news in it, so to speak. On the one hand, there is no perfect style, one that works all the time. That means you cannot hope to find it. On the other hand, your core style is likely to have, because of this very point, upsides and downsides.

It seems that you will be well served if you have a core style modulated by a style repertoire—like a role repertoire. It is quite possible for IdeaManagers to vary the kinds of presentations of self that they make, at least within some range. These variations can occur in different situations, with different people, and as the conditions under which one works change. In point of fact, we probably do this anyway. Most of us act differently when we are "out with the girls" or "out with the guys" than we do at home. What the IdeaManager and IdeaLeader must particularly avoid, however, is to get into a stylistic rut in which he or she is always the same—or always appears to be the same—regardless of the conditions and situations. I have already talked about the observing ego and the way in which one tries to observe oneself adjust. That concept can be usefully applied here, as well, in terms of the development of differing styles. Think of yourself as an actor on a stage, playing different roles. Sometimes you may need a tougher, more directive role. At other times you may need a more understanding role. Though it may not be possible for individuals who are oriented in the directive direction to shift into an understanding direction very easily, there might be times and situations when this new style could be tried out.

Good and Bad Styles

While there is no best style, that does not mean that there are no bad styles. Style can be seen as an eggtimer, laid on its side. The narrow neck is a kind of "zero" point; moving to the right and fanning out are ranges of good styles. Moving toward the left are different kinds of bad styles. There are many ways to be bad, and these styles should be avoided, just as there are many ways to be good, and these styles should be embraced in one's repertoire.

Bad styles are, generally, those which demean people; which are hostile, sarcastic, and abusive. Consider one executive who brought a water pistol into staff meetings, squirting those with whom he disagreed. Styles which humiliate others are bad styles. These points may seem obvious, yet for IdeaManagers and IdeaLeaders anything that creates distance between and among people reduces the idea readiness and idea production of the organization.

Good styles are those that are people enhancing; that help individuals manage flow and move up the level of complexity. Good styles do not have to be "soft" or have no standards. That mistake is a common one. Jackie Spinner (1997) discusses this very point in her article on drill sergeants: "What's the difference between discipline and humiliation?" she asks. All too often, humiliation passes for discipline: discipline, accomplishment, standards, and toughness are all good; humiliation is not.

Types of Good Style

There are two key aspects of style: *character and level*. Character addresses questions about what kind of style you have; level addresses questions about how good you are at what you select. Let us look at character first.

The character of a style refers to certain choices about approaches that an individual IdeaManager or IdeaLeader might make. A key point to consider here is that styles exist in a dynamic tension; picking one means that you have to deal with the other one also. For example, there are participative versus directive styles, bossy/autocratic versus democratic styles, task-oriented versus people-oriented styles, fixed styles versus situational styles, reading versus talking styles, forest versus tree styles, and solo versus group styles. These are among the most common tensions, though it is certainly possible to identify others. The problem is that picking one part of a style pair to emphasize means that you have to express, at times, the subdominant element as well.

1. A participative style is one that involves a wide range of organizational members in problem solving. Involvement is not based upon position but on knowledge and involvement in the problems in question. An advantage is involvement and buy-in; a downside is that it takes time.
2. A directive style centers the responsibilities for these tasks in expertise. A positive is that knowledgeable people are providing guidance. A downside can be the tunnel vision that technical people have at times.
3. An autocratic style is position based, and centers responsibility for decision making in a small executive cadre or, even more restrictively, with a particular individual (often the CEO or boss). A plus is that higher levels of the organization are involved. A negative is that ignorance may be higher (recall the principle of uncertainty absorption).
4. A democratic style, like a participative style, involves many individuals in decision making, but the involvement tends to be on the basis of prior decisions about entitlements rather than relevance and appropriateness, which are implicit in the participative mode.

5. A task-centered style focuses on accomplishment often specified in very specific terms (e.g., "the bottom line"). Press to achievement is a plus here; ignoring people is a downside.
6. A people-oriented style assesses organizational activities in terms of the personal impacts on staff, customers, clients, and local communities. Allegedly narrow and mechanical definitions of organizational purpose and measures of that purpose are rejected.
7. A fixed style is one that is invariant and repetitive regardless of the particular conditions. Consistency is an advantage; inappropriateness is a disadvantage.
8. A situational style is one that may vary considerably with those same conditions. A situational style, therefore, might be autocratic and democratic, participative and directive, and relatively untroubled by the apparent conflict among these various styles. Customization is a strength here; a negative is that there may be no sense of a "core" style on which people can depend.
9. A reading style helps those who like to read things first, then talk. An advantage is that colleagues get things down on paper, which creates specificity. A negative is that the spontaneity of conversation is often constrained by the text.
10. A talking style is for those who like to talk first, and then get things onto paper. A plus is that a lot of ideas can come out in this mode. A negative is that they keep on flowing, and never get past the talking stage.
11. A forest style involves getting the big picture first, then filling in the details. A strength is the big-picture view; a weakness is the absence of significant details.
12. A trees style is for those who like to start with the smaller pieces of a problem and work up, or build up, to the big picture. Care and precision are benefits here; lack of overall perspective can mean that one focuses on unimportant and insignificant details.
13. A solo style is for IdeaManagers who like to think things out a bit on their own first, and then touch base with others. The good news is that they have a clear idea of what is needed; the bad news is that it might be clear, but wrong.
14. A group style is for IdeaManagers who like to start by tossing an idea around to help prime their pump. Positives here include a broad range of ideas and approaches as well as involvement; negatives can be that you never get past this stage, or that the IdeaManager goes off in some other direction, leaving those involved feeling shut out.

Since each style has pluses and minuses, you can see that using only one is something of a problem. Even the situational style can be too situational. A mixed style, built around a core style, still seems to be overall better strategy. Particular emphasis should be given to the linked style to your core style.

Level of Style

You can also think of style as the level of performance, regardless of the particular character of any particular style. When someone says, "He has a great deal of style," the reference is to level rather than to character. You can have an authoritarian style and still carry it off with aplomb. You can also have a wooden and jerky authoritarian style. The same is true of each of the others. The five-stage hierarchy of leadership competence that Dreyfus and Dreyfus (1986) suggest fits in well here. These serve as generalized, developmental foci through which we all progress, whether the focus is on IdeaManagement and IdeaLeadership, tennis, chess, or fly fishing. Dreyfus and Dreyfus identify the following levels of competence:

1. the Novice Stage
2. the Advanced Beginner Stage
3. the Competence Stage
4. the Proficiency Stage
5. the Expert (or Master) Stage

Like character, the level of skill performance is also an aspect of style. Regardless of what you may know in the intellectual or interpersonal area, you must somehow give expression to your knowledge. Furthermore, it is not only a matter of giving expression to your competencies, you have to do it reasonably well. It is always true that stylistic assessments involve not only describing what one has chosen ("she plays badminton better than tennis"), but how well the game is played ("and she plays tennis outstandingly well").

The point here is that most of us, in most things, are at the middle level, so there is always room to improve. On the other hand, we can get very good at our core style and be good enough at other styles to use them. One does not—as the perfectionists insist—have to be a master at everything to have it be useful and satisfying.

THE "ELEMENTS OF [GOOD] STYLE"

Whatever style you adopt, there are some common elements that IdeaManagers and IdeaLeaders should seek to infuse in that style, elements that seem more likely than not to be associated with the production of new ideas for products and services and their implementation in the workforce.[3]

People Enhancing

I have already mentioned a bit about this point. The first element is to adopt (or try to) a people-enhancing posture. There are many ways that this can be done. Supporting people does not mean that you are a wimp. There are different ways of communicating encouragement and backing. There are tough coaches who are hostile and negative, and there are tough coaches who are supportive and positive. There are laid-back individuals who provide support directly, and there are laid-back individuals who provide support more distantly and removed. Because the IdeaManager and IdeaLeader depends on people for ideas, it is imperative that he or she adopt a people-enhancing, people-supportive style in order to permit new ideas to be developed and shared.

Creativity

The IdeaManager and IdeaLeader needs to exemplify and model creativity as an aspect of his or her style. This means physically doing different things in the organization. Staff get messages from a wide range of sources; and if the IdeaManager and IdeaLeader asserts new things, new ideas, and new products and services but never gives any evidence of trying anything new, that is construed as a double message. Usually, in a double-message situation, individuals select the message that is potentially least harmful. In this case, not doing anything seems closest to the winning strategy. Creativity also needs to become an ongoing part of the IdeaManager and IdeaLeader's life. Thus, attempting to be creative in some comparable area (such as an artistic or sports arena) keeps the creative juices flowing and keeps the problems and difficulties of creativity squarely before the IdeaManager and IdeaLeader. If an IdeaManager and IdeaLeader can demonstrate creativity, this will attract others who are also creative and liberate the quasi-creativity in the rest.

Optimism

The IdeaManager and IdeaLeader needs to bring a certain optimism into his or her style. The reason for this is straightforward. In the new idea, product, or service game, everything is uncertain or ambiguous and looks odd. Discouragement, defeat, and withdrawal always seem just a step away. When an individual is proceeding into the unknown, he or she needs hope: hope that the idea will work, hope that the new product or service will be successful, hope that others will see the possibilities. It is this impetus that the IdeaManager and IdeaLeader needs to provide. The provision of hope is not blind, however. The IdeaManager and IdeaLeader is continually questioning the new idea, putting it in different contexts, and seeing how it might work under varying conditions. But these are positive tests that any new idea initiator expects and accepts. If the new idea for a product or a service does not meet these tests, then hope of a different sort must be provided: hope that the next idea will be successful or hope that this idea, when certain other developments have matured and can be combined with it, might at that later time be successful. Hope is a great stimulus and should be a part of the style repertoire of any IdeaManager and IdeaLeader. It involves focusing on the possible while planning around the potentially problematic.

The Ability to Doubt

As important as the ability to hope is, it is no more important than the ability to doubt. Hope tends to be expressed toward the new product or service. Doubt tends to be expressed toward the existing product or service. The reasons for the latter are the inverse of those for the former. In the new area, we tend to look for the possibilities. We stress these while keeping the problems in view. But we do not permit problems to be completely determining. We already know the possibilities for the existing product or service. Therefore, doubt, questions, or wondering about whether that particular product or service is actually doing all that it possibly can should take precedence.

A second element of doubt has to do with established wisdom. It would be too strong to say that IdeaManagers and IdeaLeaders should reject established wisdom, but it is fair to say that breakthroughs have occurred over history in exactly the areas where what people said could not be done, was done. The IdeaManager and IdeaLeader, therefore, must keep working at an open-minded approach. It is helpful to remind participants that most things we are now certain cannot be improved on, will be improved on shortly.

It follows, then, that the IdeaManager and IdeaLeader must readily give permission to question established wisdom. It is in this easy grant of permission to question that doubt has its most effective stylistic impact. Picture yourself in a marketing team meeting of some sort. A new staff team participant suggests that a new and different (from that firm's point of view) market segment be targeted for the firm's product or service. The other staff members in the team meeting—old hands with your organization—say something like, "We've already tried to crack that group and failed. It cost us a bundle before. It would just be pouring money down a rat hole now. Everyone knows that they (whoever they are) aren't going to buy our electric fork."

Now is your chance to prove what a solid IdeaManager and IdeaLeader you are. You can certainly agree with the established wisdom. That will close a potential line of inquiry, and there are times when that is the right thing to do. This is especially true if recent studies of the market have just been done and the data are fresh and persuasive. There are also times when going with the flow of established wisdom is not the appropriate course. Indeed, more often than we care to admit in situations like this, the hard data are old and stale—or worse, there are no hard data, only lore. Conviction is high that the old situation still prevails, but evidence is slim. When that is true, you should adopt a somewhat different scenario in your IdeaManager and IdeaLeader role; namely, hedge your bets. In other words, adopt the prime directive of bureaucracy: When in doubt, equivocate. Respond with something like, "Well, it's been a long time since we've looked into this. There's a lot of change going on. Maybe it would be worth taking a look at. If we were to take another look at it, what are the kinds of things we ought to keep in mind?" This is an opening, freeing the kind of response that does not necessarily agree with the new employee's proposals but does validate the idea of the proposal and gives permission for the group to begin to think about it. That is the power of doubt.

Be Curious

Another crucial element of style to be mentioned here is curiosity. Curiosity involves asking questions: Why is that? How can we explain this result? What do you suppose was going on there? These simple questions, especially in a group context, are enormously powerful. They become yet another way to cut through established wisdom.

As humans, we are always simplifying and shortcutting causal relationships in our environment: this causes that, gods are bowling and cause thunder, lightning is the spear of the gods, and so on. Throughout history, quickie explanations of this sort have been the staple of many. A more select few, however, have asked additional questions. Some have even gone so far as to fly a kite in the rain to see whether or not electricity would come down the wire attached to the kite.

Curiosity, as an aspect of style, is so very important because, like doubt, it is liberating. It opens things up for investigation. It suspends prejudgment and, thus, allows new ideas, new procedures, and new approaches to enter the system.

Listen

One of the most important aspects of style, as Robert Bolton (1979) says in his book, *People Skills*, is the ability to listen. McCormack (1986) agrees. All too often, managers find themselves directing rather than receiving, instructing rather than absorbing, commanding rather than consulting. IdeaManagers and IdeaLeaders in particular need to listen. All too frequently, we miss the key points that others are sharing with us because we are already preparing our reply. Listening involves focused attention on the speaker. It involves setting aside one's own thoughts, wishes, and desires to get into the conversation or put the speaker down. It requires interaction, but of a very special sort. Some listeners use greatly specified and highly detailed questions as an apparent listening device when, in fact, it is an attacking device. Questions are important to clarify, to probe, and to reformulate, but not to trap or to corner speakers. If you listen, you not only gain the ideas that are being shared in the exchange but an extra positive benefit as well: the interpersonal respect that arises toward the listener from the speaker.

Think, for a moment, about the last time someone really listened to you. It was probably a terrific and memorable experience. Whatever the style that the IdeaManager and IdeaLeader uses, or whatever range of styles are selected, listening should be an extremely important part.

CONCLUSION

Style remains an elusive concept. Though all seem to understand that it is the way individuals go about achieving their goals, the very concept of style seems to have resisted attempts to provide a complete list of style alternatives. It may be that the elusiveness of the concept itself accounts for the fact that rather different styles are found to be both successes and failures, depending on a range of antecedent and subsequent conditions and, possibly, the skill of the individual person in displaying the style. The conclusion suggested here is that, rather than seeking one successful style, IdeaManagers and IdeaLeaders should cultivate a range of styles or a range of ways in which they can present themselves that will vary, depending on the situations in which they find themselves. Given that difference, however, some common elements of style, aimed specifically at the encouragement of new ideas for products and services, have been suggested.

NOTES

1. Bass (1981) provides a particularly good summary.
2. These popular initials refer to different orientations toward people. Theory-X managers assume that individuals do not wish to work and have to be watched, pushed, and checked. Theory-Y managers believe people want to work and need to be directed and guided. Theory-Z managers (Ouchi, 1982) are some combination of them. For a complete list of alternative styles, see Bass (1981, 289). For a sample assessment chart developed by Likert, see Bass (1981, 31–34).
3. The title comes from a famous book on writing (Strunk & White, 1979) which makes the same kind of point; that is, that there are some basics that run through all the main kinds of good writing.

Chapter 16

Creating Organizational Subculture

Organizational culture is the set of ideas—values, visions, missions—that characterize an organization. Subculture is the particular set of those ideas which characterize a particular organization or its subparts. Cultures and subcultures serve as the integrating centers for skills and style on the one hand, and strategy, structure, systems, and staff on the other. IdeaManagement and IdeaLeadership is crucially concerned with crafting an appropriate subculture, not only because of those integrating properties, but also because the belief system of an organization inspires and vivifies organizational participation.

WHAT IS ORGANIZATIONAL CULTURE?

In his book on organizational culture, Schein (1985) defines organizational culture as "a pattern of basic assumptions invented, discovered, or developed by a given group, as it is learning to cope with its problems of external adaptation [what we have called context] and internal integration—that has worked well enough to be considered valid, and therefore to be taught to new members as a correct way to perceive, think, and feel in reaction to these problems" (p. 9).

He describes a three-element definition of organizational culture. The first element deals with basic assumptions. These are "taken-for-granted" and "preconscious" points of view. These are the ones that are often revealed in an analysis of organizational assumptions. The second element centers on organizational values. These are built on the basic assumptions and enjoy a more general level of awareness. The third step involves artifacts and creations.

These are products of basic assumptions that Schein (1985) speaks of as being "visible but not decipherable," at least without reference to some understanding of those values and assumptions. I include organizational policies in this last group. Policies are a product of assumptions and values and represent a solidification of organizational ideas and foresight.

Culture can be managed and created. Small towns do it. Propaganda is an example of how societies do it. Public relations is an example of how organizations often do it. Much of cultural management at the moment, however, is episodic and unfocused. A cult may be one example of culture that is so powerful when managed and focused that individuals are captured totally. Brainwashing, which is probably an appropriate word for what occurs there, requires deprogramming in order to bring the individual back to a culturally realistic view of the world around them. But what is managed for evil purposes can be managed for good, as well. Organizational cultures can enhance and inspire us. They can remove us from the boxes and traps in which we exist, making our lives richer and giving meaning to our daily tasks. It is this that we have in mind as the goal of cultural management. The payoff, of course, will be an excellent and successful organization. That organization will be characterized by an adequate supply of new ideas and a set of norms that is receptive to trying those new ideas, playing with them, and seeing which ones make sense and which ones do not.

Let us consider some of the kinds of each of the elements of culture.

KINDS OF ASSUMPTIONS

Assumptions are the basic ideas that organizations hold about the way the world works. Assumptions about supply of goods, people, and money; about the values for which people work; and about the things that are needed to motivate people are examples of kinds of assumptions. One kind of assumption set can be called *metavalues*. Metavalues are general values that would serve any organization. Commitment to quality, presence of a work ethic among staff, integrity, loyalty, and so on are among the overall values you would probably want to espouse.

Managing Assumptions

Assumptions are usually managed through testing. They are tested by the context. When auto manufacturers assumed that Japanese cars were no threat (and almost died in the process), they were acting out of an assumption base. Assumptions need to be tested regularly through some kind of environmental scan. They are also tested through question and challenge. The IdeaManager and IdeaLeader is an assumption crystallized (someone who lays out the assumptions implicit in values and action) and asks if these assumptions are truly still valid (recall the French Vintners mentioned in Chapter 14).

Context and questioning are most often likely to reveal a very important feature about assumptions: We often hold conflicting ones. The problem with assumptions and metavalues is that they often conceal as much as they reveal. Many people see values, and talk about them, as if they came in some kind of list. However they are more likely to come as a set of conflicting commitments. Let us look at international (America versus Japan) and national (within U.S. organizations) examples.

KINDS OF VALUES: GLOBAL DIFFERENCES

Cultures differ, of course, on a worldwide basis. Countries have different cultures, and regions (Western and Eastern, and, within that, Nordic, Middle European, Mediterranean, Latin, Japanese, Korean, Chinese, etc.). *Riding the Waves of Culture* is a wonderful book that provides a lot of insight into global differences in culture (Trompenaars, 1994).

One way to think of the matter overall, however, is to compare Japanese and American organizations to derive a sense of the overall differences in emphasis and approach. In any such comparison it should be understood that we are dealing with what Max Weber (1930) called "ideal types." When looked at in any real detail, there are a lot of variations within each. Furthermore, whatever is dominant in one culture is certainly subdominant in the other. Thus, Japanese characteristics can be found in all American organizations, though they are usually not as prominent. Conversely, American characteristics are to be found to some degree in all Japanese organizations. Nevertheless, it is possible to get a sense of stylistic difference from such an overall comparison.

To begin to understand the difference between Japanese and American organizations, look at the differences between Japanese and American rice. If you have eaten both kinds of rice, you will instantly recognize the important differences. Japanese rice sticks together in big clumps. It is quite possible to eat it with chopsticks, because it packs together so well. You might say that Japanese rice has a "collective orientation." American rice is just the opposite. Each grain fights for its own independence. A fork full of American rice results in most of the rice falling back into the bowl. As a metaphor for the different orientations of the two countries, rice paints a picture as well as any: collectivism versus individualism.

A second aspect of culture can be seen in the contrast between the bonsai and the burger. The bonsai tree is one that requires meticulous care and a long length of time to produce. The burger, in contrast, is the center of our fast food industry—made within seconds and often consumed even more quickly. These contrasting elements express the long-term orientation of Japan relative to the short-term orientation of America.

A third point of difference is in the mode of expression. The alphabet used by Americans is, in its way, a marvel of economy. All our words are made using combinations, and some of those letters are used only rarely. All languages are not this way, including Japanese. Japanese uses three separate writing systems to communicate, including a large number of borrowed Chinese characters. Thus, to be moderately well educated in Japan, one needs to know about 1,200 of these separate characters; to read the paper, about 2,000; and to be literate, a good deal more than that. There are, to be sure, some commonly used characters. But these number in the hundreds. The implications of these differences are stunning. One is that there are no typewriters capable of handling the entire range of the written language. No keyboard is extensive enough to hold even the common characters (though today, LED keyboards are moving in that direction). Given such a system, interpersonal communication in great detail is almost a necessity. These cultural differences are the springboard for some organizational differences. They are best summarized by Ouchi (1982, 48–49), as shown in the following list. While a few years old, and changing somewhat, Ouchi's work is, to me, an excellent summary. The work of Benedict (1946) and my own observations are also included.

A Summary of Japanese and American Organizational Differences

Japanese Organizations	North American Organizations
Ouchi	
Lifetime Employment	Short-Term Employment
Slow Evaluation and Promotion	Rapid Evaluation and Promotion
No Specialized Career Paths	Specialized Career Paths
Implicit Control Mechanisms	Explicit Control Mechanisms
Collective Decision Making	Individual Decision Making
Collective Responsibility	Individual Responsibility
Holistic Concern	Segmented Concern
Benedict	
Shame Orientation	Guilt Orientation
Tropman	
Sticky Rice	Independent Grains
Bonsai	Burger
Last Name First	First Name/Nickname
Talk/Write	Write/Talk/Revise

Naturally, these distinctions are oversimplified, but they do provide a sense of the way in which Japanese organizations may differ from American organizations. It may well be that a combination of these two rather opposing styles would be most productive. Ouchi (1982) comments as follows:

In a Type Z company, the explicit and the implicit seem to exist in a state of balance. While decisions weigh the complete analysis of facts, they are also shaped by serious attention to questions of whether or not this decision is "suitable," whether or not it "fits" the company. A company that isolates subspecialities is hardly capable of achieving such fine grained forms of understanding. Perhaps the underlying cause is the loss of the ability for disparate departments within a single organization to communicate effectively with one another. They communicate in the sparse, inadequate language of numbers because numbers are the only language all can understand in a reasonably symmetrical fashion. (p. 61)

What Ouchi is suggesting is, in effect, competing orientations, competing styles. Emphasis on a single set of values is likely to become problematic. The very best IdeaManagers and IdeaLeaders are able to produce combinations of styles within their organizations that meet evolving needs. A mix of Japanese and American styles may be one step in this direction, but other combinations may also be appropriate. While nations and regions have cultures, there are blends; what is dominant in one is not absent from the another, but it might be subdominant.

KINDS OF VALUES: THE CLASH IN CULTURE/SUBCULTURE

A good of value conflict within American society is presented by Lawrence Miller (1984) in his book, *The American Spirit*. Miller himself does not use a value-conflict perspective per se, but he was only one step away. With a little modification, his alternatives fit very nicely the purposes here. They illustrate the kinds of choices that all organizations continually need to make as they create their cultures. They also exemplify the need for balance. In no case, from this point of view, would you pick only one of Miller's alternatives. You would, rather, seek to emphasize one over the other while taking account of the one being underemphasized. He calls them "primary values." With some very slight modifications, Miller's list consists essentially of the following:

1. Multipurpose versus Unipurpose
2. Comfort and Satisfaction versus Excellence Ethic
3. Unity of Interest versus Class Interest
4. Personal Purpose versus Organizational Purpose
5. Command Decision Making versus Consensus Decision Making
6. Empirical versus Qualitative Decision Making
7. Disposable Labor versus Intimate Concerns
8. Expediency versus Integrity
9. Performance-Based Rewards versus Power/Tenure-Based Rewards
10. Career versus Job

Let us take a brief look at each of these.

Multipurpose versus Unipurpose

Miller's discussion of these two values was originally titled, "Purpose Driven versus Lacking Purpose." The clear choice here is between organizational purpose and no organizational purpose. For most organizations it is not simply a case of one or the other. Rather, the difference is between having a single, overriding organizational purpose and multiple purposes. What is actually required is a blend between a single overriding purpose and the many other purposes that organizations have to accomplish. The single, "no diversions permitted" orientation is certainly to be valued. Such singlemindedness of purpose, however, can often lead us to ignore other strategic goals.

The IdeaManager and IdeaLeader, therefore, must create a balance between the single overriding purpose on the one hand and other organizational purposes on the other. Frequently, of course, setting priorities, selecting goals, and goal refurbishment are what are needed. Even if you do have a single purpose, it may change due to environmental shifts, internal composition adjustments, and so on. To the extent that purposes are expressions of values, however, discussions of purposes, selection, articulation, and the setting of priorities are in fact discussions of values and their orchestration within the organizational framework.

Comfort and Satisfaction versus Excellence Ethic

On one hand, most of us are committed to excellence and superlative performance whenever possible. On the other, we recognize that that kind of perfectionism can destroy a corporation or an individual if pushed to extremes. It is not possible to be excellent day in and day out in every product line or innovation. Similarly, it is important to have some things that one does well enough—not necessarily as well as others or the very best but a place to relax a bit and to enjoy the fruits of previous labors. As Miller (1984) suggests, the question here has more to do with the dominance of one or another of these ethics rather than the choice. Most of us would recognize the need for both.

But the areas one selects for excellent performance are important, and the measurement systems one sets up are crucial to consider. Certain areas may be set aside as "good enough" areas of organizational performance. It is certainly not shameful to recognize that both values need expression. The question is how to accommodate them. Sometimes simultaneity is the way; that is, some products are selected for excellence, others to be satisfactory. Most manufacturers of consumer products, for example, manufacture products according to a hierarchy of excellence. For the most part, VCR manufacturers offer a basic line that is inexpensive, offers minimal features, and is built to minimum acceptable standards. They also offer progressively more expensive and feature-laden models, culminating with a top-of-the-line model that is very expensive (relative to the cheapest model), is manufactured according to the highest possible standards of engineering and quality control, and does everything but provide a critique of the videotaped material one plays on it. Virtually all car manufacturers do the same thing.

Another way is sequence. For a while our product will be the best. Then others will take over while we retool, at the same time maintaining a good level of product or service. We will then compete for excellence once again in the market.

There may be other ways. The key point, however, is the *balance* between excellence and comfort and satisfaction, rather than total dominance of either. If comfort and satisfaction become dominant, the organization is in a dangerous position. Comfort and satisfaction levels have a tendency to sink, at least with respect to product quality. "Good enough" becomes acceptable; then "poor" takes over. Specific measures of the levels of product-service performance, therefore, should be set for both the comfort and satisfaction value area and the excellence value.

Unity of Interest versus Class Interest

One view of organizations, celebrated a bit in the Japanese management tradition, is that organizations are like families or tribes. They secure the same kind of commitment and the same kind of participatory involvement that would occur in a family or tribal situation. Others view organizations as loosely coupled systems, full of diverse interests, class conflicts, and competitions. Conflicts between blacks and whites, for example, or conflicts between men and women, or conflicts between those who are getting ahead and those who are not are typical.

One would expect, we suppose, that the organizations that serve a country would reflect a country. If, as in the case of Japan, there is a greater degree of homogeneity and commonality among the citizenry, then one would expect commonality and unity, to a degree at least, to be characteristic features of that country's organizations. Likewise, organizations that serve a divided society might well be expected to be divided themselves. Thus—again, to some degree—American corporations are microcosmic exemplars of the society as a whole. In this particular situation, culturally dominant values become organizationally dominant values. The job of the IdeaManager and IdeaLeader is to seek to act as a counterweight or counterforce (much as an outrigger on a Polynesian canoe is used to create balance) which will allow for accomplishment and achievement. The job of the IdeaManager and IdeaLeader within the American context, therefore, is to find bases and realms of unity, communality, and similarity so that to some extent the differences can be submerged or at least set aside while attention is paid to the organizational purpose and the activities that will serve that purpose. However, in a firm where a unity of interest is the dominant theme, emphasis on the creating of some diversity, heterogeneity, and internal organizational friction is required in order to get the supply of new ideas required for continual achievement.

Personal Purposes versus Organizational Purposes

The value conflict that Miller (1984) attempts to define with his "Purpose Driven versus Lacking Purpose" value pair also defines a conflict between organizational goals and personal ones. We can think of this conflict as one between commitments to the organizational purposes, missions, goals, and orientations on the one hand, and personal purposes on the other. These words are all plural, because organizations do not have single purposes any more than individuals. To be sure, the IdeaManager and IdeaLeader must help the organization clarify its own purposes and give them proper priorities, but he or she must also help individual staff members to do the same. The balancing functions require the creation of a proper articulation between organizational purposes and personal purposes. One way to achieve this balance is to create a fusion between some organizational purposes and some personal purposes. Some Japanese managers do this by taking the family on a company-sponsored vacation. This probably would not fly in an American context, but there may be other ways to achieve a configuration that would be positive and useful.

Command Decision Making versus Consensus Decision Making

It is popular today to think that decision making loosely described by the phrase "consensus decision making" is the way to go. It is thought that consensus decision making involves participation at all levels of the organization, brings in a variety of perspectives, and secures agreement from those who are required to carry out a particular business strategy before making an actual decision. Participation, at least, if not consensus entirely, certainly seems to be the wave of the future.

Consensus does not work in all kinds of situations. Sometimes in emergency and very difficult crisis situations a command mode is appropriate. When time pressure or other kinds of stresses are besetting the organization, command may be appropriate. Furthermore, there are individuals who are at different levels of stakeholding commitment to the organization. The founder–owner, for example, may take a dim view of consensus on the simple ground that he or she was the individual who put up the money and energy to make the organization start and, therefore, should be able to say what happens. Whether one calls this command or not, it may closely approximate it.

Once again, the issue is not either command or consensus but, rather, the conditions under which consensus or command are appropriate and the styles through which command or consensus are carried out. An important point about decision making is that it has less to do with a style of command versus consensus than with the setting and structure (organizational team meetings) in which the decisions are made. All too frequently, organizational staff do not have the skills to manage the decision-making system teams and team meetings. Thus, both command and consensus fail because, at some point, both require some kind of group activity.

Empirical versus Qualitative Decision Making

In his original discussion, Miller (1984) labeled "non-rational" what I call "qualitative." Unfortunately, his word skews the case badly. Clearly, organizations need an empirical base for decision making. They need to know the kinds of numbers that they have to generate, and all employees within the organization need to be aware of what these numbers mean and for which ones they are responsible. We should never forget, however, that numbers can be assessed in the same way we assess computer programs: garbage in, garbage out. The most sophisticated analytic techniques will not provide the right answers if the wrong questions have been asked. There is room, therefore, for qualitative discussion and sharing within the framework of question building and number orchestrating.

Moreover, there are certain kinds of questions that numbers cannot answer at all. How many people, for example, would respond affirmatively to a market survey about a new product that they have not yet seen, used, or contemplated? What if a market survey had been done on Post-it™ Notes before they were available? Even if people could conceive of a semi-sticky paper, they would not have much of an idea as to the kinds of uses to which it might be put. Were we to rely on empirical methods—in this case a market survey—with respect to this particular product, it is very likely that the results would be sadly different from those we have today.

To a certain extent, the qualitative side of a decision-making system brings judgment, product knowledge, and immersion to the particular product in a service industry. These are nontrivial, and a complete decision system should blend both. The difficulty is, of course, that qualitative judgments tend to become entrenched. The facts cannot change them. This is a point made by Henry Rosovsky (1987), former Dean of the College at Harvard, in an article he wrote about being a dean. He cautions leaders never to underestimate the permanence of perception against facts. To the extent that qualitative approaches to decision making reject entrenched features, permanent views that are simply declared over and over again, such as the one Rosovsky is referring to, it is a poor method. But that is not because it is qualitative. There are also poor methods of empirical decision making. The IdeaManager and IdeaLeader needs to create a culture in which both numbers and judgment are respected. Each must be used to challenge the other. Each must supplement rather than supplant the competing method.

Disposable Labor versus Intimate Concerns

Organizations can have different values regarding employees. One of them is that the employee is a quasi-family team participant of the tribe; a person for whom one has some kind of deep concern and to whom one has a personal commitment. Alternatively, the employee can be viewed as little more than a human analog to an interchangeable part. When one breaks down, get another one that works. In the industrial society value system, the disposable labor focus was clearly the key element. It is against this perception that labor unions have labored long and mightily. It is against the cavalier and insensitive approach to individuals as human beings that they have fought significant battles. In the coming social structure of the information society and high tech–high touch, individual workers become more important, if for no other reasons than for the knowledge and skills they have already learned and the difficulties that are involved in replacing those skills and that knowledge and getting quickly to the same level of functioning that a firm was at before in its business.

Concern for individuals is appropriate and necessary. IdeaManagers and IdeaLeaders must be aware of and sensitive to the crucial role individuals play in the development of a product or service. At the same time, concern for individuals (as all parents know) does not translate into a lack of standards, quotas, and job requisites. Therefore, managers need to strive for a blend of both orientations toward employees.

Expediency versus Integrity

When Rosabeth Kanter (1983) speaks about a culture of pride, she means in part focusing on the fun and good feelings one has in being associated with a "winner" in a product or service. Beyond that, the culture of pride also includes working for an organization that both has and manifests integrity. It is associated with an organization that gets things done. Integrity involves open communication, open feedback, and visible demonstrations that the organization is honest and above board in its dealings with its employees, its customers, and its community.

It sounds strange to speak of an alternative to integrity, and alternative may be the wrong word. In the main, the pursuit of profit is an "end justifies the means" activity. It appears that organizations need to be watched so that they do not become overzealous in their pursuit of profit. The problem is to not allow one value to be an excuse for the other—not to allow the pursuit of profits to be an excuse for a lack of integrity or to stand on one's integrity to the point where appropriate action is delayed.

Performance-Based Rewards versus Power/Tenure-Based Rewards

In a "can-do" society characterized especially by organizational activity, the thought is always that rewards should go to people who "can do" the job. The operative cry, then, is "What have you done for me lately?" Clearly, it is important to reward people who accomplish significant organizational achievements. It is also important not to forget that most employees most of the time will not fall into that category. Though it is true that leadership can exhort individuals to exceptional achievement, there still needs to be a group of standard-bearers who do the various jobs of the organization regularly and reasonably well and who are characterized by organizational commitment and loyalty. Tenure, therefore, represents an amortized commitment, to some extent at least, and thus can be recognized.

Though Miller (1984) lumps power and tenure together, I am inclined to distinguish between them. Power, as a basis for reward, certainly has a long history. And it may well be appropriate to reward individuals of greater power differentially, more on the grounds, principally, that such individuals have greater responsibilities.

The problem, particularly with power and tenure, is that these bases for organizational compensation and other rewards become entrenched and separated from performance. Therefore, IdeaManagers and IdeaLeaders interested in creating a proper and viable organizational culture should seek to have differential bases for rewards, including at least the following three elements.

The tilt should be toward performance. Notwithstanding that belief, power and tenure are important values. In your organizational management activities, you might want to give serious consideration to dividing raise allotments into fractions for each. Alternatively, different kinds of rewards might be given for different types of contributions. Tenure, for example, might be rewarded in part by money and in part by organizational celebrations (e.g., prestige). To some extent, access to further resources might be a reward for power. American executives in particular are now receiving astronomical compensations. Unfortunately, due to competition among executives for such rewards, the cost is high; and the feelings of self-worth and reward become minimal. As in most armament races, additional increments of compensation to top-flight CEOs only serve to cancel out the premiums paid to other CEOs. A more variegated compensation system, basing itself on different values rather than on a single value, could be a great step forward.

Career versus Job

Miller (1984) does not talk specifically about a conflict of values between career orientation and job orientation, but it is an important one for us to keep in mind. IdeaManagers and IdeaLeaders are career oriented. Frequently, they will invest a lot of their own time and energy in the development of products or services in the hope of developing gain later in their career. They hope, of course, that the organization will be receptive; and indeed it is a part of their job to make the organization receptive (both in the sense of "force" and "prepare"), but if that cannot happen, they move on. One of the problems that IdeaManagers and IdeaLeaders often face is that others are not as committed or as farsighted. This is particularly true of employees. Entrepreneurs may find that employees are less willing than they to put in fourteen-hour days, to work weekends, and so on. Rather, the employee may take more of a job orientation; that is, "I'm here to do a specific set of tasks for a specific salary:

Give me the tasks, and let me go to work, and at five o'clock I'm out of here." Entrepreneurs need not only to be aware of the differences in attitudes that employees take but also to adjust the jobs and rewards—at least to a certain extent, depending on these two orientations.

MANAGING VALUES AND THEIR CONFLICTS: CULTURAL MIXING AND PHASING

Looking at Miller's (1984) list of cultural conflicts overall, several general points need to be made. To begin with, the value dimensions on the left-hand side (multipurpose, comfort and satisfaction, unity of purpose, personal purpose, command decision making, empirical decision making, disposable labor, expediency, performance rewards, and career) tend to be the ones that have characterized business organizations in this century. A cultural analysis of American business today would yield the legitimate conclusion that it is less the values of business that have caused the problems than the unbalanced emphasis on more dominant values that have been problematic. Overemphasis on expediency, empirical decision making, personal gain, disposable labor, and so on may well have caused problems. And the question would arise: What about performance? Surely, performance cannot be faulted. We do not fault it, but there is an essential point that must be made; namely, as a solo basis for evaluating an employee, performance does not represent the total picture. Loyalty, for example, is very important. The fact that an employee has contributed over a number of years is also worth taking into account. This perspective does not mean that there are not parameters of performance, only that we recognize in business what we recognize in life: There are various bases that combine in a variety of ways to make a particular type of decision. This observation leads to our second major point. Cultural management is really the management of cultural balance. Organizations, like people, sometimes go crazy. They become unbalanced when only one part of these cultural dualisms are recognized. Quinn (1979) points this out eloquently. It is the blending and melding of these various value packages that is the real test of organizational management. Sometimes consensus needs to be generated, but sometimes it is command. Sometimes performance needs to be emphasized, but sometimes it is power and tenure. Sometimes satisfaction needs to be emphasized, and at other times the emphasis must be on excellence. The point of all this is simple: You cannot always do one thing or the other. Conditions change. Personnel change. Variety is required.

Values Management: Some Strategies for Blending

Though it may appear difficult, it is in fact possible to manage culture. If the focus is on blending and melding, there are several possible courses available as options. Sometimes both values can be honored, as in the different levels of products mentioned in the excellence versus comfort/satisfaction dilemma. Another strategy is *averaging*. This simple expedient involves taking some of the influence of one value and some from the other value and splitting the difference. If some command and some consensus is needed, then an acceptable average is worked out.

Often, however, as in the case of command and consensus, averaging is not the best option available to you. Sectoring or sequencing may be better ways to proceed. Sectoring involves picking those particular areas where command is to be used and other areas where consensus is to be used. The very inconsistency is actually a refreshing bit of freedom from the unanimity of all one or all the other. Sequencing involves alternating value bases over time, as opposed to the use of other conditions. You may decide that none of these meet your particular need at a particular point in time. You still have *counterbalancing* available to you. With counterbalancing, the IdeaManager and IdeaLeader seeks to provide the alternative perspective; if everyone is interested in consensus, he or she may seek to involve a command orientation; or, if everyone is command oriented, then the IdeaManager and IdeaLeader might try for a consensus orientation.

It is crucial for the IdeaManager and IdeaLeader to be aware of the need for flexibility within the value matrix. A great number of values are required in any culture to keep it current, fluid, and relevant. Herbert Kaufman (1985) points out that organizations decline because they have problems with resources. They have problems with resources, he argues, because they are unable to adapt themselves to the changing environmental conditions. Though he does not use this particular term, it is possible to think of such organizational inertia as a *values ossification*. This means that if one particular set of attitudes, ideas, and beliefs that have characterized an organization over time continue to dominate, the organization ultimately finds itself out in left field and then out of the park.

Value Management: Crafting the Vision, Mission, and Goals Package

I have used an illustrative set of values to bring home the idea that competing emphasizes the need for balance. It should not and does not mean that these are the only sets one could come up with. Rather, it simply means that through working with employees, consultants, supplies, and customers (as well as former customers and customers-to-be) a package of values is developed that can attract and retain the commitment of all throughout the organization.

Organizations typically use words like "vision," "missions," and "goals" to signal their values. Vision is the broadest statement of the purposes and commitments of the organization. One popular example, "The Golden Rule" vision, is timeless, until changed. Mission derives from vision and introduces some goals or targets; it is semi-timeless. The Ten Commandments are something like this, except that they tend to be on the proscriptive side; we are told what not to do. We also need to be told what to do. Goals represent more specific, timebound injunctions or suggestions. Church rules might serve as an example. Creating, rewriting, and reenergizing these values is a job for the IdeaManager and IdeaLeader.

Values Management: Culture as a Reward

Employees work for money income; they also work for psychic income. Psychic income is the emotional reward of working for a particular place. These rewards are usually seen as a kind of "values alignment." Some people are "greens." They look for companies with the most positive environmental record. Other people are committed to prestige; they want to work for the "best" company in their area, (and some of these kinds of firms exploit this reward by paying less.) Other employees want a good attitude and friendliness in the workplace (remember that the top dissatisfiers at work are other people—bosses, peers, subordinates, etc.). Crafting and articulating values can actually be a form of "cultural compensation," and should be attended to with that in mind. For the organizations of the twenty-first century, receptivity to and appreciation of ideas for the new and different will be a key kind of cultural compensation.

Value Management: The Firm Logo and Motto

Given all these conflicting orientations, it is necessary to pull all of these things together into a coherent and symbolized culture. One of the best ways to do this is through an organizational logo and motto. Every organization, no matter how large or small, should have both a logo and a motto. Attention to these should at least occupy the central attention of the top individuals and, at best, of everyone connected with the enterprise, rather than being something delegated to a lowly subordinate. The logo in body symbolizes and represents the organization, and the few words that make up the motto symbolize the fundamental essence of the firm. Many profitable discussions about organizational culture have come from attempts to either refurbish or generate a new logo and motto. When one is forced to say in a few words the essential focus of the organizational effort ("Quality is job one," "The mark of excellence," "Better things for better living"), it stimulates and gives concrete reality to thought. It forces organizations to answer these questions: What business are we in? How can we communicate that? (Naisbitt, 1982). Often, people think the communication is only to others. This is not so. Communication via logo and motto is first and foremost to the organization itself, and seen as an economical reminder of what the organization stands for and promises.

In defining a logo or a motto, care must be taken to embody both sides of the competing value frameworks. Overemphasis on a single value (excellence, for example) is likely to create a climate in which that promise cannot be sustained. This causes members of the organization to fall further short than they would have if a more balanced approach had been taken.

KINDS OF ARTIFACTS AND CREATIONS

Schein's (1985) third area of culture was artifacts and creations. Policy, as mentioned, is one kind of creation. One can discern values through an examination of policy. Hence, one needs to be sure that policy as it is developed expresses organizational assumptions and values. Other kinds of artifacts are cups, jackets, clothing of any sort, designs, mementos, or laminated cards with the company motto on it, any and all of which serve to embody publicly the values and subculture of the organization.

Finally, recognitions, ceremonies, and rituals are organizational artifacts. Recognitions (worker of the week, employee of the day) embody preferred organizational values and call attention to those which are more desired. Ceremonies are public, group-based recognitions which commemorate and honor events and people important in the firm. Rituals are ceremonies (like a wedding) which not only commemorate but also transform individuals, departments, or products from one organizational status to another. IdeaManagers and IdeaLeaders create and encourage recognitions, ceremonies, and rituals as a way of managing values.

MANAGING ARTIFACTS AND CREATIONS

Policy, of course, is one way in which culture is made manifest within the organizational context. Because they also serve to direct the specific day-to-day activities of the organization, policies represent a concrete point of the cultural fulcrum: the transition matrix between ideas and actions/directions. The conditions and contingencies often specified in policy can be understood as attempts to explain to policy implementors the different value conditions under which different actions are permissible, desirable, or required. It is true, however, as Schein (1985) suggests, that values and assumptions are often implicit in policy rather than stared directly. Therefore, the IdeaManager and IdeaLeader who approaches policy needs to be analytically discerning—there is more there than you might think. Since values are hard to manage directly, they are often managed through questions raised about policy, the words expressed in policy, and actions which policy directs.

CONCLUSION

Organizational culture is a powerful—perhaps the most powerful—integrating force within the organization. This is especially true in a society like America, where there are wide diversities and many different orientations, backgrounds, and interests. An important task for business is to provide a ground where these can be temporarily set aside. One of the best ways to do this is to provide a belief system to which a wide range of diverse individuals can subscribe, at least for the time during which they are associated with the organization in general and, more particularly, during the time they are at work. The difficulty, of course, is that there is not a single set of beliefs or values that will serve this purpose. Rather, the values of any corporate culture are a blend of conflicting dispositions that, if left to themselves, may happen to work out all right or may happen to clash so much that they cannot be overcome. These clashes can be very costly. Consider, for example, acquisitions and mergers, where two different cultures are suddenly brought together under the same corporate umbrella. Too infrequently, as many failed partnerships attest, a split is necessary; the differences are simply too great.

I am not suggesting that culture management can overcome all of these potential problems. Attention to culture as a specific and integrating force within the organization is a good place to start. One can ask about the kinds of culture one needs and about the kinds of values one wishes to embody. One can then systematically go about seeking to incorporate them. Organizational ceremonies are an important part of culture management. Ceremonies convey to employees what is important and what is valued, and, as Schein (1985) suggested, are part of the way that we respond to external problems and the environment.

Chapter 17

Creating Idea-Driven Strategy

Organizations need a guidance system. The ideas contained in the values subculture, expressed in vision, mission, and goals, are that guidance. Strategy, in a general sense, is a structure of organizational expectations and a guide to action. Strategy focuses time-limited energy to solving organizational problems. Strategy is the organization's approach to doing the right thing, while tactics is the organization's approach to doing things right. Strategy helps you work smart while also working hard. It involves, of course, selection and choice.

WHAT DOES STRATEGY LOOK LIKE?

Strategy is an organizational policy. As such, it has several features common to all policy:

1. It is derived from vision, values, mission.
2. It is written.
3. It is a guide to action.
4. It is approved by legitimate authority.

What this means is that strategy is fundamentally connected to who we are and why we exist as a company. It means that you cannot have a strategy that is fundamentally opposed to your *raison d'être*. Strategy is an extension of, and a vehicle for the enactment of, vision and values. A will, for example, is a personal strategy for distributing personal assets. It reflects the values and commitments of the maker.

Strategy is not strategy if it is in our heads. Some executives talk about "enacted" strategies. That just means they do not want to write anything down! Strategy, like a will, has to be written. The writing is "God's way of showing us how sloppy our thinking really is." The writing also is the mechanism through which choice and decision is expressed; somebody gets the house, somebody gets the car, and so forth.

Also like a will, strategy tell us what to do, what to emphasize, and how to approach things. "Making money" is not a strategy. It has to be a bit more specific than that.

Strategy has to have backing. It cannot be something that one or two people work out. Once it is written down, it has to be approved by the principals of the organization, or its board (if it is overall organizational strategy) or subunits (if it is a subunit strategy).

All these things flow together in a strategic plan. A strategic plan tells us how we are going to go about achieving our goals. It is a touchstone document for all in the organization. It need not—should not—be long. But it needs to provide the direction employees need to carry out the business. If vision and mission provide answers to the questions, "What business are we in?" and "Where are we going?" then the strategic plan provides the road map.

A CACOPHONY OF CRITICISM

There has been a lot of criticism of "planning," especially in America. The criticism is of several sorts. One line of attack argues that something like a five-year plan is just too rigid in today's fast-moving world. A second criticism argues that it is impossible to know enough to plan. A third criticism argues that plans are too rigid and do not allow flexibility (see Mintzberg, 1994). All these points, and others, are reasonable, and should be considered. But my view is that these criticism throw the baby out with the bathwater, in much the same way that criticism of committees winds up celebrating working alone. Obviously there are problems with committees, just as there are problems with strategic planning. From my point of view, this orientation is wrongheaded and regrettable. The answer, however, is not to get rid of either one of them, but to fix them.

The real basis for much of the criticism is, I think, cultural in nature. American society particularly is something of a do/plan culture rather than a plan/do culture. Plans seem like nonaction. It is based on the idea that plans are somehow fixed, immutable cages from which you cannot escape. To me, plans are flexible. (One of my favorite phrases comes from Groucho Marx: "You don't like my principles? I have others.") Plans are dynamic. They provide direction but can be altered—should be altered—as conditions permit. The fact that one changes one's will as family conditions change is no argument for having no will. The fact that one may adjust a dinner party menu as one finds out about the preferences of guests is no argument for having no menu at all.

Strategy is a more formal kind of map building, which, through writing, exposes many hidden assumptions and metavalues for analysis, deals with the contradictions inherent therein, and develops a guide for the near future. And it can change. Overall, the man or woman with the plan wins. For the IdeaManager and IdeaLeader, strategy is where all the ideas actually come together.

THE STRATEGIC QUARTET

The strategic plan is really a complex document that provides answers to four kinds of questions:

1. Where are we going—the substance of success
2. How are we going to get there—the path to success
3. What are the acceptable means of getting there—the parameters of success
4. How can we create a system and culture which continually energizes and refurbishes 1–3—the system of success

The idea-driven company of the twenty-first century will have a dynamic strategy. Successful companies will be characterized by really good strategic ideas. The IdeaManager and IdeaLeader needs to work on developing the ideas. As a goal or end, strategy deals with an answer to what we are trying to achieve in the next period of time: secure market share, developing a certain ROI, experiencing a certain growth in stock price, retaining certain contracts, and so on. And these strategic goals must be ideas of the highest quality—sensible, thoughtful, and fact based. This is the substance of success.

Strategy also talks about the paths to success, rather than the results of success. We will secure an increased market share by doing this or that. These are the means of success. Strategy also deals with the parameters. Part of strategy sets the conditions for success, rather than the substance of success or the means of success. It outlines some ways that we will act in seeking these goals. We will offer quality service, for example, or we will be a family-friendly company. Suppose "excellence" is one of the parameters you wish to employ. Then you could do no worse than look at the "several excellencies" that Peter Vaill (1982) suggests. He gives a number of alternative criteria which can be used alone or in combination to assess excellence. Organizations are excellent when the following are true:

1. They are performing excellently against known external standards.
2. They are performing excellently against what is assumed to be their potential level of performance.
3. They are performing excellently against where they were at some previous point in time.
4. They have been judged by informed observers to be doing substantially better qualitatively than other comparable systems.

5. They are doing what they do with significantly less resources [sic] than it is assumed they needed to do what they do.
6. They are perceived as exemplars of the way they do whatever they do and thus become a source of inspiration to others.
7. They are perceived to fulfill at a high level the ideals for the culture within which they exist.
8. They are the only organizations that have been able to do what they do at all, even though it might not seem that what they do is a difficult or mysterious thing.

To these I would add the following:

9. They provide values in products and services, and add value to the system.
10. They accomplish these tasks without exploiting workers or the environment.

What Vaill (1982) is really talking about are measures that could be applied to any organization, if it wished to adopt them. I have added a couple of my own. Number 9 says that a strategic parameter of your organization might be that it really has to add value to the system through new products and services. This avoids the charge of "churning the system" and "paper organizationalism." I am also suggesting (Number 10) that a strategic limitation be the avoidance of exploitation of people or the environment. In my ideal company, you cannot make money through child labor or through dumping your externalities in Lake Michigan.

Finally, strategy suggests processes for strategic renewal. The strategic ideas mentioned in these points (1–3) suggest that success goals, success means, and success parameters must be continually regenerated, reinvented, and refurbished (recall the Five-C Conference). Strategic ideas must be improved, updated, and recrafted, often quickly. Part of strategy is designing a system for strategic production.

TYPES OF STRATEGY

Miles and colleagues (1978) developed four organizational response styles: (1) the Defender, (2) the Prospector, (3) the Analyzer, and (4) the Reactor. They offered these as ways organizations respond to environments in each of these areas.

The first of these, the Defender, needs to secure a market on an institutional basis. On a managerial basis, the Defender needs to maintain organizational control and to insure efficiency. On a technical basis, the Defender produces and distributes goods efficiently. Organizational strategies for the Defender will focus on solving these problems.

The Prospector, on the institutional level, seeks ways to locate and exploit new opportunities. On a managerial basis, the Prospector wishes to facilitate and coordinate diverse operations. On a technical basis, the Prospector seeks to avoid long-term constraints of a single industrial program or process.

The Analyzer seeks to find and develop new organizational opportunities at the institutional level. At the same time, the Analyzer wishes to maintain a traditional base of customers and products. At the managerial level, the Analyzer seeks to design organizational systems that can accommodate both regular and innovative elements. At the technical level, the problem is how to stimulate both efficiency and stability. The Analyzer is a fairly good example of value dualism, as discussed in Chapter 16. Both innovation and stability are sought, and developed and attended to on a recognized simultaneous basis.

The Reactor has no real strategy at the institutional level. At the managerial level, management seeks to retain the "same old stuff" and retains old strategies and systems in spite of large-scale changes in the environment. At the technical level, production continues as it did in the past. Because there is no strategy to which technical changes can be fit, the inertia of history becomes dominant.

If one steps back a moment and looks at these four types—defense, prospecting, analysis, and reaction—one can see they comprise fairly general response modes to changes in the environment. At one level, one can ignore the external environment and react only when prodded and forced. A more adaptive strategy is defense; seek to locate oneself in a reasonably safe environment, fortify one's products and services, and wait out attacks. The Analyzer strategy is more venturesome and allows one to retain anchors in traditional products and services while at the same time beginning to prospect for new and additional ways to penetrate the market.

The most venturesome (or risky) of these strategies is the Prospector strategy. It focuses resources entirely on the development of new and innovative products.

STRATEGIC DICTA

In the creation of organizational strategies, there is a powerful set of strategic dicta—systematic ideas, if you will—that should be taken into account. Whatever the nature of your business or assignment, these ideas will help.

Strategy Differs Depending on Stage of Growth

Pay attention to what stage your firm is in. Organizations go through stages of growth. First there is the new organization stage. Then, implementation follows. Next comes growth or expansion for those fortunate enough to survive the first two phases. The fourth stage is consolidation, and the fifth is renewal. Strategy needs to be adjusted to the stage.

Strategies Differ as the Organization Grows

The Parts of Your Firm Are Different

Take account of the different parts of the firm. Harvard sociologist Talcott Parsons (1960) provided a second insight into organizational strategy when he pointed out that organizations have three levels or parts. These levels are only loosely connected each to the other. The three sectors he saw were as follows: (1) a technical sector, which involves production and the actual "work" of the organization; (2) the managerial level, which involves the decision-making and directing segments of the organization; and (3) the institutional level, which involves making connections with the wider environment.

Three Parts/Three Problems

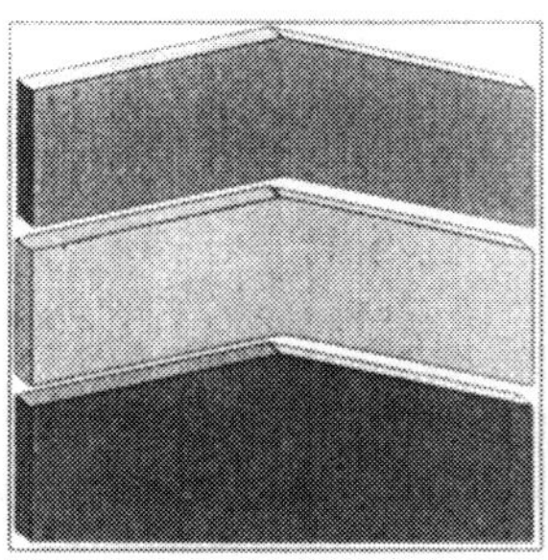

It is quite likely that these three sectors will not necessarily grow at the same speed or at the same rate, nor have the same sets of issues and concerns; problems and phases may be rather different for each. While the overall organization is characterized in one way, the subparts may actually have their own trajectories and these may be inverse to the overall one. Thus, the technical part has one set of issues, the managerial part another, and the institutional part a third. A second aspect of strategy, then, is to have somewhat different substrategies for the different subparts of the organization.

The Problems of Your Firm Are Different

Miles and his colleagues (1978) looked at organizations as problem sets, rather than parts. They identified three orientations that are quite similar to the Parsonian trilogy. They talk about organizations having an organizational problem (which, because it focuses essentially on links with the environment, is similar to the institutional one), an administrative problem (which links to the management aspect that Parsons discussed), and an engineering problem (which focuses on the technical level). Thus, the third strategic dictum is to design substrategies appropriate to each of the three problem levels within the organizational structure.

There Are Big Gaps between and among the Parts of Your Firm

There are cleavages between the parts of the organization that are not easy to cross. Indeed, parts of the organization do not necessarily lead logically from one to the other. Organizations are like deserts: From a distance they look seamless; closer in, there are big canyons. Those skilled in technical materials are not necessarily skilled in managerial matters, as anyone who has seen an excellent teacher, professor, or player become a bad principal, dean, or coach can attest. Similarly, good managers (principals, deans, or coaches) do not necessarily make good CEOs (school superintendents, college presidents, or athletic directors). The "Peter Principle" (Peter, 1970, 1972) ("Individuals tend to rise to the level of their own incompetence," or "You will be promoted from what you do well into something new until you screw up, at which point you will remain") is a perfect example of this organizational observation in operation. The skills required at the next major level of the organization are rather different and may even be at variance with those at other organizational levels. A fourth aspect of organizational strategy—the fourth strategic dictum—is to prepare for intraorganizational stability and transition. This simultaneous strategy allows those individuals who are skilled within a particular level to remain and advance there, while simultaneously identifying those who are able to move and take on other responsibilities and preparing them for that.

Mix and Phase Strategic Approaches

The best way to design strategy is to have a blend or mix. First, it is important to see that variations occur within the developmental area of the organization. Hence, a different mix of these strategies may be used at different times in the organization's history. At a very beginning phase, for example, a Prospector strategy is appropriate. After all, there are no old products or services within which one can maintain a firm anchor. In the renewal phase of the organization, however, an Analyzer strategy might be important. There are variations over time. Part of the job of the IdeaManager and IdeaLeader, and the skills that person possesses, involves reconfiguring the strategic matrix such that the appropriate dominant strategy can be operationalized at the appropriate time.

The idea of dominant strategy suggests that there might be several, because to some extent these strategies, like values, exist simultaneously. It is not a question of having only one and not the others. Rather, it is a question of which is prominent and dominant at a particular point in time. Indeed, their simultaneous presence acts as a plus for the organization.

For example, even the Reactor strategy—hardly one that seems terribly elegant when studied in and of itself—might well have many benefits when present simultaneously with a Prospector strategy. The converse can be true as well: The Reactor and the Prospector, working together, may act as simultaneous controls on each other. The problem, of course, is when one becomes totally dominant. Then the company ceases to prospect at all if the Reaction strategy is the victor. In this case, the company becomes or can become merely a shell of its former self. On the other hand, without the Reactor, the Prospector may plunge headlong into a range of activities that prove to be unwise. Similarly, the Defender and the Analyzer strategies may work in tandem. The Defender, moving more toward security and entrenched positions, and the Analyzer, recognizing virtues in that but moving out, can balance each other reasonably well.

It is not necessarily true that every part of the organization has the same strategy at any given moment in time. We all tend to talk as if that is so. One speaks, for example, of the X Company as having an aggressive strategy, or the Y Company as having a conservative strategy, and so on. And yet, on further examination and after more detailed scrutiny, it turns out that the X Company and the Y Company are collectives of strategies. It may well be the case, for example, that the technical level has one particular strategic trajectory, the managerial another, and the institutional yet a third.

Part of these differences may depend on the nature of the environment. In the high-tech area, for example, the technical level may be prospecting constantly while the managerial level may be seeking a defensive position with respect to products already established. The institutional level, represented by the Board of Directors, may be seeking an Analyzer strategy. Because different parts of the organization interact with and deal with different parts of the environment, it is rather likely (wise or not) that they will formally or informally undertake different strategic directions. Managerial orientation, for example, is heavily intraorganizational. Their primary focus is dealing upward with the institutional level on the one hand and dealing downward with the technical level on the other. They tend to be more insulated from external pressures, either from customers (as the technical level would) or investors and general environmental politicians (as the institutional level would). Many at the managerial level, therefore, are more likely to adopt either the Defender strategy or the Reactor strategy, in part because they are not confronted with the issues and problems as directly as the other two levels.

Part of the job of the IdeaManager and IdeaLeader, therefore, is to understand what the strategic imperatives are at each level and to seek to orchestrate and fit all the parts and elements together. This task is not an enviable one, nor is it easy. It is for this reason that the creation of organizational subculture becomes important as an integrating tool. If all of the organizational elements and parts at least have the same set of values and orientations, it is possible to use these as a jumping off place for strategic articulation.

The first step, of course, is recognizing the likelihood that there will be different strategic points of view at the different organizational sectors. Considering the concept of the strategic matrix, it is quite possible to fit different strategies within a matrix and yet maintain an overall orientation or perspective toward one's line of work.

There may be times, however, when an IdeaManager and IdeaLeader wants to stimulate differences in strategic perspectives. If, for example, the entire organization is dominated by a Reactor or Defender strategy, then one might seek an organizational niche where a Prospector or an Analyzer strategy could be introduced. Successful development of this strategy within a limited organizational domain will hopefully begin to create sufficient interest and envy to cause the generation of organizational change. Indeed, the virtue of simultaneous strategies with prominence and dominance rather than solo occupation of the strategic slot once again becomes evident. It is only with the friction generated by questions and hesitations that even a good strategy can become better. Without internal strategic competition as an ongoing part of organizational life, the likelihood of successful strategy for dealing with the external environment is diminished.

Strategy in organizations involves articulating compositional and contextual elements in a process of mutual adjustment, such that their evolving needs and demands mesh. It is imperative not to see the context as a neutral thing to which one must respond, but, in principle at least, as an element that one may shape to some degree. Phrases like "market creation" speak to part of this issue. Furthermore, strategy involves structuring and smoothing sprints and pauses so that the benefits can be gained from this unevenness, rather than the problems. Cycles of heavy activity and rest can be beneficial if properly tuned. Then, as suggested earlier, it involves linking different strategies with the different phases. One might concentrate on implementing more of a Prospector strategy during a sprint phase, for example, and more of an Analyzer strategy during a pause phase. Finally, it involves planning, configuring, and orchestrating the activities of distinct organizational components to create mutual support. In this sense, strategy implies and requires the creation of structure.

CONCLUSION

Strategy—the structure of expectations and the provision of guidelines—is an important starting point for individuals who want to introduce new products, services, and ideas. This is true whether they are seeking funding for an original idea or they desire to introduce that idea into an ongoing concern. What is important to keep in mind is that "strategies" (like decisions) is a collective noun. There are likely to be collections or packages of strategies. Overall, this is what Hamel and Prahalad (1989) call "strategic intent."

There may be dominant strategies and subdominant ones. IdeaManagers and IdeaLeaders have four tasks here. One is to stimulate the ideas that drive strategy and become strategy. The second is to get the ideas translated into strategic policy; that is, to get them written and approved. The third is to assist in customizing strategies for the problems and parts of the organization. The last is to manage the strategic package so that there is articulation and coherence among the substrategies. In this respect, the IdeaManager is like an orchestra conductor, paying attention to the various different sections with their own idiosyncrasies such that the total sound is wonderful, coherent, and pleasing.

Chapter 18

Creating Idea-Driven Structures

The more efficient an organization is, the dumber it is.

—Richard Greene (1986)

Structure matters. Every routine has a route. The way a house or an organization is laid out influences the efficiency with which it works. It has been suggested that form follows function; the function of a thing should dictate the form it takes. In the same way, structure should follow strategy. Once the organization has outlined the strategic elements that it wants to pursue or achieve, it moves to the next step of designing structures to articulate these goals and objectives. Helping this to occur is one of the jobs of the IdeaManager and IdeaLeader.

A second type of structural job is to sponsor, create, and encourage idea-generating structures, whatever the overall organizational structure turns out to be. Let us begin with the problem—pressures on the organization and the new things that are happening—and then move on to idea-generating structures.

PRECIPITATING AND PREDISPOSING PRESSURES

Organizational structures today have two general forces working on them: *predisposing* and *precipitating*. The predisposing factors are influences driven by the environment and the times—essentially forces coming from superordinate culture and structure. Precipitating factors are those which relate to the organization itself. The tasks of IdeaManagers and IdeaLeaders here are challenging.

One set invites them to propose ideas to update structure or create a structure that provides fit among and between predisposing factors and precipitating elements. As the following illustration suggests, there are multiple forces pressing in upon the organization. Structure needs to be such that it can accommodate the internal and external elements in a balanced, articulated fashion.

Precipitating and Predisposing Factors (Arrows) Pressing onto/into the Organization (Box)

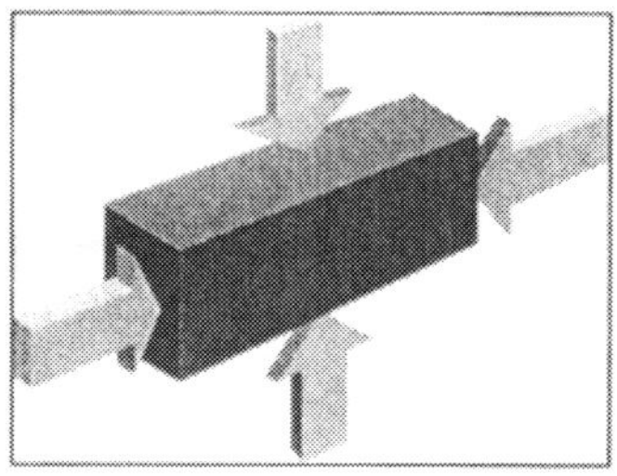

A second challenge is to imbue substructures within whatever organizational design is selected that stimulate the flow of ideas. Structures are needed, because otherwise there are no "drivers" within the organization.

Predisposing pressures will be considered in greater detail in Chapter 21 on superordinate structure and culture. For purposes here, I would like to talk about the general results of those pressures in terms of their impact on organizational structure. That impact has been profound. Let us begin by looking at some of the problems organizations experience structurally, and most often fail to address.

STRUCTURAL PROBLEMATICS

At the end of the twentieth century, organizations in the developed world are facing many structural problems. The events of the middle part of the century—war, massive production—accentuated the "machine model" of organizations, a hierarchical pyramid which has a protected center and a thick barrier separating it from the outside. Most often it was vertically integrated, with direction flowing down and information flowing up.

The Old-Fashioned Organization

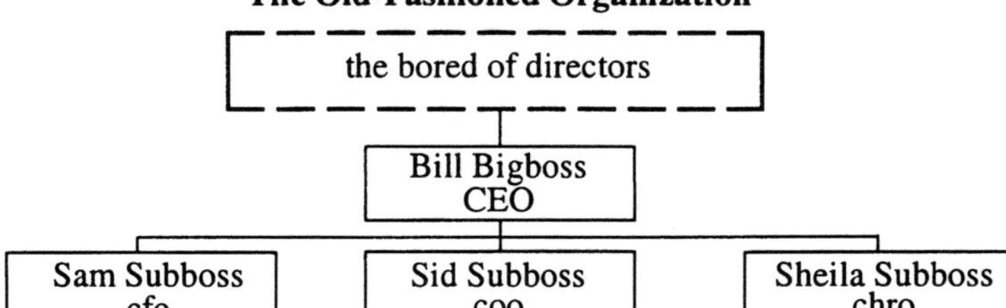

In theory, this kind of organization should work well. In practice, it developed many problems that were forcing it to change.

Insularity

The historical structure insulated the organization from customers and top staff from the employees of the organization. Figure 18.1 shows this structure, as described by Tom Peters (1988).

Bad Fit

A second failing of organizations is that they only have a tenuous relationship between their strategy and structure. Many structures are driven by, well, who knows? Here are some of the more problematic ones. It should come as no surprise to anyone that the forms of many organizations are outdated with respect to their functions, their desires, their goals, and their strategies.

The Jerry-Built Structure

This problem of badness of fit leaves many organizations looking as though they had been designed by Rube Goldberg (the man whose name has come to be synonymous with very complex structures used for solving simple problems). We have all seen the occasional building that has passed through numerous hands and that has been added to and changed somewhat by each owner. Lacking elegance is too kind a description. It is a Jerry-built structure with gables sticking out here, extra rooms there, a parapet or two, staircases that lead to nowhere, sundry connections to various outbuildings, and so on. In short, it is a mess. And then some chief executive officer is surprised when the structure does not function well.

The Overly Complex Structure

Another problem is the too complex organizational structure. Peters and Waterman (1982) speak of structure in their injunction, "Simple form, lean staff." Though there are a lot of ways that injunction can be made operational, the general perspective is a good one. Complexity of structures decreases organizational elegance and compounds the difficulties organizations have in accomplishing their goals and solving their problems. Someone once defined elegance as being equal to the number of variables divided by the simplicity of solution. It is this goal we are trying to achieve in designing organizational structures. Many organizational charts have lines, and then dotted lines, and then other lines, in a gnarled attempt to illustrate how the organization really works. The complex situation creates rigidity and slowness to respond.

Figure 18.1
The Inflexible, Rule-Determined Mass Producer of the Past: All Persons Know Their Place

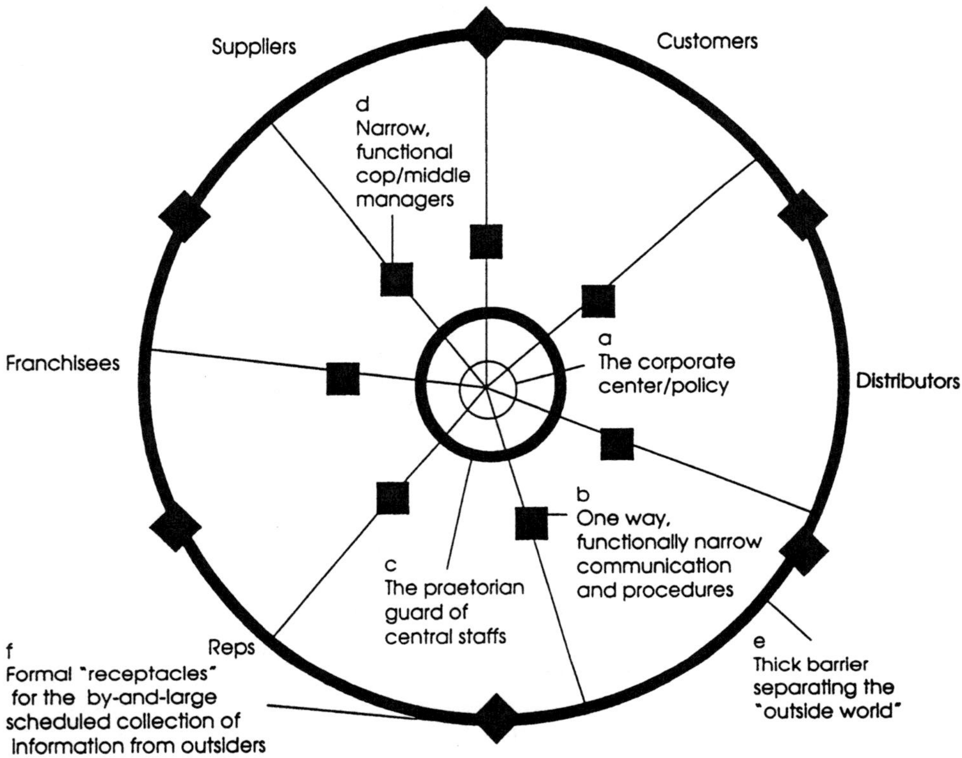

Source: Tom Peters, "Restoring American Competitiveness: Looking for New Models of Organizations," *Academy of Management Executives* 2, no. 2 (May 1988): 103–107. Reprinted by permission of Academy of Management.

Note: Start with (a), the corporate center/policy. This is the traditional, invisible, impersonal, generally out-of-touch corporate hub. The tininess of the circle representing the corporate center suggests both tightness and narrowness of scope; communication to the outside world (in or beyond the firm's official boundary) is usually via formal declaration—the policy manual or the multivolume plan, by and large determined on high—and communicated via the chain of command (i.e., downward). Within this tiny circle lie the "brains of the organization." It is here, almost exclusively, that the long-term thinking, planning, and peering into the future take place.

Repetitive Redundancy

Complex structures engender complex systems. This means that there are often multiple pay systems, promotion systems, evaluation systems, and so on. They become convoluted, overlapping, and redundant.[1]

Plumposity

Organizations are supposed to be revolving doors: employees moved in, moved up, and moved out as they and the firm changed. As it happens, many organizations have a door that only opens inward. Staff size and costs begin to grow and the organization becomes less and less efficient.

"Undiversity"

As the workforce changes and the nature of the employees' needs changes, organizations do not. The top team is usually made up of white males, regardless of the nature of the employee mix or customer mix. Women are working in increasing numbers but are underrepresented in top team positions. As one woman said, "Want to know how we feel? Cut your salary by 45 percent, for starters!" And companies are going global with an ethnocentric mentality and staffing pattern.

WHAT'S NEW?

These pressures have been building and have resulted in profound changes in organizational structure. Popular phrases like downsizing, resizing, and rightsizing allude to the drop in head count (addressing plumposity), but also signal other changes as well. Organizations are being pressured to be more networked, flexible, diverse, and global. How is this happening?

One way is to move from the vertical organization to the horizontal organization. In the horizontal organization, subprocesses are parts of larger processes—from the beginning to the end—rather than functions, as in the older organization chart (see Figure 18.1). Consider the following illustration.

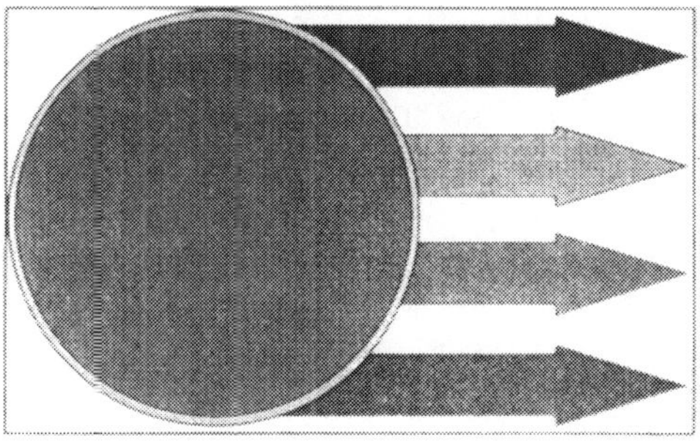

In this organization, let us say there is some central intake or entry point (the circle) out of which flow four key processes. If this were an auto dealership, it might be new cars, used cars, parts, and rentals. The difference is that the new care buying process is followed from beginning to end—from marketing and advertising to financing to selling—and the customer is followed by the same person instead of being handed off from one department to another. The same thing could be true in a hospital, where one doctor integrates everything that you need from all other specialists. Processes are organized around the flow of the customer, and, as such, structures become aligned with systems, as will be discussed in Chapter 19 on systems (also see Stewart, 1992).

Process structures deal with problems like the following: The April 1987 catalog of the Lands' End direct-mail merchandising company contains a quote from a man who runs a laundry business in Chicago, complaining about the lack of process structures. He said,

> You have hit my pet peeve. I can't think of another industry where designers communicate so little with service people. They [shirt manufacturers] taper their shirts so they don't fit our [launderers] presses, then put too much fabric in the collar so it doesn't iron flat. Sometimes they even use a collar liner made of a different fabric so the collar shrinks but the liner doesn't. Or put in nonremovable collar stays that show through the collar when it's ironed. They don't even know enough to cut the sleeve gussets long enough to go over the presses. This shirt can be ironed perfectly. (p. 112)

Lands' End did not have this particular problem. That is why they mentioned it.

This particular example is of an interorganizational system; but, obviously, it would be to everyone's advantage in that business to try to come up with some common definitions, sizes, and procedures and have a seamless process from the beginning to the end. Managers here, sometimes called process owners, try to see that such seamlessness occurs.

Peters (1988) also has a description of what is new. In this rendition (Figure 18.2), in contrast to his earlier drawing, boundries are thin, managers are wandering around, and suppliers are entering the organization; it is very different from the historical model.

Other phrases are creeping into the argot concerning structure. Sometimes the process (horizontal) and functional (vertical) organizations are run simultaneously. This is called a matrix. In a matrix structure, any worker has two bosses, one for function and one for process. Many say it is unnatural to have two bosses; this is bunk in my view—most have two parents! The problem is that companies create two bosses but leave one salary, one performance appraisal, and one promotion route. So there are really not two bosses; there is a "real" boss (the one who controls those things) and a "fake" boss. Matrix can work if time and salary are divided between the two bosses. Employees often resist this, though, because it adds uncertainty and leaves the job of integration, to some extent, with them. Career ladders are being replaced with career lattices.

A matrix design, though, no matter how many bosses one has, is still an alignment of vectors. Suppose we move away from the box design completely, and use another kind of metaphor for the organization. A solar system would do nicely. We can start by moving from box to circle.

Figure 18.2
The Flexible, Porous, Fleet-of-Foot Organization of the Future

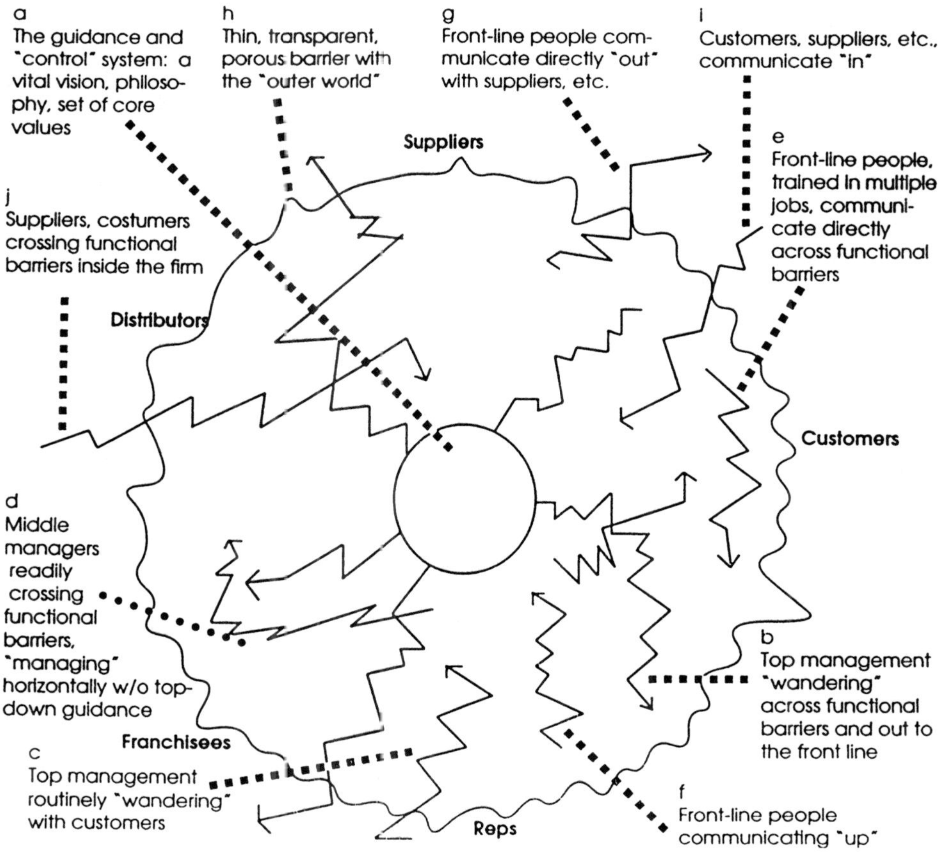

Source: Tom Peters, "Restoring American Competitiveness: Looking for New Models of Organizations," *Academy of Management Executives* 2, no. 2 (May 1988): 103–107. Reprinted by permission of Academy of Management.

Note: Every person is "paid" to be obstreperous, a disrespecter of formal boundaries, to hustle and to be engaged fully with engendering swift action.

The first of these involves a mental image. Think of taking the two ends of the bottom row of the theory "pyramid" organizational chart, one in each hand, stretching them out, bending them around, and attaching them at the top. In other words, create an organizational circle. There is no particular reason why an organizational chart could not be redrawn as an organizational circle. One possible representation of the idea is given in Figure 18.3. Now let us consider the implications of the organizational circle.

Figure 18.3
The Organizational Circle or Solar System

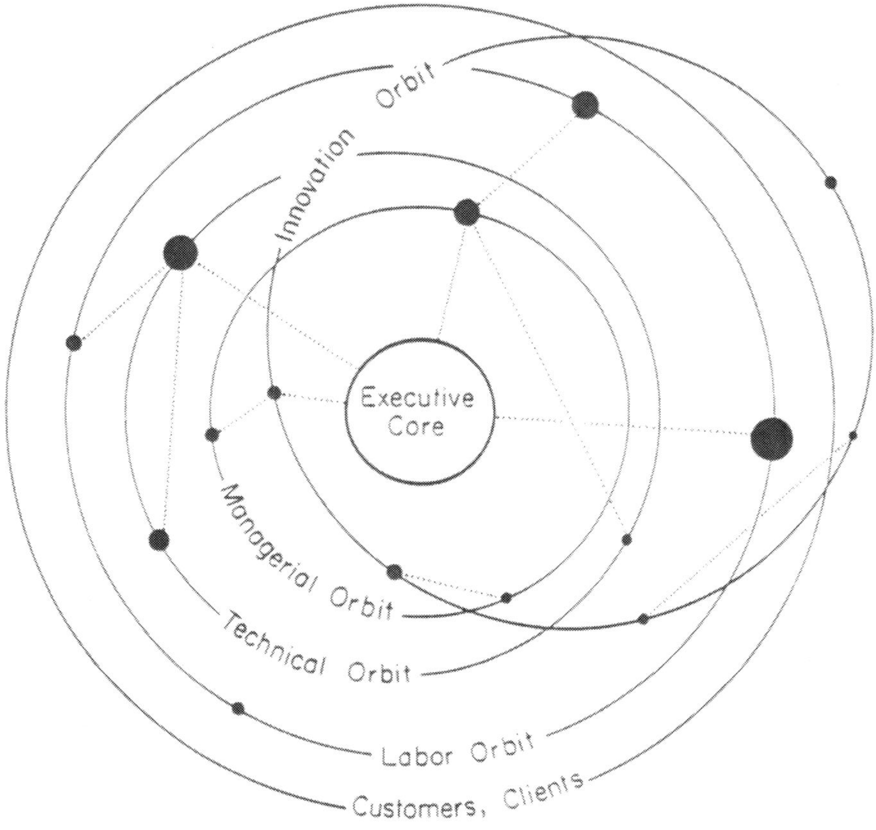

To begin with, the hierarchy becomes flat. There is less up and down and a great deal more back and forth. The organizational circle concept reframes and refocuses our orientation toward authority. The "higher-ups" no longer exist above anyone; they are, however, central to the organization. Now, the center of the organization is a kind of fulcrum that creates organizational balance and that can redirect its energies, as they are needed, to various parts of the organization.

A second thing that happens is that contact between the center and the second, third, or fourth levels becomes easier. In fact, levels do not really exist anymore, because hierarchy has become flattened. They are replaced by orbits. Following Parsons's (1960) ideas, we can hypothesize three main orbits: the institutional (executive, central) orbit, the managerial (second) orbit, and the technical or operational (third) orbit. We could also add another extraorganizational orbit to represent customers, clients, suppliers, and so on. One can see radii going from the center to the very edge without necessarily going through some of the spheres of activity that exist in the surrounding orbit. The organizational circle and its attendant orbital structure tend not to define things as being "beneath" other things (which in and of itself might be sufficient rationale to adopt it).

A third aspect of the organizational circle is that it is possible to locate experimental spheres without necessarily putting them at the "edge" of the organization or having them bumping into other spheres. We call these *incubator programs* (they represent experimental activities being undertaken by the organization that are being watched closely by the central office; they may be expanded to full divisions or other organizational entities, or they may be closed down). Galbraith (1982) calls these "reservations," but the concept is essentially the same. They are places where new ideas can be tried, and they can be located wherever it is convenient within the organizational circle.

Fourth, the organizational circle seems to emphasize the unity and interconnectedness of organizational parts rather than their distinctness and their difference. A greater emphasis on blending and oneness seems to emerge. You might find it both fun and enlightening to attempt to present your organization as a circle rather than as a set of boxes.

The next logical step is to create the organizational sphere. This is accomplished by the simple process of drawing an imaginary diameter anywhere on the circle and spinning the circle around that diameter. The result will be a ball or a sphere. In recognition of the dynamic character of organizations, think of it as an organizational gyroscope. Orbits are now not only moving out from the center like rings on a plate; they may move in both horizontal and vertical directions—just as they do with a gyroscope.

The organizational gyroscope concept further opens up the organizational structure, now allowing for a wide range of placements. Not only can organizational centers or subspheres be located on the orbits, but the orbits themselves can he designed in a variety of ways to cut across each other. Centers may exist where orbits cross, and such loci may be sources of innovative ideas as individuals who work in such centers are forced to come to grips with conflicting sets of problems, demands, expectations, and responsibilities.

The point of the organizational gyroscope is that it allows us to rethink the kind of organizational structure we have, to diminish hierarchy, and to emphasize commonality. Furthermore, it provides us with a location where we can place fledgling ventures, to allow them to incubate and to develop a bit while having some independence on the one hand and some oversight on the other. From an idea-generating point of view, this represents a much better way of thinking about structure than the old tree-and-branch method, because of its emphasis on innovational location. IdeaManagers and IdeaLeaders have the role of helping organizations to restructure so that form, indeed, does follow function.

IDEA-GENERATING STRUCTURES

Whatever model of organization a particular firm chooses—and let us hope it is a modern, useful one—there is still the need to create a situation in which there is structural support for new ideas. This means that structural change is a constant process: macro-, meso-, and microstructures need to be addressed, linking structures established, and evaluation structures put into place.

Structural Change

Organizations, therefore, periodically need to go through structural reconfiguration. In a sense, at least, this perspective justifies some aspects of reorganization that some people find difficult. Because it is designed to accomplish certain aspects of the organization's goals, each structure retards the accomplishment of other goals. Centralized organization may favor some organizational outcomes over others, whereas decentralization favors still others. Reorganization, reconfiguration of structure, or restructuralization, therefore, always attempt, at minimum, to solve those organizational problems that have been generated by and are unattended to by the extant structure. However, if that is all reorganization does, it is insufficient.

Every reorganization should seek not only to solve those problems left unattended by the current organization, but should also retarget, refocus, and recalibrate organizational efforts toward their markets, suppliers, customers, and so on. We refer to the problem of outdated structures as structural lag, and call problems surrounding Jerry-built, inelegant structures "Rube Goldberg's Disease."

A third structural problem that organizations experience in designing and articulating their operations is the thought that somehow organizational structure refers only to the organization itself, that it begins with the CEO and ends (probably) with the janitorial service. A related problem is the conceptual frame of reference that suggests that all of the organizational substructures add up to one per unit. Some substructures are overlapping and intersecting but, hopefully, not redundant. In general, there are three organizational structures that are of particular importance: (1) the macrostructure, (2) the mesostructure, and (3) the microstructure. The macrostructure refers to the large-scale organizational environment and the impact that that structure has on the organization, itself. Macrolinking structures are those aspects of the organizational structure that have as their chief function articulating with macrostructures. The Board of Directors is an example of a macrolinking structure.

The mesostructure (or the in-between structure) of the organization really refers to what we typically think of as the organizational chart. It is the mesostructure that is often changed when reorganization is undertaken. As we suggest, however, shuffling the mesostructure without appropriate adjustments in the macrolink and microlink structures will not be helpful in achieving the desired organizational goals.

The microstructure refers to the work space and work station area. These contain the individuals with whom we interact on a daily basis. This is the part of the office complex that forms the bulk of our daily routine. Microlinks are those microstructures that primarily serve the organizational job of linking with customers, clients, and markets. In a restaurant business, for example, the owners and their lenders form the macrolinks; those who serve food to the customers form the microlinks.

I have already addressed to some extent the linking structures. Microlinks and macrolinks are two types of structures that perform boundary-spanning activities; they link the organization to the external environment. Intramural structures (including legal, financial, office management, and other offices) are those that seek to serve the organizational purpose of keeping parts of the organization informed about what the other parts are doing and/or thinking—what the organization is up to, in general. Sometimes, as with the Personnel Office, they service the organization, itself. Other times, as with the Customer Relations Office, they provide some microlinking functions and try, as well, to provide intralinks to other parts of the organization based on the information that they receive (properly codified and assembled) from the whole set of customer complaints, queries, and so on. In some sense, then, structural change will need to be a process, not a point.

USING THE MACROSTRUCTURE TO GENERATE IDEAS

The macrostructure is really the institutional level of the organization. It encompasses the top team, the board, and key stakeholders, which together provide the guidance system of the organization. IdeaManagers and IdeaLeaders have several structural tasks here.

Create and Enhance Environmental Scanning Structures

Firms need structures that are constantly scanning the extraorganizational environment; that is, those things happening outside the organization that are of importance to and focus on activities of the organization. IdeaLeaders and IdeaManagers personally engage in and otherwise support constant environmental scanning to find out "what's out there." The sonar specialist on a submarine performs this kind of function, continually sweeping the sea above, below, and around the submarine to check on what elements are in the environment and to attempt to assess their impact upon the boat. Futurists, idea speculators, and demographic number crunchers are all invited, in one way or another (in person if you have the resources, through books if you do not), to suggest environmental changes that the firm needs to deal with.

Create and Enhance Stakeholder Involvement

IdeaManagers and IdeaLeaders need to create ways to touch base with key stakeholders on an ongoing basis. Some of these will be on the board. Others will not. Yet there may be issues, interests, and information that is important. Settings meetings and creating advisory groups, focus groups, and so on are ways that the larger compass of interests are heard.

Energize the Board of Directors

One of the most important macrolinks is the Board of Directors. This crucial macrolink deserves a special comment. There seems to be a general consensus evolving that corporate boards are not doing the job they need to be doing in any of the areas just discussed.[2] Rather than living up to their names as directors, members of corporate boards seem more to view their posts as sinecures, rubber stamping much of the material presented to them by the administration in cooperation with the "inside directors."

Directors often seem to be the last ones to know about new directions for an organization, rather than being among those groups that initiate periodic organizational review and refurbishment of mission and role (Haft, 1981). The power and influence of inside directors often leads to meetings that express a high degree of self-satisfaction. American business is replete with stories about questionable practices of board members and problems of omission and inattention, as well. The inside–outside dichotomy has, in many cases, led to boards that know too much about current business and that are overinvolved (e.g., through bonuses) in improvements in the quarterly profit statement. On the other hand, it has led to boards that do not know much about the organization at all and may thus feel at a loss with respect to strategic and other organizational initiatives (Patton & Baker, 1987). Any change in American productivity needs to focus not only on American workers and American managers, but also on American directors as the models, leaders, and macrolinkers. They are the pattern setters. They are the ones who should be crying, "Follow me." At present they appear to spend altogether too much time sitting around asking, "What's new?"

IdeaManagers and IdeaLeaders, especially those in CEO spots and top-team spots, need to encourage a vital, exciting, energetic board. There is a paradox here. Many CEOs think that a quiescent board, one that does what they suggest, is best. While it may make less work for the CEO, it is not good for the organization or the CEO. Boards test CEO ideas and approaches. Boards bring ideas to the table. IdeaManagers and IdeaLeaders need to work constantly to encourage the board to link to the external environment (bringing the outside in) and assist the firm in that environment as needed and appropriate (taking the inside out).

Encourage a Vital Top Team

All too often top-team members—CEO, COO, CFO, CHRO, CIO, corporate counsel, and so on—work more as individuals than as a team. While there is obviously individual work to do, there is also a great deal of need to coordinate and consolidate efforts. IdeaManagers and IdeaLeaders at the top level need to encourage regular top-team interaction and brainstorming to provide ideas that can then be explored by other members of the organization.

USING THE MESOSTRUCTURE TO GENERATE IDEAS

The mesostructure is the organizational chart. Creating an idea-generative climate involves attention to a number of factors.

Encourage the Clash of Ideas

Firms and ventures that want to encourage the supply of new ideas must also encourage the clash of new ideas. It is in this clash of ideas that problematic aspects of new ideas are uncovered and set aside. Strength does not occur through support: Support permits risk in the first place; the strength of the idea then develops through testing. Most firms understand the concept of product testing. A new car, a new drug, or a new package is sent to the lab, where it is jumped on, pounded, torn apart, ripped, and generally abused. Stress reveals flaws, and weaknesses show up very fast. The same must be true of ideas. One common problem is that idea development is located somewhere off in the corner in its own structure. As important as an idea-generating structure is, it should not allow—as it has in some instances—the rest of the organization to be careless and lackluster about its interest in the development of new approaches, concepts, and services. Activities that seek to reduce organizational hierarchy and encourage both the development and challenging of new ideas are key aspects of an idea-fertile mesostructure.

Create a Climate of Creativity

The accomplishment of these objectives will move a firm toward the achievement of a climate of creativity. Some organizations always appear to be bubbling over with new trials, half-baked idea boards, and so on. The creativity may even extend to decorative and structural features of the firm. Other organizations convey the sense that they are not eighty or one hundred years old but one year old repeated eighty or one hundred times over. A climate of creativity is one that tilts in favor of new ideas or approaches on a trial basis and one that has set up structures—including testing and trial structures—to test new ideas. It is a part of the ongoing set of activities that characterize the organization.

Set Aside "Special" Rooms

One technique worth considering is to set aside a special room for idea testing and challenging. There should be a large, sliding nameplate holder on the door. When ideas are to be challenged, the title "Devil's Advocate Session" is listed on the name plate. Individuals—the presenter and all others—who come to any team meeting in that room at that time know that the purpose of it is to challenge, critique, kick, grind, shake, rattle, and roll the idea to see how it holds up. There is another nameplate that may be used on other occasions: "Angel's Advocate." When that sign is in the nameplate holder, the norms are now for support instead of attack. People are required to bend over backward to see how the idea can be made to work: what is good about it, what are good extensions and side points of it, and so on.

All ideas must go through both advocacy activities. The sequence is also important. At the very beginning of idea evaluation, an angel's advocate session is scheduled—on the assumption that support is necessary during the birth phases. Too much criticism too early may cause premature rejection. During the middle phases, devil's advocacy comes into play. This is then followed by another angel's session, and finally another devil's session. This alternation provides both criticism and support. The alternation is crucial. The result of this process is an idea that has support and commitment and fewer problems than usual.

Set Up Idea Departments

Idea departments are important aspects of organizational structures. Even a small organization can have one, though it may be a role for a period of time rather than a whole department (i.e., a person assigned to perform this function). The role or department becomes the center for the pulling together of the various relevant new ideas. It also circulates them throughout the organization. A little effort in this department will go a long way and achieve astounding results for most organizations. Idea departments or roles may also be responsible for holding a Five Cs Conference. Such a conference—focusing on the characteristics, competencies, conditions, contexts, and change needed for new ideas—can provide the regularized stimulus for total organizational involvement and growth. The Five Cs Conference represents a temporary aspect of the mesostructure. Managers should not believe that all aspects of organizational structure are there forever. A temporary conference, for example, is a good way to reshuffle organizational allegiances and interactions without proposing that such a reshuffling be permanent or fateful.

Use Champions

The product (or project) champion is another example of a temporary role that can be used to good effect. Daft and Bradshaw (1980) pointed out the importance of the champion concept. The organization should not sit around waiting for a champion to surface. Rather, to the extent possible, they should identify one or two open slots into which product champions can be fit. When an individual has a particularly good idea, there is already an existing organizational niche into which they can be placed for a period of time in order to develop their innovation.[3] In an ideal situation, the champions in an organization should be individuals preselected for their skill in material research and in presentation and to whom the organization accords enormous prestige. Champions should be assigned to promising ideas (and their idea generators), without regard to their personal feelings about those ideas. The task of a champion is to defend an idea as effectively as possible, in the same way a lawyer defends a client without regard to that client's innocence or guilt. Many organizations, particularly very large ones, have something like champions, though they probably do not recognize them as such. Most large universities, for example, have special offices dedicated to assisting faculty members and research staff to prepare the most effective grant proposals possible without regard to the nature and quality of the idea that generates the proposal.

It is also possible, on a temporary basis, to engage an organizational design specialist. There are, after all, architects for organizational structure just as there are for physical structure. It would be hazardous for anyone, in advance of any particular strategic information, to try to find out, predict, or suggest what would be the most appropriate organizational structure in any particular situation (apart from sharing some general perspectives about the nature and characteristics such a structure might have). An organizational design specialist can assist the organization in reconfiguration. Such individuals draw on both the best of the best organizational design literature and on specific knowledge of strategic goals and objectives.

USING THE MICROSTRUCTURE TO GENERATE IDEAS

Many organizations that spend a lot of time in mesostructure reorganization pay no attention at all to the microstructure of daily work. Whatever the gratifications are in working for a large, prestigious organization, most of one's daily work life is spent within small confines: one's own office, a suite of local team meeting rooms, a cadre of people with whom one spends a lot of time, or, thinking of the famous Scott Adams (1995) nemesis, the cube. The microstructure is where the "rubber hits the road." The exemplary hotel–motel service that so struck Peters and Waterman (1982) in Washington (discussed in their introduction) is an example of a microstructure of the front-desk work area. It is there where courtesy is or is not extended. It is there where customers' needs are or are not met as they register and check out. For these reasons, attention to the microstructure is not only necessary but crucial.

It is within the microstructure that hierarchies can truly be flat. Though limited change may be possible in the overall structure of the organization for a whole host of reasons, within the particular microstructure status differentials can be reduced, power relations eased and tempered, gender differences made moot, and communication channels opened. Relationships can be developed that are mutually supportive but can also have assessment and evaluative aspects. It is within the microstructure context that quality circles are instituted—and they, indeed, represent one form of microstructure with which much experimentation is now going on. Whether you wish to move all the way to quality circles is somewhat beside the point. The key element is that there is participation and review. The staff team meeting takes on new and important dimensions.

Create a Fun Setting

It is within the microstructure that fun and work are most likely to be combined. Some executives think of fun as those rare organizational opportunities such as a picnic or Christmas party when everyone gets together. Most employees do not find these fun. Rather, such activities represent just one more aspect of "work," in which formal relationships are dominant, status recognition is key, and the perils of screwing up are enhanced. What the employer may think of as fun may be in actuality a gut-wrenching, anxiety-generating period for the employee.

The introduction of new ideas and the trying of new approaches, on the other hand, is frequently viewed by workers as "fun." There are some requisites, of course. There has to be some organizational support for the time and energy these activities take. In addition, there has to be sufficient planning and organization. A new idea dropped on individuals at the last moment with the injunction "Make it work or else" is not what characterizes good organizational management. If other aspects of the organizational microstructure have been set up in the ways suggested, however, it is unlikely that poor planning will characterize new idea introduction.

Decentralize to Work Stations

The microstructure is also a location where supplies, equipment, and other material aspects of doing a job may be located. Here again, the IdeaManager and IdeaLeader can make use of this obvious fact as a way to stimulate innovation. Try to find ways to devolve control of supplies to the local microstructural units. In a small office, this may simply be accomplished by giving the secretary a budget plus permission to make a range of decisions about the kind of supplies, their nature, their storage and distribution, and so on. Allowing people to have control over a certain aspect of their microstructural environment enhances their own feeling of self-worth. It also provides training in the thinking process. When organizational analysts talk about decentralization of decision making and delegation of authority, there is a temptation to think of it in terms of big subunits and major organizational decisions. That can be a focus, of course, but what is often overlooked is that there can be delegation of authority and decision making even within the microstructure itself. The rule of thumb here is that everyone in the microstructure ought to have some realm or area over which they have decision-making power and on which they can report—rather than for which they need to check.

We are not suggesting that these decisions be made in the absence of an overall guiding policy. Quite the contrary. In the context of organizational policy and microstructural policy having been set up—on equipment and supplies, let us say—an individual can then be delegated to proceed and do the job, reporting back and seeking reactions.

The availability of this grant of power is high. Its rewards are incredibly great, in terms of accomplishing the job, making the task more meaningful, and training people in responsibility and decision making. It is a key aspect of microstructure that should be attended to by IdeaManagers and IdeaLeaders.

Reduce Exploitation

One final point about microstructure is important to bear in mind. Exploitation of some members of the microstructure is to be avoided at all costs. We all know the importance of avoiding status differentials that inhibit communication, and to some extent the injunction to avoid exploitation falls within that principle. Microstructures are small, organizational work teams. Our experience tells us that there are people in organizations who work hard, and there are others who do not work so hard. This differential is already the beginning of exploitation potential. Hopefully, in discussions and team meetings within the microstructural work group, differences in production trajectories can be discussed at appropriate intervals. But the problem of exploitation is more serious than this. It involves individuals of lower status being used, coerced, or made to feel guilty for naught; pressured into doing more than they really should for the pay that they are getting. Secretaries often fall within this category, working extra-long hours doing extra typing, filing, and so on for minimal salaries. In this example bosses reap the benefits in terms of the additional free time, and secretaries wind up giving their time for free.

There is a great deal wrong with this. Though it is true that we want to get the most out of everyone, it is the whole that is important here. The culture of a microstructure is like that of a high school play staff. Everyone in the play works together: the actors, the director, the stage managing crew, the costumer, and so on. It is true that some people have roles that are more prominent than others—the actors, for example—but it is very clear to everyone in the production that everyone is needed. Even the small jobs have meaning. Everyone has to do his or her job so that the total play will come off smoothly. When this happens, people will frequently work long and hard to contribute to the common weal. But the stage manager does not work harder so that the actor can work less. When that happens, the culture of the work group is soured and poisoned. Though one may coerce larger work efforts out of some individuals through exploitation, the troubled culture saps achievement motivation and engenders overall lackluster performance.

To sum up, then, microstructure is the stuff of daily work life. Strangely, and because of its commonality and familiarity, it has escaped serious attention as a locus of IdeaManagement—or any management at all, for that matter. It is in the microstructure context that new ideas are developed. In that context, too, new ideas must be implemented. Hence, for both reasons, it is important to have a well-organized and smoothly functioning microstructure. Without it, few ideas will be generated and almost none will be implemented well.

CREATING AND USING EVALUATION STRUCTURES TO GENERATE IDEAS

Evaluation structures are extremely important for big and small organizations. The market itself is one evaluation structure, but the market often gives ambiguous messages, and the messages tend to come after the fact. Sometimes the market does not know where to give a message. Consider the case of the bad fit of the manufactured shirts cited in the Lands' End catalog. The poor fit did not affect the customer, it affected the launderer, but when the customer gets a shirt back that is badly ironed he or she may not know quite how to express dissatisfaction. In short, market information frequently has clear results but unclear meaning.

The market tends to give whatever it gives in terms of information on products rather than people (except for the CEO). Thus, reviewing the accomplishments and concerns of people becomes important. Current performance appraisals (often called "pains in the ass") are frequently ill-equipped to support ideas and learn from failures. Most often they quash ideas and assign blame for failure. IdeaManagers and IdeaLeaders need to attend to a series of evaluation structures so that both success and failure can become teachers.

In any evaluation system the participation of those who are to be evaluated is important. Such participation starts, as always, with an understanding of what the goals are that are to be achieved. Strategy sets these goals. Then structural elements are put into place that allow those goals to have a chance of being achieved. Evaluation structures are also developed to check on attitude and speed (monitoring), make course corrections (oversight), change flight paths or trip sequences and routes (assessment), and scrub flights (appraisal). Because different strategic goals will require different evaluation structures, those involved in goal accomplishment should have a hand in designing the elements within each evaluation component.

Evaluation structures try to prevent both acceptance and rejection errors (see Chapter 4) and to perform a number of other important organizational equilibrating tasks. Such structures are needed that do more than feed *back*. They must get information in such a way that a feed *forward* system can be introduced. Michael (1980) introduces this concept as a way to anticipate problems and solve them before they affect operations. Somehow, evaluation, as it is often discussed, is a reactive and sometimes posthumous activity. As such, incidentally, it is not necessarily bad. You can, for example, develop a post-project audit system. Select one or two projects a year that have been completed and perform an audit/autopsy of them. Review project records, interview project personnel, look at project outcomes and results, and so on. This can prove to be salutary, because the entire organization is informed about the findings, and no doubt some are positive and some are less so. The overall purpose should not be to assess blame but to find out what was good and how it can be repeated and what was bad and how it can be avoided. The difficulty with such a system lies only in its uniqueness. It should, in fact, be only one of a series of evaluative structures that should be set up from an IdeaManagement and IdeaLeadership point of view. But proactive strategies are better still. In general, there should be four components or substructures to every evaluation structure. They are different in purpose and orientation, they occur with differential frequency, and they have differential fatefulness for the products and services they are looking at. They are (1) monitoring, (2) oversight, (3) assessment, and (4) appraisal.

Creating Monitoring Structures

The first evaluation structure, and the one on which all others are subsequently based, is monitoring. Monitoring is some type of frequent assessment, designed appropriately for the product or service in question. By frequent, we mean daily or weekly reviews of what is happening. In car manufacturing, for example, daily figures on problems and flaws in car production should be available. In an auto dealership, any sales should be posted and so should daily figures on number of cars repaired, types of repairs, general level of satisfaction, and so on. The monitoring system is the "pulse-taking" feature of the organizational evaluation structure. Without the database that it provides, the remaining evaluative elements—oversight, assessment, and appraisal—cannot go on effectively.

Creating Oversight Structures

Oversight is the second echelon in the evaluation hierarchy. It involves review of daily or weekly service figures, and it seeks to assure that relevant targets, trajectories, and dates are being met. Overseers are able to make adjustment in the system of service or product delivery such that the previously agreed upon targets, trajectories, dates, and so on are more likely to be met. It is anticipated that such oversight reveals essential minor fluctuations in the production/service schedules. Should major departures from such schedules be revealed, emergency team meetings may need to be called, and such a situation may indicate other problems as well. The oversight is simply an organized way of reviewing the data put together by the monitoring system.

Creating Assessment Structures

Assessment may occur at monthly or quarterly intervals and can involve fateful outcomes for the product, service, and people. An assessment review, as opposed to a monitoring and oversight review, can generate change of the system rather than change in the system. Though monitoring essentially reviews descriptive statistics, assessment begins an intensive analytic process, often using rates, ratios, and comparisons. So, for example, the question of car manufacturing errors in an assessment may be proportionalized and then compared to such proportions at other plants, at other times of the year, in other sectors of the same plant, or with external standards or measures known to be valid for the particular case in question.

Similarly, in the car dealership example, the number of new cars sold per day can be subjected to some intensive analysis. How many sales were made in proportion to the number of individuals who came in and looked at cars, for example? How does this particular showroom floor compare with others? How many calls of inquiry were made, and how many of these calls resulted in subsequent sales?

The list of proportions and comparisons can go on and on, but the point is made. Assessment can reveal comparative flaws in the system. If the evaluation structure is set up properly and properly linked to other organizational structures, it will be able to initiate changes of the production/service system that will increase the good things that have been discovered and decrease the disappointing and difficult ones. Sometimes additional information is needed in an assessment. If in the case of the car dealership, for example, there are a low number of sales per visitor, then further information must be sought in order to determine why this might be so. Once reasons are discovered, appropriate changes can be considered.

To put things on a very basic level, using something we have all had experience with, monitoring is the rough equivalent to taking daily attendance in the classroom. Oversight involves periodic testing, such as might be undertaken by pop quizzes and homework review. Assessment represents the midterm and final exams. Appraisal involves the summation and judgment of all of these factors taken together in the assignment of a final grade.

Creating Appraisal Structures

Appraisal is the coming together of many factors in a final judgment. Judgment is crucial in appraisal and is, finally, what appraisal involves. Like fixing the sale price of a house, it is based on a host of hard data factors developed during the monitoring, oversight, and assessment processes. In appraisal, however, a final reckoning is accomplished, and this reckoning can be extremely fateful for products, services, and people. Appraisal may involve a judgment of failure and, as a result, product discontinuance and the liquidation of supplies, accounts, equipment, and job positions.

Appraisal is usually done on a yearly or multiyear basis. As in the stock market, time is needed for cycles to express themselves. It is inappropriate to rush in (short of some emergency) and make "crash" appraisals. Often the data are not present for such an undertaking anyway.

Using the Evaluation Structure and Substructures

Evaluation structures and substructures have two functions: (1) personal purposes, to assist individuals and teams; and (2) organizational purposes, to assist the organization. IdeaManagers and IdeaLeaders work on setting up improvements in the evaluation structures. But as important for the organization, they seek to do something very few organizations actually do at all: organize and harvest the evaluation elements for organizational as well as personal information. Performance appraisals usually end with the person. What a shame. As an organization looks over many such measures (at one time and over time), patterns will emerge which might stimulate pattern recognition and lead to changes in training strategy, recruitment, deployment, and so on.

CONCLUSION

Structure matters. Older vertical structures have had many problems. Among other things, they lacked flexibility, diversity, and a global view, and they were higher and unconnected. Form became disconnected from function and strategy. Firms are now being reorganized into structures that address some of these issues, and IdeaManagers and IdeaLeaders help with this. Organizations are going to look a lot more like bubbles than boxes.

At the same time, IdeaManagers and IdeaLeaders are looking to create structures—or use updated existing structures—to better advantage in the idea-generating department. The board of directors will remain an important organization structure, but the unit needs to function more imaginatively. The same can be said of the organization of the top team—there is no organization of the top team in many cases. And finally, organizations engage in appraisals for many individual purposes. With a little tweaking, they could service organizational purposes as well.

NOTES

1. Though we use the word "redundant," we want to alert readers to the fact that there are times when redundant systems are needed; for example, safety measures and computer controls. If a redundant system is generated by design, that is fine. The ones we are referring to occur simply because they are added to the ones already extant.

2. While this consensus is more recent, analysts were alert to this problem twenty-five years ago (see Bennis, 1978, 1979; Carroll, 1981; Groobey, 1974).

3. If this concept has a familiar ring to it, it should. It is not entirely unlike the notion of a "Fair Witness" that Robert Heinlein (1963) conjured in his classic science fiction novel, *Stranger in a Strange Land.*

Chapter 19

Creating Idea-Driven Systems

Organizational systems are those organizational features that link the substructures together and make the organization a whole, over time. Systems operate in time and over time; structures tend to operate at one time. The horizontal organization, as discussed in Chapter 18, is an attempt to capture systems and make them work. Metaphorically speaking, systems represent the blood vessels and nerves of the organization (the structure of the system) and that which flows through these blood vessels and nerves is information (the content of the system). If structures are boxes or bubbles, then systems are pipelines and their contents.

Systems allow the organization to act over time. We are all aware of organizations (especially but not exclusively large ones) in which the left hand does not know what the right hand is doing. System failures present an additional problem when the first stage does not know what the second stage needs or wants (recall the discussion of process owners and the shirt maker in Chapter 18). Failures of coordination, control, and direction—of sequences—are failures of systems rather than failures of structures. Systems, then, represent the dynamic aspect of organizations. As opposed to the more static structural features, they represent the process aspects of organizations. And, as in the case of nerves and blood, they not only embody flows but exchange: exchange of information, exchange of energy, and exchange of resources. Finally, they embody transformation: That which flows through the system is different when it comes out.

THREE SYSTEM PROCESSES: FLOW, EXCHANGE, AND TRANSFORMATION

Organizational systems are characterized by flows: Flows of information from one place to another, flows of authority, flows of energy and resources, flows of customers, and flows of raw material. In thinking about the organizational gyroscope, what systems add are the threads of interconnections between the nodes and the orbits. This image can be amplified by considering the threads to be of different colors, indicating different systems. Flows mean that whatever is in the system is moving, over time, from one place to another from one status to another. Sometimes what flows (what is in the system) is materials. One calls this a materials-processing system. Sometimes what flows is people (jails, colleges) and one can think of a people-processing system. At other times, what flows is ideas, and one can think of an idea-processing system.

Part two of the system is exchange. As the content moves through the system it loses some properties. A mail carrier moves through a building, receiving mail to go out and "losing" mail as people pick theirs up off the cart.

In this exchange, transformation, a third aspect of systems, occurs. As students flow through college they are transformed into more capable persons (one hopes). As raw materials flow over the line they are transformed into products. Sometimes, information is turned into power and resources are turned into products, just as plants turn sunlight into energy. At other times, information is traded for resources, resources for products, and so on.

The IdeaManager and IdeaLeader, thus, have three related tasks: establishing systems, preventing their breakdown, and enhancing their function. In attending to these the IdeaManager and IdeaLeader need to focus on the three crucial elements of flow, exchange, and transformation.

ESTABLISHING IDEA-GENERATING SYSTEMS

Creating and establishing idea-generating systems is not that different from establishing systems in general. For every organizational chart, circle, or gyroscope, there is a book of procedures. It is essentially the creation of these organizational procedures that is involved in the establishment of organizational systems.

Procedures involve sets of directions and specifications for the handling of people, ideas, money, material, and so on. Personnel systems focus on the set of procedures required for the handling of people. Financial systems focus on the set of procedures required for the handling of money. Materials handling systems and other handling systems focus on the procedures required in the processing of materials. The IdeaManager and IdeaLeader will need to establish these sets of procedures. The difference in the organizational systems is that there is special attention paid to the idea-handling system. Most organizations do not have a special system for handling, sponsoring, developing, processing, or otherwise generally dealing with ideas. It is here that the

IdeaManager and IdeaLeader work especially hard, to be sure that the existing systems, in addition to performing their functions, are moving ideas through the organization.

Fixing Broken Systems

IdeaManagers and IdeaLeaders must be concerned with the breakdown of various systems. Breakdowns occur in each of the three areas that are central to the system concept: flow, change, and transformation.

Consider first the case of flows. Flows cease or become inadequate: The flow of information is too late, too early, or wrong; or the flow of resources and authority may have problems. This occurs because flows in organizations become obstructed, or they become uneven, or there are leaks. What is sent out from the front office, for example, may arrive only in small amounts in the field. There are blocks and turns in the flow process that decrease its velocity, force, and timeliness. Though procedures can be set up to work, the question of whether they do actually work requires constant scrutiny. Exchanges can be botched as well. Even though the flow of information, people, and money arrives at the proper place at the proper time, there may be difficulties in utilization. Sending structures may not know what to send or how to send it. Receiving structures may not know what to ask for. The languages and subcultures, even within a small organization, may differ so significantly that communication breaks down. Transmissions may become garbled, and the organization may face the problems of uncertainty absorption and authoritative augmentation. Uncertainty absorption, of course, occurs when certain problems and unknowns that perplex those at the bottom get systematically removed as the information about these problems is passed to the top executives. Similarly, a simple suggestion by a top executive is interpreted authoritatively by individuals lower down, and the negotiation that might occur is thus forestalled.

Finally, the transformation system can work poorly or work when it is not supposed to. Considering this latter point first, sometimes information is transformed when it is just supposed to be exchanged. Recall that when I discussed uncertainty absorption, I described a situation in which uncertain information was transformed into certain information as it moved up the hierarchy. Also recall how with authoritative augmentation a query from the top becomes an imperative by the time the request gets to the bottom of the organization pecking order.

Other times, transformation does not occur. Many executives complain that they receive undigested "messes" of facts, reports, and "stuff" from subordinates—subordinates who are supposed to process and digest these diverse pieces of information and present syntheses of them to higher ups. I should note that even the word "process" provides linguistic protection against system failure. Process implies something happens, but does not tell us, really, what that something is. For example, a jail or prison is a people-processing system, but it really should be a people-changing system, and the people should change in a positive direction. Calling things "processing" is a mask behind which too many of us, too often, hide.

I give the prison as an example because it has a positive goal, or an asserted positive goal for the inmates. The fact that inmates change in the wrong direction ought to call a big halt to things until we put in a fix. But it is ignored. Indeed, for people-processing systems in general there is what someone called the "paradoxical law of counterproductivity." You go to jail and you become a better criminal, you go to school and your IQ slips, you go to a mental health clinic and you get mentally sicker, you go to a hospital and you get sicker. There is something odd here.

Sometimes, the structures of systems are wrong. Other times, what is in the system (the content of the system) is not right. In either case, the IdeaManager and IdeaLeader seek to create a smooth system. However, assisting in the operating and improvement of extant systems is not enough. New systems specifically designed for ideas often need to be created. Idea gathering and idea processing are two good examples.

Establishing Idea-Gathering (Intelligence) Systems

Intelligence systems are procedures for not only gathering information and establishing its importance, but assuring its reliability and validity. A lot of data flow into an organization. Much of them are, no doubt, chaff. Other parts of those data though, are important and need to be dealt with. Scott Adams, of Dilbert fame, has an electronic mail system that prioritizes the hundreds of messages he receives each day. That is one function of an intelligence system. It involves (as does the rule of halves) sifting and sorting. IdeaManagers and IdeaLeaders work to establish guidelines (confidence intervals) for senior management, or, if they are senior management, insist on ratings of confidence along with the information they get.

Creating Idea-Processing Systems

The idea-processing system, as opposed to an idea-generating structure, is a set of processes for moving ideas through the organization from art to part, from concept to customer. Through the creation of an idea-processing system, with the concomitant establishment of an IdeaManager or a policy manager or an idea champion, the IdeaManager and IdeaLeader signals and models the importance of new ideas to the venture or enterprise. The idea-processing system establishes a regularized procedure for all new ideas developed within the organization.

The idea-processing system may, itself, be a source of new ideas to its own system. In the main, however, the idea-processing system takes ideas generated from other parts of the organization and begins to move them through a predetermined set of steps. These involve examination, testing, checking, sharing, and ultimate decision making.

A special idea-processing system is necessary, because without it most ideas are either lost at the time they are thought up—like our Neanderthal innovator with the needle—or they have no particular place to go (and so are lost). You will find it a useful exercise to think about organizations you are involved with, and ask yourself these questions: What if I had a new idea? Where would I take it? When we have asked these questions in organizations, the most common answer is "the boss." For many individuals in moderate to larger organizations, this is not only scary, it is not even totally clear who the relevant boss might be. Sub-bosses often resist passing on new ideas on the grounds that it might make them look bad to *their* bosses because they, as sub-bosses, had not thought the ideas up themselves. Similarly, because many people in many organizations have several bosses, it is not always clear which of them is the appropriate one to receive new ideas. These are two of the reasons why ideas become stalled. Doubtless, you can add more reasons of your own. In any event, unless we happen to link into an influential sponsor, or unless the idea is just so spectacular on its face that it sweeps away all opposition, the idea is in all probability simply doomed. Therefore, in order to free up what is already present in the organization, the IdeaManager and IdeaLeader needs to establish an idea-processing system and to set down procedures and steps that guarantee all new ideas will receive attention and careful review.

Many of those new ideas will not pan out. However, do not discard them. You can never tell when an idea that initially appears ridiculous or outlandish may turn out, in whole or in part, to provide a solution to some future problem or become the spark for some new fabulously successful product or service. Every idea, therefore, should go into an organizational inventory which is itself reviewed from time to time. At a later point, components of these older ideas, when combined with still newer innovations, may become fantastically profitable. It is this way that the idea-processing system stimulates a concept bank—just like a staff or a personnel bank (e.g., the steno pool) or a bank account. The idea-processing system, like other systems, focuses on the flow of ideas from one place to another, the exchange of ideas from one unit to another, and the transformation of ideas, finally, into legitimate and useful products and services. This process goes on informally in many organizations. Like so many other aspects of organizational life, however, once one knows about it, attends to it, and helps it along, its impact is increased a thousandfold.

System Review: Enhancing System Functioning

Establishing and maintaining systems is crucial to the continued good health of an organization. So, too, is upgrading, improving, and enhancing those systems. Failure to do so—being content with the status quo—risks letting the firm fall behind its competitors in the marketplace who are constantly modifying and improving their established systems for the better. "If it ain't broke, don't fix it," is a popular notion with some politicians and a great many business people. The fact of the matter is, however, that we must constantly "fix" things that are not broken—in the sense of modifying, upgrading, or replacing them with newer models—in both government and business. What destroyed the American steel industry, once the most successful in the world? In the main, it was a failure on the part of the steel companies to invest on a continuing basis in new plants and new processes. What made such a shambles of the American automobile industry? To a large degree it was insistence by management and union leadership on work rules and practices that were no longer practical for rapidly evolving, high-technology manufacturing environments; blind adherence to organizational structures that were no longer appropriate; and denial by the large car companies of the evidence of their own market research systems.

To improve their existing systems, IdeaManagers and IdeaLeaders have several avenues open to them. The first is regular system review, in addition to regular structure review. Time after time, organizations can be observed calling team meetings of divisions, departments, and so on. Much more rarely are those individuals who are implicated in systematic procedures called together. Consider it a truism: Organizations are made up of both structures and systems. It makes as much sense, therefore, to call all of those together who are concerned with a particular process as it does to call those together who are associated with a particular part.

The process and procedure review team meeting is a special kind of team meeting that asks about the functions of specific processes within the organization. These may be sales, marketing, finance, customer or public relations, client processing, and so on. Typically, the individuals in those team meetings will not know each other well, even in moderate size organizations. This is because systems are strings that move out over different organizational parts. That is their nature. Rarely, however, do the individuals involved have a chance to get together. The process and procedure review team meeting is a useful technique for accomplishing this, for solving problems, and for making and implementing improvements.

Sometimes systems need to be reconfigured. Certain crucial features may have been left out of the circulating loop that a particular process required. As organizations grow, especially when they grow quickly, the links and coordination provided by systems may lag. In some ways the rapidly growing organization is like the lanky adolescent whose progress through the day is more characterized by lurch and stumble than by the smoothness of well-greased bearings, because the coordination of all the new parts is not yet totally in place.

ESTABLISHING INFORMAL SYSTEMS

System improvement can be attained by the development and use of informal systems present in all organizations but rarely thought about consciously. Informal systems are those sets of flows, exchanges, and transformations that occur spontaneously. The classic water cooler provides a good example. Individuals standing around the water cooler (or having a cup of coffee somewhere else) are exchanging information about the organization, its problems, and the things that may impede it from achieving its goals. Typical managers are forever chasing people away from these sites on the grounds that they are not being paid to stand around and shoot the breeze. Actually, those people are working and, without knowing it many times, very likely in the best interests of the firm. They are engaging in information exchange in ways that are most certainly beneficial to the overall organization in both the short and long runs.

For this reason, IdeaManagers and IdeaLeaders should consider creating informal systems, especially those where employees of different ranks, levels, positions, and locations within the organization have a chance to get together. In the smaller organization—the two-, three-, or four-person organization—these kinds of contacts occur automatically. That is the very nature of such small businesses. But as the organization grows to several members with different responsibilities and commitments, it becomes hard to get together to share information, perspectives, and solve problems. It is only necessary to recall the typical family with teenage children and two working spouses to know that even a five- or six-person organization can have trouble making linking structures work.

A variety of other informal activities, therefore, can be helpful, especially when combined with management by walking around (MBWA). Through MBWA, IdeaManagers and IdeaLeaders can get a firsthand look at the actual operating conditions that staff have to deal with. MBWA is much better than getting reports. It can substantiate certain claims and create questions about others. Semiformal or quasiformal occasions, such as breakfast or lunch with employees, allow at least the conditions to be created for the expressions of views, complaints, and perspectives across all levels of the organization, including going right to the top.

Information garnered through the use of the informal and intelligence systems is unlikely to be able to be totally processed by the IdeaManager and IdeaLeader. It can, however, be turned over to the idea-processing system for further exploration. Then the IdeaManager and IdeaLeader can get back to whomever it was who raised the issue with a more concrete response.

Part of the informal system is not only to get employees to talk to the IdeaManager and IdeaLeader, but to talk with each other. An organizational celebration is a good time for this to happen. People have often said about dinner parties, for example, "It's really the chance to get to meet people rather than the actual dinner that I find beneficial." Similar comments often accompany conferences. All too common is the observation that people at a conference meet others from the same town, or even from the same organization, whom they have not seen in a considerable time: "Isn't it amazing, Joe, that we both had to come all the way from Quinter, Kansas, in order to get to talk to each other." Promises are made that this will not be permitted to happen again. The promises are inevitably broken, because the power and domination of organizational structure over organizational process tends to recreate the same conditions as before. All organization activities allow people to get together on some regular basis, enjoy themselves, and remind themselves of the work they have to do with other individuals at some future date.

CONCLUSION

The IdeaManager and IdeaLeader, then, is responsible for the establishment of idea-generating systems, for detecting and correcting problems in them, and for improving the way they function. For the IdeaManager and IdeaLeader, there are several key systems. First is the establishment of an idea system, so that ideas within the organization do not get lost and there is a common set of procedures for handling suggestions, rather than letting the suggestions surface or not depending on the energy of a particular employee at a particular point in time.

Second, intelligence systems need to be created by IdeaManagers and IdeaLeaders. It is through the intelligence system that system functioning can be assessed and structural problems identified at an early stage. When emergencies occur and surprises develop—and they will—the question should never be whether it happened or not, only how often. Once is fine. Twice suggests that the real problem is that the IdeaManager and IdeaLeader does not have an adequate intelligence system. A good one, therefore, needs to be established and made operational.

Third, work must be done toward the development and enhancement of informal systems. These already exist within the organizational framework, but they are frequently viewed negatively and hostility as occasions of "not-work" or "time wasters." Leaving aside the valuable contributions to organizational culture that informal interaction creates, it becomes a time to reinforce organizational values and to provide nonroutine occasions for people to get together and meet.

Finally, system review is a more formal way of bringing people together: the process and procedures review team meeting. This team meeting is designed to bring together individuals from different structures with natural linkage to one another. These people need to know each other to be aware of each other's problems and perspectives.

There was one system—the reward system—that I did not mention here. I will provide some detailed discussion of it in Chapter 20, because it pertains so much to staff.

Chapter 20

Creating an Idea-Driven Staff

We need others. Organizations really are wagon trains. In any of our achievements, in fact, others play a crucial and frequently seldom recognized role. A familiar illustration of this is the typical award show "thank you" speech. Almost without exception, not only do the recipients accept their awards on behalf of themselves, but on behalf of a long (sometimes an interminably long) list of others, all of whom made some contribution. For most of us involved in complex projects, those kinds of thank yous are entirely appropriate. We recognize at once the essential correctness of the statement, "I couldn't have done it without you; the team; the coach; my family; my staff; and so on."

THE STAFF OF ONE

Unfortunately, the most dominant American values, focusing on independence and "macho boss" orientations, tend to support individualism, and to work against teams and against the larger staff interdependence frequently needed to achieve results. We are, on a world scale, very far down the individualistic side of the curve. The Frank Sinatra song "My Way" is almost a second national anthem.

There are important and negative consequences for staff development here. One of the most important is the devaluation of others, both a cause and a reflection of individualism. It involves the subordination of talent and credit. The Lois Lanes, the Tontos, and the Bumsteads all play crucial roles in the development of the enterprises of their bosses and masters. Yet they rarely get the recognition they deserve. In fact, it is easy to think of the concept of "sidekick" as a sort of nonessential, tag-a-long person. That may be true in some instances, but it is far more likely the case that sidekicks are essential partners in the accomplishments of the idea-driven organization.

A second negative consequence is that we often view people as replaceable parts, rather than valuable resources. Staff remuneration is seen as a "cost" (to be minimized), rather than an investment (to be nurtured).

A third consequence is the denigration of the human resources function in most organizations. Almost no one can get to be CEO without some financial experience; if they have not had human resource experience, that can be learned "on the job." Routes to the top go through finance and production, not people.

STAFF AS A RESOURCE

IdeaManagement and IdeaLeadership, then, require that the firm be staffed with the appropriate individuals. It also means recognizing what is required and both seeking the kinds of people who are needed from outside the firm and developing those who are already employees of the firm. All staff must have the opportunity for advancing with the development of the firm. Without an adequate staff, no strategy, no structure, and no system will work at all.

Much has been said about staffing (attracting, recruiting, hiring, retaining, promoting, demoting, firing, etc.), and I do not need to go into great detail here. But in my judgment there are six elements or dimensions that are important and should be taken into consideration by IdeaManagers and IdeaLeaders as principles of developing an idea-driven staff:

1. Recognizing the need for others.
2. Recognizing the kinds of staff conditions that are relevant.
3. Recruiting the appropriate staff.
4. Inspiriting new and old staff, which almost always must include their family members to some degree.
5. Rewarding performance.
6. Evaluating the staff.

Let us now take a detailed look at each of these six elements.

Recognizing the Need for Others

An initial step in the staff development process is a recognition that staff are crucial, and that it is the totality of people working together that makes the enterprise successful. There is a story about the organizational researcher illustrating the absence of this recognition. The researcher was asking individuals in a many-layered company the following question: "If technology permitted it, at what level do you think this company could, really, be automated?" The answer was the same from every level of the organization: "below me." Each respondent was convinced of his or her own importance and viewed those below as "merely" technical. It is this kind of attitude that has brought the productivity problems to us that we experience today.

Recognizing Relevant Staff Conditions

The second step in the staff development process is recognizing the crucial nature of staff and taking inventory of the current staff. In a small organization, this will not take long. In a larger organization, more time will be needed. This process is called *profiling staff demographics*. It deals with the degrees and backgrounds of staff. It also deals, to the extent it is possible to know, with interests, goals, and so on. If you depend on a group of individuals to assist you in carrying out your venture, then it is important to know who they are and what they are like. This demographic profile, alone, allows some questions to begin to be asked: Do we have the kind of staff that is going to meet the needs that we are going to be facing? Do we have the kind of staff capable of dealing with the strategies and tactics that we are developing? Negative answers to these questions do not automatically mean that you must fire everyone. Instead, you must now begin to ask further questions about how the current staff can be brought to the level or area of competence that is needed. This is what Andy Grove (1983) calls "task relevant maturity."

A crucial point of recognition is that jobs today are much more complex and multifaceted. This is especially true in the existing organizational venture and very much the case in the new organizational venture. There, everyone is doing everything. Specialization and focus are out the window (if they ever came in the door). People do what has to be done. Job descriptions are ambiguous, if they exist at all. It is this complexity that makes individuals difficult to replace.

The IdeaManager and IdeaLeader, therefore, take inventory of the staff available. He or she recognizes that members of the staff are valuable, contributing members of the venture.

Recruiting the Appropriate Staff

IdeaManagers and IdeaLeaders always need to be in a recruiting mode for staff. Few processes are as crucial, and there are limited resources available. Some of that will go to pay the staff you select. How should you proceed?

First, you—and all IdeaManagers and IdeaLeaders—should keep a private list of individuals they know, with whom they have worked, and with whom they would like to work again at some time. These people may be anyone from persons who do cleaning, persons who do accounting, or effective salespeople, to company pilots and so on. This list should consist of individuals who have impressed you, and who represent a sort of fantasy team. As you contemplate starting a new venture, you begin with a list of a number of individuals whom you have observed work and produce and who are available to start. Obviously, you probably will not get all of them. You might not even get any of them, but the list provides a place to begin. And frequently, individuals whom you appreciate and admire know other individuals whose work you might also appreciate and admire. Those on your list, then, can be an invaluable source of recruitment leads, and as you talk about your idea with them you receive good advice.

Implied in this suggestion is a deemphasis on the interview process for hiring employees. The interview process is one fraught with difficulties. It is a tense time, both for the interviewer and the interviewee, at which neither may be at their best. It often does not ask the interviewee to actually perform the tasks for which the interviewee might be hired. Rather, the prospective employee is invited to talk about the kind of performance that might be involved. The test, therefore, is indirect at best. Instead, you should seek work samples and attempt to judge as much by the past as possible.

IdeaManagers and IdeaLeaders should also seek varied backgrounds and boundary-crossing activities. The very kinds of things that are often discounted in a resumé or record, are from an IdeaManager and IdeaLeader's point of view, likely to be pluses. Individuals who have done different things have a range of perspectives. They are likely to be more adaptive, more flexible, and more willing to try new things than those with more singular backgrounds. Those who have been involved in boundary-crossing activities, in particular, would be especially good at systems design and implementation, as they have had the experience of different business cultures and the impacts that these different cultures have on work styles and interpretations.

As you hire, you should not only look at people, but also at roles. The idea-driven staff plays a variety of roles. It needs idea-generator roles to be filled. It needs champion roles to be filled. Indeed, IdeaManagers and IdeaLeaders need to be sensitive to the whole range of competencies when thinking about filling any particular slot.

If you are looking for innovative individuals in particular, some of the best advice comes from Galbraith (1982), who says, "The best idea sponsors and idea reservation managers . . . are people who have experienced innovation early within careers and are comfortable with it. They will have been exposed to risk, uncertainty, parallel experiences, repeated failures that led to learning, coupling rather than assembly line thinking, long time frames, and personal control systems based on people and ideas not numbers and budget variances" (p. 23). As Galbraith points out, they can either be recruited or developed from the inside. In either case, some inspiriting is necessary.

Inspiriting New and Old Staff

The inspiriting process encompasses the ways in which IdeaManagers and IdeaLeaders get individuals to do the will of the organization. In some respects, the problem is a simple one, because there are only three strategies available: force, inducement, and commitment. These are broad, general strategies that completely encompass the available techniques to secure compliance. In force, individuals are simply ordered to undertake certain tasks. Force is the backbone of the Theory X. The problem with force is that it generates resentment and does not invite employees to think of ways they might independently and innovatively contribute to organizational mission and purpose.

Inducement, the classic economic cash reward, suggests that if one accomplishes a particular task, one will be paid. Unfortunately, this reward system tends to develop commitment to the reward rather than the organization. Thus, if another organization comes along and offers a larger reward, the very reward system teaches the individual to jump ship and move to the more lucrative location.

The third area, commitment, centers on the inspiriting process. The IdeaManager and IdeaLeader will use command (force) and consensus (commitment). Because of the uncertain nature of the venture, however, and the possibility or actuality of rapid growth, commitment of individuals to the venture is needed if stability is to be achieved and if a marketable service or product is to be provided.

Commitment is built through interpersonal interaction and support. The IdeaManager and IdeaLeader, therefore, must first model the kinds of behaviors that he or she expects from staff. If long hours are part of what is to be important, then the IdeaManager and IdeaLeader must model that kind of commitment. Modeling is the first step in the inspiriting process.

Coaching is a second step. It is often difficult for those individuals who know what to do in a particular case to let others do it. Asking one's child to help around the house with some task is a good example. One arrives on the scene, finds the tasks half done, and jumps in to finish up. Unfortunately, when this happens, the child never learns to complete the task. The same is true for the employee who starts but is not allowed to complete an assignment. That employee feels the anger and disappointment of not finishing, but never the satisfaction of completion. For sports teams, the role of the coach is crucial in most cases for determining how well the individual players and the team as a whole play and, to a large extent, whether the team wins or loses. A coach cannot jump into the game and play it. Whatever playing is to be done must be done by the players. In many respects this analogy translates well into the business enterprise. Many business tasks must be done by the employees. The IdeaManager and IdeaLeader cannot run around delivering pizzas, making hamburgers, installing circuit boards, or licking envelopes. It is the employee who is the fundamental actor. Recognition of this fact gives meaning and value to the coaching concept.

A third step in the inspiriting process is to explain strategic direction and to provide tactical directives. To be sure, the overall organization has a strategy. It is often unclear to an individual employee how what he or she might be doing in a particular case relates to that overall strategy. This interpretation needs to be made by the IdeaManager and IdeaLeader and reinforced continually. This reinforcing is especially important when the tasks do not seem terribly meaningful in and of themselves. Washing dishes in a restaurant, for example, must seem like a terribly unimportant task until the dishwasher fully understands the health implications of dirty dishes, the restaurant's commitment to quality as evidenced by the cleanest possible dishes, and the devastating public relations impact on a restaurant's reputation when a customer receives a dirty dish. Such concepts need to be bolstered periodically.

In relation to strategic interpretation, there needs to be tactical direction. In the case of a restaurant, for example, tactical direction refers to the way the restaurant's commitment to excellence is translated into reality through the kinds of things done by each employee. This reinforcement must be provided on an ongoing basis by the IdeaManager and IdeaLeader.

Rewarding Performance

Rewards play a crucial role in the idea-driven staff process and, indeed, in the whole firm. It is crucial that there be a reward system in place. Similarly, the process of reward allocation must work smoothly, getting rewards to those individuals for whom they are designed.

In the past, rewards have tended to mean salary and merit raise, with some benefits thrown into the picture. Staff costs were viewed as costs, and tended to operate independent of the production of the organization (with staff costs simply added to price). All managers faced the "annunitization" problem: Salary costs just keep going up.

In current thinking, what is often called "new pay" takes a different approach. Salary is being minimized; variable pay is being strengthened (variable is bonus, gain sharing, and pay for performance on a one-time basis—each year—but you can, of course, get it [or more] next year as well) (Schuster & Zeingheim, 1992). Gone too is the entitlement mentality which calls for annual raises. In its place is the need to earn one's right to competitive pay.

The IdeaLeader can introduce, and the IdeaManager can implement, a new pay system described by the following equation:

$$TC = BP + AP + IP + WP + PP + OA + OG + PI$$

where TC means total compensation, BP means base pay, AP means augmented pay, WP means workspay, PP means perkspay, OA means opportunity for advancement, OG means opportunity for growth, and PI means psychic income. In this total compensation equation—which is a new idea in and of itself—I have put all the things that the IdeaLeader and IdeaManager has to work with.

There is, of course, base pay, but the importance of that is decreasing in overall importance. In the future, employees might be guaranteed only a proportion, perhaps 80 percent, of their base pay. The rest might be earned through various contracts within the organization.

Augmented pay, a variety of one time payments for this and that, is an area of growth. It is in this area that one may add to the base pay contract and go above base pay, in addition to overtime, bonus, gainsharing, pay-for-performance, stock options and grants, and so on. The important piece here is that they are one-time payments. You may get them in a second year, but that depends on conditions at that time.

Indirect pay, or benefits, is in the process of being trimmed after a period of growth in recent years. Cafeteria benefits is one of the big areas of growth.

Workspay is the money firms make available to you for tools and equipment that you need to do your job. Firms differ a lot in this area, and many employees wind up resourcing themselves, thus cutting their own income.

Perkspay, the status differentiators, are also on the decline, but important in some firms (e.g., most firms give employees a discount on their product where the employees could use the product). Given the flattening of organizations, traditional special perks (executive dining rooms, etc.) are mostly a thing of the past.

Opportunities for advancement are a crucial part of the reward system. Upward mobility, with its attendant psychic and financial rewards, may well be the best package of all. The attendant financial rewards promote an "up for bucks" mentality that keeps people seeking promotion for both money and power. However, advancement opportunities are on the decline for a number of reasons. Many firms are small with few positions to advance into. And, again, with the flattening of organizations, the number of positions "higher up" is declining.

Opportunities for growth, acquiring different skills and competencies, are replacing opportunities for advancement to some degree. Individuals choose some jobs because the learning opportunities—formal and informal—are excellent. This particular area is a goldmine for the IdeaManager and IdeaLeader. He or she can promote opportunities for growth which appeal to the employee, and at the same time make the employees more idea interested, and more idea ready. Indeed, training programs, if the trainee is invited to report back and train others, can be one of the greatest investments organizations can make. The idea-driven organization of the next century will be, in many ways, a teaching/learning institution.

Psychic income involves the emotional rewards of the workplace. It can be positive or negative. Positive psychic income creates what some call the "employer of choice." Part of what is desired here is recognition. The late Aaron Wildavsky (1960), a famous professor of political science, once said that he once saw three churches of the same denomination in a town so small that it struck him one would have served quite nicely. But he observed that if there were three churches, there were also three presidents of the church boards, three sets of church boards, three vice presidents of church boards, and so on.

In other words, IdeaManagers and IdeaLeaders can create niches, titles, and assignments that gratify employees' cravings for special recognition and upward mobility on the one hand, and, on the other, help the organization by further specifying and locating the work to be done. In no sense is the creation and development of the positions and assignments fake. Rather, they represent attempts to focus the work and to provide recognition for it.

Something else that is important is a rewarding and gratifying work environment, and a chance to be centrally involved in a developing project of great importance.

Another very important point—and increasingly recognized as such—is time. Especially today, when more women are in the workforce and where both men and women are undertaking child care responsibilities, the flexibility of time may be an almost incalculable benefit. You may very well want to look at your enterprise from the point of view of enhancing its flexibility. Many of us work from nine to five simply out of habit, and we tend to think that employees should do the same. What is really important, however, is getting a total effort out of an employee and trying to arrange the job so that it can be done by the employee. Though some situations do not have the flexibility that would allow for differing blocks of time, many jobs increasingly do. All IdeaManagers and IdeaLeaders should be alert to this possibility.

Other kinds of psychic income that workers get from an employment situation are no less important. Colleagueship—"the people I work with"—is a very important reward in and of itself. This is another reason for an emphasis on recruitment. New employees should not only please the boss, they should please other people with whom they have to work. In some respects that may be even more important, as they are not likely to work with the boss to the same extent as with the other employees. Once individuals become committed to an enterprise, their willingness to become involved depends in part on how involved everyone else is. It is at this point that hard work and team effort become fun—because of the interpersonal enjoyment each of us gets out of being involved in a key enterprise.

Compensation of the future will require more variety as well as more choice in the package. I call this approach *cafeteria compensation*. It derives, and is the same principle as, cafeteria benefits. The eight variable package described here will become the standard template. The difference will be that employees will, within certain limits, configure the proportions of compensation they want to flow through the spigots of compensation. An employee interested in security might want all his or her pay coming through base pay and benefits. The employee with an interest in high risk and high reward might want all or most of his or her compensation coming through augmented pay. There may be a range of choices among different employees at any point in time, and for the same employee over several points in time. IdeaManagers and IdeaLeaders can use the provision of choice in the creation of an idea-driven staff. And to a certain extent, the medium is the message. As employees think more about how they wish to be paid and why, they will also think more about the job itself. Thinking leads to ideas.

Evaluating the Staff

To complete the attention to staff, a system of evaluation must be present as well (it might be helpful to review the section on evaluation structures in Chapter 17). It is difficult to apply some of the other elements mentioned here (e.g., rewarding or advancing) if you do not know the past level of performance. There are many ways staff can be evaluated, and an adaptation of the structure for organizational evaluation (monitoring, oversight, assessment, and appraisal) can be used here—though the first two might be a bit much for many staff. Still, whatever the system or structure, several points need to be kept in mind.

First, understand that some system is necessary. All firms, in fact, have evaluation systems. Some people get ahead and some do not. The real questions are whether the system is the right one and whether it has the right results; people who are talented and who contribute are the ones who get rewarded. Specifying the system means that you and the staff can look at it.

Second, apply the system across the board. Often there are two (or more) evaluation systems—those that are announced and those that are operative. For IdeaManagers and IdeaLeaders, it is crucial that those who contribute innovatively will be evaluated well. This is good for the individuals, but it is also good for the organization.

Third, let the individuals have some participation in the design of the system and the actual yearly evaluation. This involvement yields great gains when troublesome findings come up.

Fourth, be proactive. Rather than evaluation after the year ends, work with the staff to set goals first. Then ask the staff to evaluate at year's end how they did. This also seems to alert the IdeaManager and IdeaLeader to resources that need to be produced if specified goals are to be met. In addition, it is always easier to do a monitoring check in June if goals have been specified in January.

Fifth, use a system of upward appraisal. A lot of time and effort is spent in encouraging supervisors to evaluate and give information to subordinates. Less to no time is spent in getting the perspectives of subordinates to supervisors. Emphasis on a 360-degree approach is taking hold (Edwards & Ewen, 1996). It means getting feedback from everyone (a complete circle). But the 360-degree approach is complex and expensive. It is not easy to use. And working against the flow of power is always difficult.

There is one method I have found that works well, is very low tech, requires no special forms, and can be used by anyone, in a variety of settings. It is KSS. What KSS means is Keep, Start, and Stop. The superior asks the subordinate to answer three questions:

Are there things I am doing that are helpful and I should keep on doing? Are there things I am not now doing I should start? Are there things I am doing that you do not find helpful and I should stop or phase out? This is about as nonthreatening as it gets, and it is a quick way to provide useful information. (It also can be used after a meeting, within a team, or even with one's spouse.)

CONCLUSION

In no sense have all the elements that an IdeaManager and IdeaLeader need to attend to with staff been touched on here. The main categories do provide a sort of checklist that you may wish to use in order to see if you are covering some of the most crucial bases.

Management is often thought of as "productivity through people." The people are the staff, the team, the employees, and the colleagues. Without them, the venture will not succeed. Only through them can goals be reached. The first step in understanding this process is understanding thoughts and truth. Without that recognition, very little else that you do will make a great deal of difference. With it, attending to matters of recognizing, recruiting, inspiriting, rewarding, advancing, and training staff will pay great dividends.

Chapter 21

Staying Ahead of the Curve

Certainly, for the field of business it would be extremely helpful if we could discern some of the shape and texture of the future to prepare ourselves better for what lies ahead. This is particularly important for the organization of the future, because it is emerging trends that represent the market niches open for new products and services.

Too often, in the crush of daily business, we do not look ahead to reflect on what may be in the future. We give little thought to how we can best adjust ourselves, both to prepare for what is coming—in terms of structural changes and changes in values and beliefs—and to take advantage of it. On those rare occasions when we do find ourselves anticipating our journeys on the road ahead, all too frequently we see trends and developments that we do not like or that we find difficult to accept. But by orienting ourselves to change now, we can prevent precisely those kinds of developments that we believe will be troubling, and we can take advantage of those trends and developments that are coming whether we like it or not. IdeaManagers and IdeaLeaders are seldom more important than here, bringing the future into today.

THE TWO DIMENSIONS OF CHANGE

There is no question that our society—indeed, the world—is changing rapidly. Those changes can be divided generally into two major kinds: changes in social structure and changes in social culture. Changes in social structure are concerned with changes in the patterns of things we do, the laws we have, and the way we act. Changes in the "hard" side of life are structural ones. There is, however, a "softer" side of change. Changes in social culture center on the things we believe, the values we hold, and the attitudes we profess.

TENSIONS WITHIN CULTURAL AND STRUCTURAL SYSTEMS: CULTURAL AND STRUCTURAL CACOPHONY

There are, as always, tensions. There are tensions within the cultural and structural systems—something I call *cacophony*. All the elements of the structure do not point in the same way or go in the same direction any more than is true in the culture. Populations are changing in different directions at the same time. Values point in different directions (more independence, more family). IdeaManagers and IdeaLeaders need to be aware that summary measures are averages of conflicting trends. This is an obvious point, but one worth keeping in mind. Environmental scanning should be attuned for variance as well as uniformity. Diversity, rather than uniformity, characterize these two systems.

TENSIONS BETWEEN CULTURAL AND STRUCTURAL SYSTEMS: CULTURAL AND STRUCTURAL LAG

Beliefs are thought to guide actions. Actions are thought to be consistent with beliefs. And this, perhaps, should be true, but it is not—at least not always. Sometimes beliefs change quickly, and practices (structures) remain in a traditional mode, that is called *structural lag*. At other times, structure moves ahead and beliefs lag behind. That is called *cultural lag*. There is both good and bad news here. As organizational change agents have learned, you have to work in both systems—not just one—or the lag will cause the change to "snap back." Change culture without changing structure is as problematic as changing structure without changing culture. IdeaManagers and IdeaLeaders are aware of this fact.

On the other hand, each system acting as a drag or sea anchor as it does, the pace of change is somewhat modulated. This may allow more people to get on board, and not introduce too much at once. IdeaManagers seek to keep cultural lag and structural lag in balance. Let us consider an example.

Though it is true to some extent that actions shape beliefs and beliefs direct action, it is important to understand that the relationship between what we believe and what we do is open and conflicting. American society, for example, celebrates equality worldwide, and we are probably better at supporting equality than most other countries. In spite of that professed and supported position, racial and gender discrimination are still prominent features of our social landscape. It would seem that our values have not completely permeated our actions.

In spite of this historic discrimination (remember that slaves were counted as three-fifths of a person in the Constitution for census purposes), our beliefs in the importance of equality and equal opportunity have not dimmed much over the years, actions to the contrary notwithstanding. It is probably because we behave as though our beliefs are largely independent of our actions that we do not totally enact every belief, nor do we adjust every belief to every action. Many, indeed, are the IdeaLeaders who have gone ahead with a product or service despite a lot of negative belief about whether that product or service would actually succeed. As Lawton (1983) writes,

> The kernel of my message, however, is that the lack of predictability from one sector. . . . to another even if we reduce measurement error to its bare minimum, is the normal state of affairs to be expected for the human condition. Specifically we suggest that the relative autonomy among sectors is what makes human existence possible. If a change in one sector were to be immediately reflected in every other sector chaotic instability would be the result. (p. 355)

The IdeaManager and IdeaLeader need to constantly mine the environment for changes that both produce ideas and to which ideas must respond.

CHANGES IN SOCIAL STRUCTURE

What are the current changes affecting us within our social structure that affect organizations? I have already mentioned some of the most pressing at the beginning of this book. Let us take a longer look at some of the arms-length changes that are coming.

How does one go about organizing a look at the environment? To answer this it is useful to use the acronym POET. It points us to considering changes in four large areas—population, organization, environment, and technology—as a way to track the flow of changes and their interconnections.

Population

The population of the world and of American society is changing dramatically. There are estimates that the world population will approach seven billion people by the year 2000. Of these, about two billion will be older, richer, and in the more highly-developed countries. The remaining five billion will be poorer, younger, and in the less well-developed countries.

The population structure of well-developed countries, as mentioned, will be older, with more people over sixty-five and fewer under eighteen. In addition, they will be more well-to-do. The underdeveloped countries will have a much younger population, and one which is relatively poor. Thus, the world marketplace in the year 2000 seems to be dividing itself into two major camps: relatively small but older and richer teams of nations and people on the one hand, and a relatively large younger and poorer group of nations and people on the other. Addressing the imperatives of these markets will require a great deal of ingenuity. American society mirrors the changes of all well-developed nations. The population, for example, is aging.

Total population results from births, deaths, and in and out migrations. Each of these forces is working heavily to change the face of the American population. Births are decreasing, so the number of younger people is decreasing. (In contrast to the Baby Boom generation that followed World War II, this is sometimes called the Baby Bust generation.) Generation X is here. Furthermore, medical advances and improved diet and nutrition programs are helping Americans to live longer. So, not only are there fewer younger Americans, there is a growing number of older Americans. Immigration, legal and illegal, is also a growth factor.

The final population of any country at any point in time is like a bank account. There are deposits (births, immigrations) and withdrawals (deaths, emigrations). However, these do not totally determine the net size of the account. Just as bank accounts tend to earn interest, so too do population accounts. In terms of population dynamics, demographers call that interest the "length of a generation." It is expressed as the average age of a woman in the society when she has her first child. If women have children at young ages, the population grows faster, almost without regard to any other factors—just as a bank account grows faster with a higher interest rate. The length of a generation in American society is going up. IdeaManagers and IdeaLeaders must be particularly sensitive to the needs of the older family. If women in their late twenties and early thirties are having children, then child care at work becomes a very important factor, something that might be less true if the average age of a woman having her first child were eighteen or nineteen.

There are other trends involving the American family that are worth examining. The population of working women is up. The fertility rate is going down. The marriage rate is going up, and the median age at marriage is going up for both men and women. The divorce rate has doubled since 1965, and the number of out-of-wedlock births is estimated to be three times that of 1965. With respect to the demographics of the American society, there is so much variation that we might say variation is now the norm. Departures from the norm have become the norm. IdeaManagers and IdeaLeaders need to be aware of population trends, shifts, and movements in order to position themselves and their ventures to take advantage of new and different resources and contribute to finding answers to new and different needs.

Social Organization

Social organization reflects the way a society organizes itself to accomplish its various tasks. Several of the changes were originally discussed by John Naisbitt as long ago as 1982 (and again with Auberdene in 1990). He was really a seer. Those changes, fledgling when he first noticed them, are fully with us today. His trends range from institutional to self-help, from short- to long-term orientation, from representation to participatory styles, from either/or orientations to multiple-option ones, and from hierarchical perspectives to networking perspectives. Let us take a brief look at each of these.

Changes from Institutional Help to Self-Help What once appeared to be increasing reliance on professionals and specialists seems now to be moving back to a focus on doing things oneself. This countermove seems relatively pervasive, now encompassing self-help teams in finance, medical care, home birthing, and so on.

Changes from Short-Term to Longer-Term America has often been associated with the short-term, crisis-oriented mentality. This perspective has been widely cited as one of the important causes of our loss in product leadership status worldwide in the 1970s and 1980s. We appear to be moving from a here-and-now mentality into a longer-term perspective. This is apparent in the rise of strategic planning in business organizations. It is evident in the popularity of Individual Retirement Accounts and Keough Plans (even without tax deductibility). Indeed, much of the stock markets' long run up (as of 1998) might well be attributed to increases in interest in longer-term value. We see it, too, in career consulting services that help individuals plan for a lifetime of organizational activity, not just the next job. Unfortunately, the "We want it yesterday" mentality, and the "I don't want it good, I want it Tuesday" orientation are still very much with us. Planning, it would seem, is still not something we take very well to in our society. Still, as we are forced more into it, planning-oriented services should prosper.

Changes from Representative to Participatory Styles We have long thought of ourselves as a representative democracy, a view that has permeated our relationships to many of our institutions. In the past, we have tended not to deal directly with items of concern. Rather, we have a long tradition of designating representatives to ask on our behalf. This trend is changing. More and more we appear to want to act directly on and in our own behalf. We want to take control of those areas of our lives that are of most concern to us and that most effect us. Generation X is especially interested in control, having observed their boomer parents lose a lot of control through downsizing, rightsizing, and the like. Partly, of course, this orientation stems from a fear that our representatives often have done us dirt. Partly we want more involvement in things that affect us; after all, the Boston Tea Party (no taxation without representation) is a part of our history.

Throughout business and industry, however, the ability of workers to participate directly in the making of their product and to be valued for that participation is becoming an increasingly important focus. Organizations will need to take this trend into account, both in terms of designing and structuring employee participation plans and in setting up structures that allow for employees to contribute not only their physical labor but their ideas and perspectives as well.

Changes from Either/Or to Multiple Options American society is moving out of a posture in which one's choices are either "this" or "that," a situation where the number of alternatives is limited. The result is what decision theorists call a "zero sum game." The flip of a coin is a typical example of such a game: If we win, you lose; if you lose, we win. We appear to be moving toward a situation where we have more options available. The supermarket has many kinds of toothpaste, a lot of this and that, and even choice among dog and cat food.

In the workplace, choice is a value as well. Rigid and precise work schedules, for example, are being replaced in some quarters by "flex-time," in which the individual sets his or her own work schedule within previously agreed-on perimeters. There is also the development of job sharing, where the same job may be held by two different people for the convenience of both. Rigidly defined benefit plans are moving to veritable cafeterias of options. Indeed, the whole compensation system is moving to cafeteria compensation. The creation of multiple options implies that individuals not only have a choice of the food displayed there, but in the design of the cafeteria.

Environment

Changes in the environment, for purposes here, are changes in the locations of business and the way business is organized in the landscape. Naisbitt, in 1983 (and again in 1990), mentioned movement from north to south as a major trend; and clearly, at the time he wrote, that seemed reasonable. With changes in oil prices, however, some of the booming southern cities have now gone into eclipse. At the same time, some regions—New England is a notable example—have come back in relatively spectacular ways. Even the Midwestern "Rust Belt" may become burnished in time. Some authorities predict that in the years to come, fresh water will become an extraordinarily valuable commodity. Those states bordering the Great Lakes may then be sitting on a resource far more valuable than oil.

My point is simply that the physical environment of business changes. Sometimes resources that were once plentiful dry up. Sometimes resources, once unattended, become valuable. Particular market geographies that were once taken for granted become changed, changing marketing requirements radically. This leads logically to Naisbitt's suggestion that we are changing from a national economy to a world economy.

Changes from a National to a World Economy It is clear that America must reposition itself vis-à-vis the world economy, and is. American business must find those things that we do well and specialize in them more than we have in the past. Such specialization and differentiation is not new. It has been a constant process within the country as a whole, intranationally. Dealing internationally, however, requires us to face a number of problematic and difficult restrictions and hurdles that we have not had to confront before. Still, there are numerous opportunities, not only with respect to on-shore or offshore business occasions and their combinations and permutations, but also in business ventures assisting other businesses in developing and enhancing the necessary coping skills.

From Ecological Ignorance to Environmental Sensitivity Though our national emphasis on production and the material side of life is still extremely strong, more and more of it is accompanied by a sensitivity to the environment in which we live. There is a growing awareness of the quality of life, including not only the material things, but the natural setting in which we live our lives, as well. Slowly but surely we are taking measurable steps to improve that environment, and the pace of such improvement is gradually accelerating. In time, perhaps, individuals will come from all parts of the world to view our varied magnificent scenery and to enjoy our upgraded environmental quality. Opportunities abound in developing the products and services to service this environmental consciousness. Businesses need to take environmental concern into account. At the moment, green is good.

Technology

Basically, technology is a more efficient way of doing work. It is a pattern of transformation of materials through the use of energy. With respect to contemporary American society, changes in modes of production and in focal industrial activities are appropriately thought of as changes in technology. Naisbitt (1982) mentions three that are especially relevant: changes from industrial society to information society, changes from force technology to high technology, and changes from centralization to decentralization.

Changes from an Industrial Society to an Information Society Many years ago most Americans were farmers. Only a few were engaged in the production process. With the passage of the Civil War and the development of steam power, industrial technology (force technology) became the major mode of production. Most Americans moved into jobs in the production process, and only a minority remained farmers. As we have moved from the production of food to the production of materials, we may expect that we will next move from the production of materials to the production of information. This is what analysts mean when they refer to the movement from the industrial society to the information society. Already we have begun to see a decline in manufacturing as a fraction of our total human energy and effort and an accompanying increase in automated manufacturing plants. With the shift away from an industrial society, the new locus of activity will be to collection, storage, analysis, and dissemination of information. These will build on new computer and telecommunication technology. Making such a prediction in 1950 would surely have seemed more far out than far reaching. At that time, the computer was a room-filling, cumbersome, clumsy, expensive piece of apparatus. But all that was before the transistor, integrated circuitry, and the microchip. The home computer that Radio Shack marketed in 1979 for about $1,500 was eight times more powerful than the computer that controlled the defense of the entire United States in 1955, a computer that cost $11 million.

Organizations will surely find ways to exploit this trend toward an information society. Already, computer shopping and electronic mail are becoming relatively commonplace. The "smart" interstate highways of the future may contain a tiny band running down the center of each lane that links to and activates with on-board automotive directional computers. You will get in your car, hit the main drag, program in your destination, and settle back with a good book. Your car will slip into the ongoing stream of "car trains," controlled by computer-operated sensors. Chips containing maps of the United States will already be built into the vehicle. The automobile is only one of an almost infinite number of possibilities that will ultimately rely on new information technology.

All libraries will one day be stored on or in mass storage devices, addressable by computer and accessible from an unlimited number of computerized locations. Apart from the storage of information and its quick retrieval, organizational premiums will be placed on mechanisms for selecting, digesting, and synthesizing this vast amount of information. After all, even with search time counted in microseconds, the amount of information on most topics will be vast. Relevance, appropriateness, timeliness, focus, and analysis will be at a premium.

And, of course, the World Wide Web is continuing to revolutionize our lives. Search facilities which organize millions of bits of data reemphasize that premium on information. Soon we will do much of our home business over the "net." So popular has it become that it is developing its own rules of courtesy (netiquette) and own ways to give offense (flaming).

Changes from Force Technology to High Tech–High Touch Contained within the change from an industrial to an information society is a shift from force technology to high technology. This shift is of considerable importance to individuals who work for any particular organization. Industrial society was the era of force technology. Physical work was their premium. In the information age, high technology is the focal element, and high technology requires a sophisticated and intelligent workforce. Workers cannot simply be replaced "willy-nilly," as so often happened in the industrial era. Leaving aside the humanitarian considerations, physical strength is easier to replace than the sum costs of intellectual development or specialized high-technology training. Given our increasingly complex computer-based technology, the amount of time it takes to train workers becomes an extremely crucial element. Organizational activity involving worker training, retraining, and so on is likely to be a burgeoning field. Having made those investments, employers will be much more wary about making employees "walk the plank." Special efforts will have to be made at coming to accommodations between management and labor, because labor is too valuable now to be set aside in a casual manner. This opens additional opportunities for interpersonally oriented organizational types in the whole area of employee relations.

The employee has finally been recognized as the complex machine he or she has always been. The throw-away society ("If it doesn't work, throw it out and get one that does"), characteristic of the industrial age, may be on the decline. In part, at least, this is because the ability to replace depends on having a stock of expensive pieces of equipment waiting in the wings. With people we do not have "extras" waiting around until one of us breaks.

Changes from Centralization to Decentralization Correlated with these two other trends is a movement toward decentralization. Movement is away from large concerns and toward smaller, more efficient units. Corporations are stressing core competencies and core businesses, and divesting the rest. In recent years, for example, we have seen a movement away from large mental hospitals toward small, community-based foster care units. People have been moving out of larger cities and into smaller, more usable spaces where individuals can relate to one another more easily. We have seen some erosion of the consolidated political power in Washington, with some influence (albeit small) flowing back to the states. Peters and Waterman (1982) anticipated this particular trend in two of the features they find characteristic of excellent companies. One, a feature that they call a "loose tight property," implies some centralized control (the tight part) with a lot of abilities to deal individually with local situations flowing to subunits (the loose part). In addition, their orientation toward "simple form, lean staff" bespeaks a similar focus. To the extent, at least, that hierarchies represent centralization and networking represents subnodules within the organizational structure, this is another version of the shift from hierarchies to networking. Doubtless, entrepreneurs will find opportunities here. These might include specially training the smaller units and working with them on an individual unit-by-unit basis to improve their efficiency and productivity.

THE ORGANIZATIONAL ADVANTAGE

Are these trends the key ones? I am not sure. Some may prove to be enduring; others passing. Trend forecasting is a risky business, especially in the area of social patterns and social behavior. To some extent, however, whether they are right or not right is beside the point. They suggest the types of changes that entrepreneurs might look for. As one begins to sit down and think about what kinds of market niches might be available in current trends, other trends, or local variations of national trends, fresh ones will come into view. The central point here is that new patterns of social behavior and social relationships create demand for new products and new services. By examining social trends proactively and by considering how you might react to them, you will automatically be a step ahead of your competitors.

CHANGES IN SOCIAL CULTURE

If changes in social structure are in the works—or likely to eventually be in the works—then it is also true that changes in the system's beliefs, attitudes, and values are likely to be occurring as well. Some, as we indicated at the beginning of this chapter, are interrelated. Others may be proceeding quite independently but are stimulating some changes.

The Patterns of Culture

One of the more important features of the value system—and the one that has not been talked about very much—is its structure. Before examining the changes, let us take a brief look at some of the features of the structure of culture (it might be helpful to revisit the section on value conflict in Chapter 16 on subculture, especially the discussion of North American and Japanese values).

Values, commitments, beliefs, and attitudes are all more than just lists. They are patterns, shapes, and structures. For every list of values—like a dictionary—there is a grammar, a set of rules for putting them together. From our perspective and that of a number of others, similar values come in sets; that is, pairs of competing commitments (Lynd, 1939; Lipset, 1963). For example, the well-known sociologist Seymour Martin Lipset sees our whole nation unfolding as a tension between values of achievement on the one hand and values of equality on the other.

An important feature of this value structure is that it is not concerned simply with two ends of a continuum: Achievement is not simply the other end of equality; permission is not simply the other end of control. It is much like the success/failure grid mentioned earlier. We must think of high and low achievement societies in the same way we think about high and low achievement individuals. Those societies and persons who are not motivated to achieve, however, are not necessarily egalitarian, either. The best way to think about these value structures is in the form of a plus with intersecting axes. This leads to a four-fold design, as shown in Figure 21.1. One axis is achievement orientation as present in a particular culture. A second axis is egalitarian orientation. Both dimensions run from high to low. What this means is that there are four cells that characterize most cultures. High–high is a culture that is high on egalitarianism and high on achievement. There are certainly companies where this is the case. There are also many cultures where neither achievement nor egalitarianism seem to be particularly prominent. In addition, we can identify companies that are high on achievement and low on egalitarianism. These display corporate cultures that are tremendously competitive and cutthroat.

There are also those companies where achievement orientation is low and egalitarianism is high. Typical of such firms and businesses are those of a lifestyle nature. Individuals enter them less to make money or achieve a high rank in society than for the intrinsic pleasure that participating in the culture provides. Many musical careers may fall into this category (though there is a considerable amount of competition in music, as well).

Finally, there are those firms low on both achievement and equality. Because they are not moving and have relatively hostile cultures, they are among the worst places to work. The fact that there are paired values within organizational cultures does not exhaust the things that we can say about them. In fact, this perspective expands our ability to understand the dynamics of organizational culture in ways heretofore only hinted at.

Figure 21.1
The Conflict between Achievement and Equality in American Values

	ACHIEVEMENT ORIENTATION	
	Low	High
EQUALITY ORIENTATION		
Low	Low E/Low A	Low E/High A
High	High E/Low E	High E/High A

Four other points are worthy of special mention. First, the achievement–equality dichotomy is only one of many. From an organizational point of view, another particularly important value conflict is between the permission to innovate and the control of innovation. In Chapter 6, we discuss a number of others. Achievement and equality is a useful and appropriate conflict for business, but competition between values of permission on the one hand and control on the other, particularly of the innovated processes and products, is another universal competitive element that characterizes a wide range of organizations.

Second, in any given pair, one or another value may be more dominant. Within American culture, for example, we might conclude that achievement is the more dominant value, with egalitarianism being a strong competitor but less prominent. It is the presence of both plus their differential importance that allows for organizational cultures to be located differentially within the value matrix.

Third, in spite of the fact that dominance or prominence of one value of the pair exists, organizational cultures change over time. Partly, this change is in response to internal dynamics; partly, it is in response to external pressures and frictions. Over time, emphasis on one value creates a tension or a stress within the organization or culture because competing commitments require that both value orientations be honored in some way and in some time. Thus, over time, attention to achievement will produce pressures to emphasize more egalitarian and democratic values. As this pressure builds up and manifestations of these values become evident, they begin to threaten the achievement values. Emphasis on them then begins to reassert itself. The dual-value framework, therefore, creates a constant friction of values internal to the organizational culture that allows for—and, in fact, requires—some degree of value change and alterations. Hence, in the value matrix described in Figure 21.1, the organization, once located in a particular position, does not remain in that position and will change over time. Any location or dot within a matrix representing a particular organization's position and a particular point of view must be seen as a stroboscopic capturing of a dynamic organizational situation in which the culture at an earlier point in time had a different position and will have a different position at a still later point in time. Societal values shift in similar ways. Any location of a society at a particular point in time on these views will be decidedly different if we look at that society at a later or an earlier point in its history.

A great economist, Albert O. Hirschman, also indicates a source of value change deriving from dual or competing value commitments. In his book, *Shifting Involvements* (1982), he points out that disappointment in particular value commitments, which is almost certain to occur, is, itself, a generative force in beginning to explore other perspectives. He talks about "shifting involvements" from public to private orientation as a particularly salient and contemporary example. This disappointment can occur both within the society at large and within any particular organizational subculture.

We have mentioned two engines of change for values: tension between competing commitments and disappointment in the achievement or the accomplishment of a particular value. But when one thinks of values as located within different organizational parts—in a society as a whole, in communities, and in organizations—then a third engine of change presents itself. Friction between organizational values and community values and between organizational values and societal values are two specific examples of that engine of change. An organization that emphasizes achievement orientation, for example, fits well in a society that also emphasizes achievement.

Finally, I am seeking to apply the concept of competition that is well understood in the business community to the area of culture. There is much talk about the marketplace of products. We even hear about the marketplace of ideas. What we need to begin thinking about now is the marketplace of commitments and, indeed, the competition for and of commitments.

Cultural conflict does not simply exist between us and some undetermined "them." Rather, it exists within our firms, within our communities, and even within ourselves. I have spent a great deal of time discussing the structure of culture and the tensions between competing values. Let us look at some specific tensions, and shifts between them.

From Public to Private Commitments

One of the great cultural changes that has occurred in the last fifty years is a change from private orientation to public orientation and now, back again, to private. Before the Great Depression and the presidency of Franklin D. Roosevelt, the federal government was a relatively small operation. The combined efforts of the social programs initiated in the 1930s and subsequent years, and the large military effort begun in World War II and continuing today, has put the government in a leadership role with respect to revenues, employment, and influence. But that period now seems to be one that is going into eclipse. Substantial doubt about the efficacy of public bureaucracies has often been voiced. Popular belief has it that there is something like "paradoxical counterproductivity," especially in the public arena. Educational institutions fail to educate; medical institutions fail to heal; institutions of criminal justice fail to be corrective. Not only are such institutions failing, but those who become involved with them often become worse: IQs fall in school; illness becomes more severe in hospitals; criminality is exacerbated in prison.

Businesses are among the major beneficiaries of this move toward privatization. There is talk of private prisons, leased by the government. Private schools are a growing area. Private social services supported by tax dollars is another example. And there are doubtless many more ways firms could exploit this trend toward privatization.

From Bigness to Smallness

Some of the suspicions of government very likely stem from a suspicion of bigness (see Lipset & Schneider, 1983). The American public is not only suspicious of big government, but of big business and big labor as well. Certainly, the giants of the American corporate world have given us every reason for suspicion and distrust. As one student put it recently, "We thought they knew what they were doing. How could we have been so blind?" A celebration of smaller but better would unquestionably benefit the organizational impulse.

From Collectivism to Individualism

In the 1950s, when William F. Whyte (1957) wrote *The Organization Man*, the popular view of the large organization was that everyone was completely the same. All had become completely "the man in the gray flannel suit." Interchangeable people, like interchangeable parts, could be substituted one for the other without anyone knowing the difference. To house these new employees, tract housing went up so quickly and with houses so similar that there were numerous reports of men coming home at night and entering the wrong house by mistake, unable to distinguish theirs from their neighbors. In response, a reaction emphasizing the individual and his or her unique aspects developed. The famous pollster Daniel Yankelovich (1981) writes about it as follows:

> By the seventies, most Americans were involved in projects to prove that life can be more than a grim chore. Americans from every walk of life were suddenly eager to give more meaning to their lives, to find fuller self-expression and to add a touch of

adventure and grace to their lives and those of others. . . . In the nineteen-seventies all national surveys showed an increase in preoccupation with self. By the late 70's, my firm's studies showed that more than seven out of ten Americans (72 percent) spent a great deal of time thinking about themselves and their inner lives—this in a nation once notorious for its impatience with inwardness. The rage for self fulfillment, our surveys indicated, had now spread to virtually the entire U.S. population. (p. 5)

Yankelovich's summary is as good as any to capture this shift to personalized preoccupation. Entrepreneurs have seized the advantage here in providing personal development courses. The whole health movement is related in part to this. Trimming up one's body, after all, is related to self-improvement and preoccupation. The shift to upscale products and high-quality goods fits in here as well. Americans, preoccupied with themselves, are no longer satisfied with shoddy workmanship. IdeaManagers and IdeaLeaders can seek advantage here.

From Instrumental to Sacred

Yankelovich (1981) also points out that values in American society are changing to put greater worth on the intrinsic as opposed to the purpose aspect. He asks, "Should we value certain aspects of nature and society—a wilderness, a vanishing species, a primitive culture, old automobiles, old buildings—for themselves, apart from their instrumental value?" (p. 7).

My answer is yes. Part of the new American cultural value system involves a reemphasis not only on the individual person but on the value and worth of that individual person independent of what he or she can deliver in the form of goods or services. There is an "intrinsicalness" worth attending to. Entrepreneurs can find numerous opportunities to assist society to manage these developing values. But entrepreneurs should also be aware that employees will think of themselves not only as units to service the organizational venture but as people with intrinsic value, not to be shuttled and shunted from here to there for the simple and often unjustifiable pleasure of the firm.

The Getting/Giving Compact

Yankelovich (1981) also discusses the "getting/giving compact" as it has historically developed in American society and as it is now changing. According to Yankelovich,

The old getting/giving compact might be paraphrased this way: "I give hard work, loyalty, and steadfastness. I swallow my frustrations and suppress my impulse to do what I would enjoy and do what is expected of me instead. I do not put myself first. I put the needs of others ahead of my own. I give a lot, but what I get in return is worth it. I receive an ever growing standard of living and a family with a devoted spouse and decent kids. . . . I have a nice home, a good job, the respect of my friends and neighbors; a sense of accomplishment of having made something of my life." (p. 9)

Yankelovich (1981) stresses the importance of this implicit contract in sustaining the American growth pattern. But it is now over. The giving/getting compact, which might be thought of as "a rising tide lifts all boats," has now been replaced with a philosophy more akin to "each tub on its own bottom."

Trouble began when the string of American victories begun in the New Deal and World War II were broken when the war on poverty failed and the Vietnam War came to a halting conclusion. Things just seemed to get worse from then on. American productivity leveled off. Very large corporations like GM and U.S. Steel ran into serious trouble. A large number of Americans were discovered to be homeless. Others were discovered to be illiterate. For the first time it appeared that parents might not be able to expect, other things being equal, their children to do better than they had done. The price of single family homes seemed to soar out of the reach of many Americans. Faced with these possible and actual problems, the future began to dissolve. Hope began to erode. Yankelovich (1981) comments, "Sensing this contradiction between their goals and their strategies and being aware of the change for the worse in economic conditions, what most Americans fear today is coming up empty handed" (p. 11).

It is in this context that innovation will surely flourish. If the giving/getting compact, which seems to have sustained a lot of self-repression over a number of years, is now being set aside, then the time is right for individuals to try to do those things they have always wanted to do. Many among us have wanted the freedom, the independence, and the self-direction of a personal venture fueled by ideas that we believe are profitably marketable, but that others have often doubted and rejected. Furthermore, dependence on self now seems much more realistic than dependence on the larger culture to produce for us. Both white collar and blue collar employees have found that organizations have short memories. When an organization is taken over, individuals who have devoted much of their lives to its development and enhancement are summarily dismissed. Sane people conclude that organizational loyalty under the conditions we observe is foolish. Relying on ourselves and our own ideas has at least one advantage: We are probably not going to take ourselves over and lay ourselves off.

The Concert of Cultures

I have spoken of large-scale trends in belief and attitude and value systems that affect the entire country. But one must approach this kind of prognostication with more than a grain of salt. After all, in a socially pluralistic society, one would expect a pluralism of values, too. That is what cacophony and diversity is all about. It is important that entrepreneurs especially recognize that opportunities lie not only in the realm of values that characterize the entire culture, but in value packages that characterize minority teams within the culture as well. Teen values and yuppie values represent two teams of values that have already been strongly recognized by the business community. Values of the black population and the opportunities they might present for marketing and sales have also been in the spotlight in recent years. Values of older Americans and regional, sectional, and other subsectional values can represent important niches in the market that IdeaManagers and IdeaLeaders can use. Faith Popcorn (1986), a consultant who specializes in keeping businesses apprised of new values, speaks in general of nostalgia, loyalty, patriotism, and family as values that will emerge within some sectors of the population. And if history is any guide, other values will emerge in other sectors and be strong. As with the social structure, the entrepreneur must be constantly alert to changes in the social culture. These changes represent both dangers and opportunities. Failure to take them into account can be quickly fatal.

CONCLUSION

IdeaManagers and IdeaLeaders need to be aware of the outer ring of culture and structure. It is the crust of the organizational pie. Things people do and actions people take interact with beliefs that people have and orientations that people profess. Changes in population, organization, environment, and technology are part of the contextual kit that creates new conditions for organizations. They require new competencies from individuals, even if the organization and the individuals in question are doing as much as they always did.

Changes in beliefs are another part of the contextual change. The system of values tends to be locked into sets of competing commitments. Commitments tend to alternate between elements in the set, even though one element may be more valued than the other. Thus, societies and organizations may swing between achievement and equality, for example, or permission and control, even though achievement and permission may be the more dominant values.

Changing conditions and values stimulate the occasion for new ideas—either inventions (things that have not been developed before) or new applications of older ideas now being shaped to new occasions and opportunities. The Five Cs Conference, in its focus on context, should pick up and reflect within the organization some of the cultural and structural shifts that are going on. It is important not only to be aware of what is happening but to adjust your own operations in order to take advantage of those shifts.

Chapter 22

Creating Change and Supporting Shift

Throughout this book I have been talking about stimulating the flow of new ideas into the firm. This is change, or to use a less emotionally charged word, shift. People react negatively to change; shift seems less threating, more palatable, more manageable, closer to the "good old ways," better, even. In this last chapter, a few additional hints and tips, woven into a discussion of change, might be helpful.

STRATEGIC TECHNIQUES FOR THE IDEAMANAGER AND IDEALEADER

There are two particular foci you might wish to consider. The first of these involves the personal presentation of self and things you, as an individual, might do. The second involves a discussion of successful organization strategies that the well-known thinker James B. Quinn (1979) compiled.

Individual Strategies for the IdeaManager and IdeaLeader

As an individual, you can take certain actions that will enhance the impact of your ideas within the community and within the organization. These will be effective whether you are starting a new business and need venture capital and other support to get it going or you are already in an excellent business and are seeking to renew or refurbish it.

First, recognize that all new ideas advance the interests of some and retard the interests of others. You should begin with the notion, therefore, that most others in the community will be somewhere between neutral and hostile. This perspective may be overly cynical, and I am not suggesting that you become paranoid about potential opposition. Instead, as indicated before, you should recognize that opposition is the most likely thing to occur and begin to seek ways to overcome that opposition. The first step is to assess it.

Assess Change Forces and Resistance Forces As mentioned, in their book, *The Dynamics of Planned Change*, Ronald Lippit, Jeanne Watson, and Bruce Westley (1958) talk about assessing the change forces (those that would generally be counted on to support you) and the resistance forces (those that would generally be counted on to oppose you). Change forces and resistance forces may exist inside and outside of organizational locations that you are seeking to influence. It is important to do an initial assessment—a political assessment, if you will—of who is for you and who is against you. Politicians do this all the time, of course. It is called counting the votes. Often, however, innovators, captured as they may frequently be with the very interest and elegance of a new idea, do not spend time thinking about who may oppose the idea and why and who might support it and why. Once you have change forces and resistance forces listed out, the next step becomes easier.

Use Techniques of Clearing, Checking, and Involving IdeaManagers and IdeaLeaders are often alone in proposing new ideas. Sometimes that is simply because they thought up the idea alone. Other times it is because they have not taken advantage of the support that is available. The list of change and resistance forces suggests a number of allies. You can check through your proposal and idea with them and try to get their endorsement. Beyond that, you should also try to get their support and active lobbying help on behalf of the idea. Part of this involves expanding your "person power." Increasing the sheer number of supporters is extremely important, for numbers make the idea less easy to reject. It is always easy to turn one person down. It is a lot more difficult to turn down several people.

In the clearing process you not only check with other individuals, but you also seek to incorporate some of their ideas into the development of your proposals. This broadens the ownership of the idea in a real sense, and it enhances commitment. Typically, this action is taken with friends, supporters (Lippett, Watson, and Westley's [1958] change forces). However, you should not rule out the possibility of converting the opposition by coopting them into the plan. We have all had the experience of seeing people turned around as a proponent goes to those individuals, takes their criticism seriously, and seeks to address it. Not only are such individuals responsive because a particular criticism has been dealt with, but the prestige and deference generated by that exchange further builds support from individuals who might have been—and probably were—opposed.

Use In-Principle and Specification Discussion Styles Two techniques are useful here: the in-principle technique and the specification technique. They tend to work together. As a strategy, the in-principle technique asks reviewers of any particular idea or plan to set aside detailed considerations and look, instead, at the overall principle: "Is this product, this direction, this service something that we wish to pursue?" You can often get an affirmative response in general without getting tied up in specifics. The problem is that new ideas often are shy on specifics. It is not that you never get to them, but it is very difficult to know whether to proceed without having some sense of overall approval.

The specification technique involves ways to address criticism if you get into a discussion of specifics (or at the time you begin that level of discussion). Opposition to new ideas is often general and vague. Sometimes you have to work with that difficult situation. Sometimes, though, in the clearing and checking process, you can address opponents in a one-on-one, nonthreatening situation, saying something like, "What is it that you feel specifically is the problem? What kinds of specific changes can be made to address your concerns?" You may get ideas about ways to improve that will both make your proposal better and increase support for it.

It is imperative that you do not wait until opposition manifests itself. Successful IdeaManagers and IdeaLeaders anticipate opposition and take steps like those mentioned to enhance support and blunt the force of negative expression.

Develop Creative Program Design There are certain features of the design of new proposals that may serve to enhance support and discourage opposition. Nobel Laureate Herbert Simon, with Smithburg and Thompson (1956), in the book *Public Administration*, deals with this problem in a set of complementary ideas: (1) make compliance easy, and (2) make noncompliance difficult. Simon and colleagues were talking about ways to implement a plan, but the advice also applies to the very beginning design of a plan. If you can set up a plan that makes agreement easy and disagreement difficult, then you are going to enhance the ability of the proposal to succeed. One example they use is the tax deduction. Compliance is easy because it is automatic. Noncompliance is hard for the same reason.

Link Your Ideas to Current Values Simon and colleagues (1956) also argued that new ideas should be linked to prevailing values. This involves securing of precedents; the general approach of putting new wine in old bottles. Linking to values, however, is a complex task; values tend to come in linked pairs. Thus, when you seek to justify a proposal under a particular set of values, you should also be aware that there is going to be a competing set of values that will also need attention. Short-term gain and long-term gain, for example, is one case of potentially competing values. Linking a program to one of them could very well cause problems with supporters of the other. This perspective does not mean that you must always compromise your point of view. If a particular program has short-term gains, however, and is silent or even negative with respect to long-term gains, then you must be prepared for that kind of opposition and deal with it in advance.

Organizational Strategies for IdeaManagers and IdeaLeaders

The brief suggestions mentioned concerning personal strategy characteristics can link with design or organizational strategy characteristics that will enhance the success of new ideas and proposals. A very useful list comes from James B. Quinn (1979).

Strong Incentives It is very important in change activities to provide incentives for establishing innovation. Without those incentives, performances tend to flatten out. This perspective does not mean that incentives have to be totally individual. They can also be oriented to group achievement. Individuals can be rewarded, but so can teams, task forces, and other organizational collectivities. Furthermore, these rewards do not always have to be money (recall psychic income). They can be, to be sure, but there are others that may be equally powerful: prestige, team meetings with the boss, praise, permission to engage in other new projects, and so on. The point is simple. Try to provide the kind of reinforcement within the structure that will support new ideas, products, and services.

Clearly Defined Need It is important that you establish the need for a new product or service and the niche that it will occupy. Frequently, the answers to these questions are so intuitively clear to the proposer that he or she does not think to make the argument clear to others. Bearing in mind that others are likely to be neutral to hostile toward the idea, the requirement of establishing the need and the niche becomes doubly important.

Multiple Competing Approaches Do not put all your eggs in one basket with respect to new products or services development or their introduction. Instead, cast as broad a net as possible. All too frequently, organizations believe that, because they have an R&D center, ideas should come from there. Certainly, a lot of ideas do come from R&D centers, but the organization has to be fairly large to even have such a center. For the most part, in smaller organizations everyone should be invited to submit and explore ideas. If an organization permits a certain amount of time to be spent on idea development and product experimentation, everyone will have a chance to have a go at developing some innovative product or service.

There are several methods worth considering. First, you might have a special telephone number and answering machine for new ideas that you promise to listen to as boss and to which you will respond. Though an answering machine might seem a bit impersonal, many individuals with whom we have worked have said something like, "I never can catch the boss long enough to tell him the idea." They could write to you, of course, but obviously they do not. This way they can tell you something using a voice communication mode that they know you will hear. This stimulates the creativity that they have, rather than waiting for the R&D department to come up with something. You can also send out a memo to staff—or if the organization is small simply tell them—saying something like, "We're having a problem with XYZ. Anyone who can solve it gets a bonus." And, when ideas are developed, synopses of them can be sent out for comment. This approach is likely to discover and, sometimes, remedy flaws.

Multiple and competing approaches might seem like a waste of time and energy. In some specific instances it is, and for some extremely large projects such multiplicity may be impractical. But the point here is to avoid getting into an organizational rut in which the same individuals who always do things continue to do things and continue to have the same perspectives, orientations, and points of view.

But more is needed than to just stimulate the input side. You, yourself, as an IdeaManager and IdeaLeader, have to commit to accepting and processing some of these new ideas. If individuals make a lot of suggestions and never see anything happening, they will come to the conclusion that you did not want the suggestions in the first place or wanted them only for the purposes of covering your own posterior. Thus, you must be willing to accept and try the best among the new ideas.

User Guidance Throughout the process of new product or service development, close interaction with potential users is an important feature. In the book publishing business, as a case in point, the use of readers, test marketing, and trial copies being used for particular classes (in the case of textbooks) all provide valuable information that allows for product shaping and sculpting, service adjustment, and refocusing. There are always voices around you that will argue that the consumer does not know what is right. None of us like evaluations that are potentially negative and critical of efforts into which we have put a lot of time. On the other hand, early feedback allows for adjustment, and that becomes crucial.

High Expertise It is imperative to involve top talent in the introduction of new products or services. In the developmental and idea stage, such top talent may be "borrowed" from books, articles, and other authorities. In other words, rather than advancing an idea totally on your own, try to find others who have similar ideas or who have offered similar or related suggestions. Keep in mind that if it is only Sam's idea, it has less credibility than if it is Sam and Peter Drucker's idea. I am not suggesting the inappropriate link-up with authorities and prestigious individuals, but, rather, doing so when it makes sense and when the links are clear.

As the product or service moves into the development and implementation stages, the best individuals in your organization should be secured to develop and run the program. The reason for this need is that there is much less known about a new product or service than about a standard one. As a result, individuals whose expertise is pretty much doing the same old thing are not the kind of individuals you need in product innovation and introduction.

Longer Time Horizon Innovations require a longer time than many people realize to finally move through the whole process from idea to popularly accepted product or service. It is for this reason that advice to entrepreneurs to "persevere" is among the most common in the organizational literature. The material in this book, if conscientiously applied, will shorten the time. Nevertheless, as an IdeaManager and IdeaLeader you need to recognize that results from new ideas, new products, and new services are likely to pay off in the longer term rather than in the immediate, shorter term. Though you should always be looking for immediate applications, total focus on that sector of the innovation pie results in relatively modest improvements rather than in larger-scale innovations.

Committed Champions In order for innovations to continue and for new products and services to be viable, individuals must be committed to the importance and need of the products or services and be willing to devote the time and interpersonal energy to push them through the system. Backers and supporters are always needed for any idea. You cannot rely solely on committed champions, however. They are necessary but not sufficient conditions for organizational excellence in the new idea, new product, and new service department. Indeed, organizational management is designed in some degree to replace part of what is usually attributed to champions. Sometimes just the enthusiasm of your champions will cause you to prevail. More often, organized and methodical management of the idea-generating and transformation system is what is needed. And, that organized and methodical management cannot be located away in some remote R&D department, but should be part of the ongoing ambiance of the organization itself.

Top-Level Risk Taking If you are a top-level manager in addition to being an IdeaManager and IdeaLeader, then you will need to model risk-taking, innovative behavior. If the CEO is always backed up against the wall, soon the staff will follow suit. It is important for top management to realize that it is perfectly acceptable for top management to be wrong sometimes. (Keep in mind that an executive is one who makes many decisions, some of which are right.) It is for this reason that top management should engage in a variety of innovative projects on different scales. Thus, a failure, particularly in a small-scale project, serves the modeling function without a great deal of loss. Large-scale loss is more difficult to tolerate. The likelihood of those losses will be sharply reduced if innovation is an ongoing part of the organization's culture.

Moral Delivery Mode Finally, Quinn (1979) suggests that innovations were enhanced and have been successful where they fell into what he called a "moral delivery mode"; that is, where the product was worthwhile, useful, made a contribution to the community, and enhanced the common culture rather than detracted from it.

Organizational Changes

Given these things that you can do to get changes implemented, how might you propose the organization actually respond. There are many approaches, of course, but here are a few suggestions.

Adjust As the changes are perceived, IdeaManagers and IdeaLeaders can help the structure change so that the the organization can adjust to those changes. Given organizational needs and a knowledge of the environment, an organization has adjustment as an option, but there are two other options that are much more appealing.

Niche-ing The firm can find a niche, those aspects of the environment that are supportive of the organizational goals and dispositions. The environment is really not all one piece. For every trend going in one direction, there are trends going in other directions. The organizational context is sufficiently ambiguous that diverse elements always exist simultaneously. In any organization, one does not have to be satisfied with what is "there," because what is "there" is often just what the observer happens to see. A more vigorous search process will produce other aspects of the environment that will be supportive. IdeaManagers help the organization to find and exploit these supportive elements.

Creation. The organization can create or develop (as opposed to find), even at a small level, the needed elements within the environment. Firms have always recruited workers from afar, for example, and have brought them to particular locales to work. They have also taken advantage of employees who have been drawn to them. Often, however, these two mechanisms have worked in tandem, because the information pathways service those teams simultaneously. If, as a firm, one finds that there are limited numbers of technically trained people in a particular area, then it may be possible to work with a local junior college or community college to provide what is needed. The organization may even sponsor part of the costs of the initial course in order to make it more appealing for the college administration to undertake the desired innovation. If government funding is not available, government funding can be created in response to pressure. One successful example of this in the nonprofit sector is in the area of programs and services for the aging. In many places, such programs and services have been lobbied for so successfully that they are now a permanent feature on local tax rolls. Businesses have had their successes, as well, influencing local government to assist them in the accomplishment of their particular organizational goals and purposes. As a result, they have benefited through tax rebates and credits, tax abatement, assistance in land and equipment acquisition among other forms of assistance, and so on. Technological changes can be stimulated. Environmental adjustments can be created or negotiated. IdeaManagers and IdeaLeaders help the organization to develop the kinds of support needed.

CONCLUSION

New ideas—you cannot live with them and you cannot live without them. The whole idea of new ideas, though, is that they are an unexploited resource for our organizations, to which we react rather than proact. In most organizations, new ideas are randomly available, episodically energized, and accidentally used. If we—in our many organizations—have been able to achieve the American standard of living and contribution by accident, it boggles the mind to think what we could do if we really put our mind to the enterprise and our shoulder to the wheel.

References

Adams, S. (1995). *The Dilbert principle*. New York: Harper Business.

Adams, W., & Brock, J. (1985). *The bigness complex*. New York: Pantheon.

Alston, J. (1986). *The American samurai: Bending American and Japanese managerial practices*. New York: de Gruyter.

Argyris, C. (1964). *Integrating the individual and the organization*. New York: Wiley.

Argyris, C. (1969). "Individual actualization in complex organizations." In *Organizations and human behavior: Focus on schools*, edited by F. D. Carver and T. Sergiovanni. New York: McGraw-Hill.

Argyris, C. (1982). *Reasoning, learning and actions: Individual and organizational*. San Francisco: Jossey-Bass.

Argyris, C. (1985). *Strategy, Change and Defensive Routines*. Boston: Pitman.

Asher, G. (1997). "The judgment of Paris revisited." *Gourmet* (January): 24, 97–99.

Autrey, J. (1991). *Love and profit*. New York: Avon.

Baker, W. (1993). *Networking smart: How to build relationships for personal and business success*. New York: McGraw-Hill.

Barton, A. (1979). "A diagnosis of bureaucratic maladies." *American Behavioral Scientist* 22: 483–492.

Bass, B. (1990). *Stogdill's handbook of leadership*. 3d ed. New York: Free Press.

Bass, B., ed. (1981). *Stogdill's handbook of leadership*. New York: Free Press.

Behn, B. (1991). *Leadership counts*. Cambridge: Harvard University Press.

Benedict, R. (1946). *The chrysanthemum and the sword: Patterns of Japanese culture*. Boston: Houghton Mifflin.

Bennis, W. (1978/1979). 'RX for corporate boards." *Technology Review* 81 (3): 12.

Bennis, W., & Nanus, B. (1985). *Leaders*. New York: Harper.

Berryman-Finke, C. (1989). *The manager's desk reference*. New York: Amacom.

Bolman, L., & Deal, T. (1991). *Reframing organizations*. San Francisco: Jossey-Bass.

Boltan, R. (1979). *People Skills: How to assert yourself, listen to others, and resolve conflicts*. New York: Simon & Schuster.
Booher, D. (1984). *Send me a memo: A handbook of model memos*. New York: Facts on File.
Brown, D. S. (1982). *Managing the large organization*. Mt. Airy, Md.: Lomond.
Burch, J. G. (1986). *Entrepreneurship*. New York: Wiley.
Burgelman, R., & Sayels, L. (1986). *Inside corporate innovation: Strategy, structure, and managerial skills*. New York: Collier-Macmillan.
Cameron, D. A., & Whetten, K. S. (1998). *Developing management skills*. 4th ed. Reading, Mass.: Addison-Wesley.
Carroll, D. T. (1981). "From the boardroom." *Harvard Business Review* 59 (5): 62–66.
Chochran, T. (1968). "Entrepreneurship." In *The encyclopedia of social sciences*, edited by D. L. Sills. New York: Macmillan/Free Press.
Cohen, M., March, J., & Olsen, J. P. (1972). "A garbage can model of organizational choice." *Administrative Science Quarterly* 17: 1–15.
Collins, B., & Guetzkow, H. (1964). *A social psychology of group processes for decision making*. New York: Wiley.
Cox, F. M., & Tropman, J. E. (1987). "Society: American values as a context for practice." In *Strategies of community organization/macro practice*. 4th ed., edited by F. M. Cox, J. Erlich, J. Rothman, and J. Tropman. Itasca, Ill.: F. E. Peacock.
Crichton, M. (1987). *Sphere*. New York: Knopf.
Cross, L. (1997). "Notes." From WQRS, Detroit, Michigan.
Csikszentmihalyi, M. (1990). *Flow: The psychology of optimal experience*. New York: Harper.
Cyert, R. (1975). *Managing the nonprofit organization*. Lexington, Mass.: Heath.
Daft, R. L., & Bradshaw, P. J. (1980). "The process of horizontal differentiation: Two models." *Administrative Science Quarterly* 25: 441–456.
Davis, S. M. (1987). *Future perfect*. Reading, Mass.: Addison-Wesley.
De Bono, E. (1970). *Lateral thinking*. New York: Harper.
De Bono, E. (1985). *Six thinking hats*. Reading, Mass.: Addison-Wesley.
DeGraff, J. (1997). Personal communication, July 8.
Deming, W. E. (1986). *Out of crisis*. Cambridge: Massachusetts Institute of Technology, Center for Advanced Engineering Study.
De Pree, M. (1993). *Leadership jazz*. New York: Doubleday.
DeVries, M. (1985). "The dark side of entrepreneurship." *Harvard Business Review* 63 (6): 160–167.
Dreyfus, H. L., & Dreyfus, S. E. (1986). *Mind over machine: The power of human intuition and expertise in the era of the computer*. New York: Free Press.
Drucker, P. (1966). *The effective executive*. New York: Harper.
Drucker, P. (1985). *Innovation and entrepreneurship*. New York: Harper.
Drucker, P. (1990). *Managing the nonprofit organization*. New York: Harper.
Drucker, P. (1993). *Post capitalist society*. New York: Harper Business.
Edwards, M. R., & Ewen, A. J. (1996). *360° feedback*. New York: Amacom.
Egan, G. (1994). *Working the shadow side*. San Francisco: Jossey-Bass.
Elkin, R., & Molitor, N. (1984). *Management indicators in non-profit organizations*. New York: Peat, Marwick, Mitchell & Co.
Ferguson, M. (1983). *The agrarian conspiracy*. Los Angeles: Tarcher.

Fisher, B., & Ury, W. (1981). *Getting to yes*. New York: Houghton Mifflin.
Fitzgerald, T. (1987). Personal communication, March 8.
Flamholtz, E. G. (1985). *How to make the transition from an entrepreneurship to a professionally managed firm*. San Francisco: Jossey-Bass.
Frost, R. (1971). *The road not taken*. New York: Holt, Rinehart, & Winston.
Fucini, J. S. (1985). *Entrepreneurs: The men and women behind famous brand names and how they made it*. Boston: Gaven K. Hall.
Galbraith, J. (1973). *Designing the complex organization*. Reading, Mass.: Addison-Wesley.
Galbraith, J. (1982). "Designing the innovating organization." *Organizational Dynamics* 10: 5–25.
Gardner, H. (1983). *Frames of the mind*. New York: Basic Books.
Gelatt, J. P. (1992). *Managing the non-profit organization in the 21st century*. Phoenix: Oryx.
Glassner, B. (1994). *Career crash*. New York: Simon & Schuster.
Goffman, I. (1959). *The presentation of self in everyday life*. Garden City, N.J.: Doubleday/Anchor.
Goldratt, E., & Cox, J. (1986). *The goal: The process of ongoing improvement*. Croton on Hudson, N.Y.: North River Press.
Goleman, D. (1995). *Emotional intelligence*. New York: Bantam.
Gordon, W. J. J. (1973). *Synectics: The development of creative capacity*. New York: Collier.
Greene, R. (1986). Personal conversation with author.
Groobey, J. (1974). "Making the board of directors more effective." *California Management Review* 16 (3): 25–34.
Grove, A. (1983). *High output management*. New York: Random House.
Haft, R. (1981). "Business decisions by the new board." *Michigan Law Review* 80:1–67.
Hamel, G., & Prahalad, C. K. (1989). "Strategic intent." *Harvard Business Review* 67 (May–June): 63–76.
Hardacer, M., & White, B. K. (1987). "How to make a team work." *Harvard Business Review* 65 (6): 112–120.
Harrigan, B. (1978). *Games your mother never taught you*. New York: Warner.
Harvey, J. (1988). *The Abilene paradox and other mediations on management*. Lexington, Mass.: Lexington Books.
Heinlein, R. (1963). *Stranger in a strange land*. New York: Putnam.
Hesselbein, F., ed. (1996). *The leader of the future*. San Francisco: Jossey-Bass.
Hirschman, A. O. (1970). *Exit, voice, and loyalty: Responses to decline in firms, organizations, and states*. Cambridge: Harvard University Press.
Hirschman, A. O. (1982). *Shifting involvements*. Princeton, N.J.: Princeton University Press.
Hochschild, A. (1997). *The time bind: When work becomes home and home becomes work* . New York: Metropolitan Books.
Holcombe, M., & Stein, J. (1981). *Writing for decision makers: Memos and reports with a competitive edge*. Belmont, Wash.: Wadsworth.
Houle, C. O. (1989). *Governing boards*. San Francisco: Jossey-Bass.
Janis, I. L. (1983). *Groupthink*. Boston: Houghton Mifflin.
Janis, I., & Mann, L. (1977). *Decision making*. New York: Free Press.

Jay, A. (1976). "How to run a team meeting." *Harvard Business Review* 54 (2): 42–57.
Jenks, C., Perman, L., & Rainwater, L. (1988). "What makes a good job?" *American Journal of Sociology* 93: 1322–1357.
Johnson, W. (1979). *Muddling toward frugality*. Boulder, Colo.: Shambhale.
Jones, C. (1979). "If I knew then . . . (a personal essay on committees and public policy)." *Policy Analysis* 4: 473–479.
Josefowitz, N. (1980). *Paths to power*. Reading, Mass.: Addison-Wesley.
Kane, J. (1970). "Dynamics of the Peter principle." *Management Science* 16: 13–15.
Kanter, R. (1977). *Men and women of the corporation*. New York: Basic Books.
Kanter, R. (1983). *The change masters*. New York: Touchstone Books.
Katz, D., & Kahn, R. (1978). *The social psychology of organizations*. 2d ed. New York: Wiley.
Kaufman, H. (1985). *Time, chance, and organizations: Natural selection in a perilous environment*. Chatham, N.J.: Chatham House.
Kaufman, J. (1997). "Gray expectations." *Wall Street Journal*, May 5.
Keirsey, D., & Bates, M. (1984). *Please understand me: Character & temperament types*. 5th ed. Del Mar, Calif.: Prometheus Nemesis.
Kerr, S. (1995). "On the folly of rewarding A while hoping for B." *Academy of Management Executives* 9 (1): 7–16.
Kidder, T. (1981). *The soul of a new machine*. New York: Avon.
Lands' End. (1987). Direct-mail catalog, April
Lawrence, J. (1955). *Inherit the wind*. New York: Random House.
Lawton, M. P. (1983). "Environment and other determinants of being in older people." *The Gerontologist* 23: 349–357.
Lessen, J. (1996). "Savoring success." *World Traveler* (October): 33–38.
Levering, R. (1990). *A great place to work*. New York: Avon.
Levinson, H. (1981). *The executive*. Cambridge: Harvard University Press.
Leyton, E. T., Jr. (1987). "The most original." *American Heritage of Invention and Technology* 2 (3): 50–56.
Lippit, R., Watson, J., & Westley, B. (1958). *The dynamics of planned change: A comparative study of principles and techniques*. New York: Harcourt Brace and World.
Lipset, S. M. (1963). *The first new nation*. New York: Basic Books.
Lipset, S. M., & Schneider, W. (1983). *The confidence gap*. New York: Free Press.
Lynd, R. (1939). *Knowledge for what*. Princeton, N.J.: Princeton University Press.
Lynn, L. E. (1981). *Managing the public's business: The job of the government executive*. New York: Basic Books.
Mackenzi, A. (1990). *The time trap*. New York: Amacom.
Malburg, C. (1991). *How to fire your boss*. New York: Burley Books.
March, J. G. (1994). *A primer on decision making: How decisions happen*. New York: Free Press.
March, J. G., ed. (1965). *The handbook of organizations*. Chicago: Rand McNally.
March, J. G., & Simon, H. (1958). *Organizations*. New York: Wiley.
McCaskey, M. B. (1982). *The executive challenge: Managing change and ambiguity*. Boston: Pitman.
McCormack, J. (1997). "You snooze, you lose." *Newsweek* (July 21): 50–51.
McCormack, M. (1986). *What they don't teach you at the Harvard Business School*. New York: Bantam.

McGregor, D. (1960). *The human side of enterprise*. New York: McGraw-Hill.
Merton, R. K. (1957). *Social theory and social structure*. Rev. ed. Glencoe, Ill.: Free Press.
Michael, S. R. (1980). "Feedforward vs. feedback controls in central planning." *Academy of Management Review* 29 (4): 465–499.
Michaels, A. (1986). *Wall Street Journal*, 12 December, 26.
Miles, R., Snow, C. C., Meyer, A. D., & Coleman, H. J., Jr. (1978). "Organizational strategy, structure, and process." *Academy of Management Review* 3 (3): 546–562.
Miller, D. (1990). *The Iscarus paradox: How exceptional companies bring about their own downfall*. New York: HarperCollins.
Miller, L. (1984). *The American spirit: Visions of a new corporate culture*. New York: Morrow.
Mintzberg, H. (1976). "Planning on the left side and management on the right." *Harvard Business Review* 56: 49–58.
Mintzberg, H. (1994). *The rise and fall of strategic planning*. New York: Free Press.
Mintzberg, H., & Waters, J. A. (1982). "Tracking strategy in an entrepreneurial firm." *Academy of Management Journal* 25 (3): 465–499.
Morita, A. (1987). *Made in Japan*. New York: Dutton.
Myers, R., Ufford, P., & Magill, M. S. (1988). *On site analysis: A practical approach to organization change*. Etobicoke, Ontario: OSCA.
Naisbitt, J. (1982). *Megatrends: Ten new directions transforming our lives*. New York: Warner.
Naisbitt, J., & Auberdene, P. (1990). *Megatrends 2000*. New York: Morrow.
National Assembly. (1989). *A study in excellence*. Washington, D.C.: National Assembly.
Neugeboran, B. (1985). *Organization, policy and practice in human services*. New York: Longman.
Ouchi, W. (1982). *Theory Z*. New York: Avon.
Palmer, H. (1995). *Enneagram*. San Francisco: HarperCollins.
Parkinson, C. N. (1957). *Parkinson's law and other studies in administration*. New York: Houghton Mifflin.
Parsons, T. (1960). *Structure and process in modern societies*. Glencoe, Ill.: Free Press.
Parsons, T. (1963). "Suggestions for a sociological approach to the theory of organizations." In *Complex organizations: A sociological reader*, edited by A. Etzioni. New York: Holt, Rinehart, & Winston.
Pascale, R. T., & Athos, A. (1981). *The art of Japanese management*. New York: Warner.
Pascale, R. T., & Athos, A. (1982). *The end of Japanese management*. New York: Warner.
Patti, R. (1983). *Social welfare administration*. Englewood Cliffs, N.J.: Prentice Hall.
Patton, A., & Baker, J. C. (1987). "Why won't directors rock the boat?" *Harvard Business Review* 65 (6): 10–18.
Perrow, C. (1984). *Normal accidents: Living with high risk technologies*. New York: Basic Books.
Peter, L. (1970). *The Peter principle*. New York: Bantam.
Peter, L. (1972). *The Peter prescription*. New York: Bantam.
Peters, T. (1988). "Restoring American competitiveness: Looking for new models of organizations." *Academy of Management Executives* 2 (2): 103–107.

Peters, T. J., & Waterman, R. (1982). *In search of excellence*. New York: Harper & Row.
Pinchot, G. (1983). *Entrepreneuring*. New York: Harper.
Pioneers. (1974). Old West Series. New York: Time Life.
Popcorn, F. (1986). "Comfort and indulgence among trends." *Entrepreneur* 14 (10): 10.
Powell, W. (1989). *The non-profit sector*. New Haven: Yale University Press.
Primozic, K., Primozic, E., & Leben, J. (1991). *Strategic choices: Success, survival or Sayonara!* New York: McGraw-Hill.
Quinn, J. B. (1979). "Technological innovation, entrepreneurship and strategy." *Sloan Management Review* 20 (3): 19–30.
Quinn, R. (1988). *Beyond rational management*. San Francisco: Jossey-Bass.
Quinn, R. (1996). *Deep change: Discovering the leader within*. San Francisco: Jossey-Bass.
Quinn, R. (1997). Personal communication with author.
Reed, S. (1993). *The toxic executive*. New York: Harper Business.
Rosovsky, H. (1987). "Deaning." *Harvard Business Magazine* 89 (3): 34–40.
Rothchild-Whitt, J. (1979). "The collectivist organization: An alternative to rational bureaucratic models." *American Sociological Review* 444: 509–527.
Rothman, J., Erlich, J., & Tropman, J., eds. (1995). *Strategies of community organization*. Itasca, Ill.: F. E. Peacock.
Rotter, J. (1966). "Generalized expectancies for internal versus external control of reinforcement." *Psychological Monographs* 80 (1): whole #609: 1–29.
Rowan, R. (1986). *The intuitive manager*. Boston: Little, Brown.
Ryan, W. (1971). *Blaming the victim*. New York: Vintage.
Sayles, L., & Chandler, M. (1971). *Managing larger systems: Organizations for the future*. New York: Harper.
Schein, E. (1985). *Organizational culture and leadership*. San Francisco: Jossey-Bass.
Schelling, T. C. (1978). "Egonomics, or the art of self-management." *American Economic Review* 68 (2): 290–294.
Schneider, B., ed. (1990). *Organizational culture and climate*. San Francisco: Jossey-Bass.
Schuster, J. R., & Zeingheim, P. K. (1992). *The new pay: Linking employee and organizational performance*. New York: Lexington Books.
Scientific American. (1987). "One hundred years ago." 256 (3): 10.
Selznik, P. (1987). *Leadership in administration*. New York: Harper & Row.
Senge, P. (1990). *The fifth discipline*. New York: Doubleday.
Simon, H., Smithburg, D., & Thompson, V. (1956). *Public administration*. New York: Knopf.
Slade, J. W. (1986). "The man behind the killing machine." *The American Heritage of Invention and Technology* 2 (2): 18–25.
Spears, L., ed. (1995). *Reflections on leadership*. New York: Wiley.
Spinner, J. (1997). "Absolute power: Drill sergeants, discipline and abuse in America's sensitive new army." *The Washington Post Magazine*.
Stechert, K. (1986). *On your own terms: A woman's guide to working with men*. New York: Vintage Books.
Stewart, T. A. (1992). "The search for the organization of tomorrow." *Fortune*, 18 May, 92–98.
Strunk, W., Jr., & White, E. B. (1979). *The elements of style*. New York: Macmillan.

Tannen, D. (1990). *You just don't understand me.* New York: Morrow.
Taylor, F. W. (1947). *Scientific management, comprising shop management, the principles of scientific management [and] testimony before the special House committee.* New York: Harper.
Thaler, R. H., & Shefrin, H. M. (1981). "An economic theory of self control." *Journal of Political Economy* 89 (2): 392–410.
Thurow, L. G. (1992). *Head to head: The coming economic battle among Japan, Europe, and America.* New York: Morrow.
Tichy, N. M. (1997). Personal communication, September 14.
Tichy, N. M., & Devanna, M. A. (1986). *The transformational leader.* New York: Wiley.
Trailblazers. (1973). Old West Series. New York: Time Life.
Trompenaars, F. (1994). *Riding the waves of culture: Understanding diversity in global business.* Burr Ridge, Ill.: Irwin Professional.
Tropman, J. E., Erlich, J. & Rothman, J., eds. (1995). *Tactics and techniques of community practice.* 3d ed. Itasca, Ill.: F. E. Peacock.
Tropman, J. E., & Morningstar, G. (1984). *Meetings: How to make them work for you.* New York: Van Nostrand.
Tropman, J. E., & Morningstar, G. (1989). *Entrepreneurial systems for the 1990s.* Westport, Conn.: Quorum Books.
Tuchman, B. (1984). *The march of folly.* New York: Knopf.
Vaill, P. B. (1982). "The purposing of high-performing systems." *Organizational Dynamics* 11: 23–39.
Vaill, P. B. (1989). *Managing as a performing art.* San Francisco: Jossey-Bass.
Vinter, R., & Kish, R. (1985). *Budgeting: Not for profit organizations.* New York: Free Press.
Vroom, V. H., & Yetton, P. W. (1973). *Leadership and decision-making.* Pittsburgh: University of Pittsburgh Press.
Wareham, J. (1991). *The anatomy of a great executive.* New York: Harper.
Weber, M. (1930). *The Protestant ethic and the spirit of Capitalism.* New York: Scribner.
Whetten, D. A., & Cameron, K. S. (1998). *Developing management skills.* 4th ed. Reading, Mass.: Addison-Wesley.
Whyte, W. F. (1957). *The organization man.* New York: Simon and Schuster.
Wildavsky, A. (1960). Personal communication.
Wolfe, T. (1984). *The right stuff.* New York: Bantam.
Wooden, J. (1986). "On staying power." *New York Times Magazine,* 8 June, 60.
Yankelovich, D. (1981). *New rules.* New York: Random House.
Zander, A. (1982). *Making groups effective.* San Francisco: Jossey-Bass.

Index

ABOUT THE AUTHOR

JOHN E. TROPMAN is Professor of Nonprofit Administration and Adjunct Professor of Organizational Behavior at the University of Michigan, Ann Arbor. He is also principal of his own consulting firm, High Quality Decisions, Ann Arbor, which offers programs and coaching for corporations, government agencies, and nonprofit organizations. With teaching experience in a wide range of subjects and fields, including executive education, organizational behavior, and human resources management, Tropman is author of many journal articles and books, including *Does America Hate the Poor? The Other American Dilemma* (Praeger, 1998) and *Entrepreneurial Systems for the 1990s* with Gersh Morningstar (1989).

CPSIA information can be obtained
at www.ICGtesting.com
Printed in the USA
LVOW08*2309251116
514341LV00003B/15/P

9 781567 201680